ZA

THE LIFE OF GIOVANNI BOCCACCIO

BOCCACCIO AND PETRARCH

ILLUMINATION FROM FRENCH MS. EDITION OF BOCCACCIO'S "LE CAS DES NOBLES
HOMMES ET FEMMES" WRITTEN IN 1409 FOR JEAN, DUC DE BERRI

THE LIFE OF GIOVANNI BOCCACCIO

BY

T HOMAS CALDECOT CHUBB

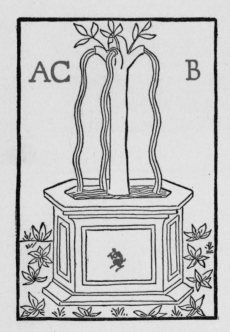

ALBERT & CHARLES BONI
NEW YORK · MCMXXX

DESIGNED BY ANDOR BRAUN
Printed in the United States of America

To
My Grandfather
SAMUEL LEE

> . . . . TE VULGO LABORES
> PERCELEBRUM FACIUNT, AETIS TE NULLA SILEBIT . .
>
> COLUCCIO SALUTATI.

ILLUSTRATIONS

* *Through the Courtesy of the Pierpont Morgan Library, New York.*
** *Through the Courtesy of the Metropolitan Museum, New York.*
*** *Through the Courtesy of the Public Library, New York.*

INTRODUCTION

IN writing this life of Boccaccio, I have tried to accomplish two things. In the first place to assemble as much of the existing knowledge in regard to the author of the *Decameron,* and in regard to his works as seems necessary for an adequate understanding of this illustrious Florentine, and having assembled it, to present it—I believe for the first time by an American author—to American readers. In the second place, to recreate—as far as is humanly possible—the complex personality of an extremely interesting and extremely human man of letters who died nearly six centuries ago.

The first of these two tasks has been largely a matter of patience. It has been necessary—merely—to absorb, and then collate sizable masses of critical information. For quite candidly, in my essay at delineating this man, it has been only in matters of interpretation that I have tried to add anything new.

The second task, however, has been considerably more difficult.

"For who," as the subject of this biography himself observed in the proem to the *Genealogy of the Gods,* one of those massive and formless Latin works with which he occupied his later years, "in our time can approach the minds of the ancients, and expose the secret thoughts of those so long gone from this mortal life into another, or rediscover the sentiments they had?"

"That certainly," he concluded, "would be more divine than

human." And with his expert judgment on this matter, I am prepared quite entirely to agree.

It is, therefore, with very actual humility that I have set down what attempts to be a portrait in full length of this serious-minded and yet gay-writing begetter of Italian prose, who looked shrewdly and intently at the multifarious scene around him, and with wit and beauty and urbanity—and with roguish and robustious humor—set down that which he saw. I hope that I have done fullest justice to a great man and a great writer, and I have already breathed more than one prayer to those Latin and Italian muses who guided him so wisely and so eloquently, that they at least look upon my pen.

For the rest, there is little to say. My method has been, I think—though with a few modifications—the modern one. Facts and dates afford a useful apparatus for measuring those small, but to us extremely important scratchings on the sands of time which we call human destiny, and they are too often scorned unreasonably by the new type of "antipedantic" pedant, but it is still to be remembered that they are merely facts and dates. Moreover, as it has somewhere been remarked, the writer of biography is but a novelist whose plot has already been drawn for him. This aphorism I have tried to keep constantly in mind as the various chapters were being written.

But I have also tried to keep equally in mind that the first loyalty of the historian—and of the biographer, who is, after all, but a more detailed and intimate historian—is to the truth. In granting to the biographer the artist's right to selection and composition, it is not necessary to admit that any untruth or, for that matter, any real exaggeration, can be justified on the ground that it makes a more sprightly and readable story.

Of course with a man like Boccaccio, there is much controversy, and since when authorities, like doctors, disagree, the patient, which in this case is the book, dies, at times perhaps I have been forced to be arbitrary. To those who find me too much so, I can only point out that at the conclusion I have indicated the more important of my sources, referring them to the same men without whose patient and unselfish work —of which I have shamelessly made use—this book could never have been written. And to whom here collectively, as there individually, I wish to express my gratitude.

THE LIFE OF GIOVANNI BOCCACCIO

CHAPTER I

ON the first day of May in the year 1308, Albrecht of Austria, German Emperor and King of the Romans, himself murderer of his predecessor, Adolph of Nassau, met his death at the hands of an assassin. The fact itself was not unusual, for violent ends were common enough in those forceful days, and but for what succeeded Albrecht might simply have been recalled as another one of those Teutonic military princes, who were made nominal sovereigns of an empire whose very existence, one might almost say, was more literary than real, and whose capital, Rome, holy and imperial, not one of them had ever visited for more than fifty years.

But such was not to be the case. A successor to the imperial office had to be chosen, and the Pope's position and influence was such that he could actually, if not apparently, name this successor. Committed by his own temporal necessities, on the one hand to a divided and republican Italy, and on the other to opposing, if only tacitly, the swift growth of monarchial France, he could not look with favor on any of the obvious candidates. A man relatively unknown must be selected. He persuaded the electors, therefore, to agree on Henry of Luxembourg. The ruler of a virtually insignificant state, this red-headed and beardless warrior whose thick eyebrows, slight squint and chaste morals so impressed contemporary chroniclers, seemed likely to fulfill all the other Papal requirements. He was a good Catholic—something to say of one of his race, even two centuries before Martin Luther

—and would not, like certain earlier and rationalistic emperors, be unaffected by exhortations emanating from the Holy Father. His French education—he had spent part of his youth in France—as well as his own personal tastes made him not unsusceptible to Gallic influences. He wore, for instance— according to Mussato, who knew him—his hair cut in the French fashion, and had the appearance of a French prince. The Pope had then, it seemed, at least moderately good reasons to expect him "to live in accord with King Philip and be Guelph in his politics." In other words, he would neither embroil northern Europe by stirring up Franco-German rivalry, nor stir up Italy to his own possible advantage by espousing the cause of the divided and disheartened Ghibellines—the pro-imperials, that is; the hard-pressed aristocrats— against the democratic supporters of the Pope.

These Ghibellines had, however, another view of the matter. Especially the Florentine Ghibellines, now for eight years banished from their city. Very likely inspired by their own hopes and desires, they saw clearly and realistically the effect of the imperial crown on whosoever wore it. If he were an ambitious man, he would come to conquer. If he were an avaricious man, he would come to plunder. If—and this seemed to be the case—he were sincere and serious-minded, he would come to organize. He would come to rule. He would come to give justice. In any case, he would descend through the jagged passes of the Alps—with his prestige, and probably—better still —with his lances. Them it was that he would rally to his standard. Long lean, they would fatten at his advance.

In consequence, there broke out an enormous pæan of thanksgiving. Dante, sharp-featured and splenetic, whose fierce and unsurmountable, if not always wise, patriotism was edged by his own personal vindictiveness, forgot complaining

and shook the acid off his pen. He then dipped it in exaltation, wrote Frederick of Sicily, wrote Robert of Naples, wrote
Roman senators, wrote dukes, marquises, and counts. "The
dawn of a new day lightens and already it scatters the shadows
of our long calamity. We shall see the joy long awaited for,
we who have spent so many nights in the desert. Rejoice,
Italy! Thy spouse, the consolation of the world, the glory of
thy people, Henry the most clement, comes to celebrate the
wedding feast!" Cino da Pistoia, poet, too, and likewise
lawyer, turned to the Bible. "Lord, now lettest thou thy
servant depart in peace, for mine eyes have seen thy salvation!"
So great was their exultation that Pope Clement was no
longed accused of lewdness and hardly even of venal cor-
ruption.

In the fastnesses of the Alps; in the great draughty halls
of stern castles perched in the Apennines; in the rugged
Casentino from whence, between silver-green olive trees, the
Florentine exiles looked down homesickly on their compact,
beautiful city; in Milan and Brescia and Verona, "cities of the
plain"; in Pisa and Genoa and Arezzo, old suits of armor
were taken down and polished, old lances were shined and
sharpened. A knight-errant had appeared on the scene, and
all of the knights-errant of the fair garden of the empire were
pricking up their ears. The old era would do battle against
the new era. Gentlemen and aristocrats—even if very frequently somewhat aging gentlemen and aristocrats—gentlemen
and aristocrats of "the good old times," then, as always, just
sinking below the horizon—would defy shopkeepers and merchants and money changers. Proud feudalism and gallant, if
hopeless, chivalry would oppose stolid democracy whose
strongest supporters were those odoriferous countrymen "from
Campi and Certaldo and Figghine" who had corrupted the

blood of a fair city like Florence, which formerly, according to the great poet of Heaven and Hell, "ran pure in the veins of the meanest artisan."

Who could doubt of the result?

And then Henry came. Hawk on arm, he entered Italy "with the pope's consent." Champing steed, plumed helmet, gleaming carapace, and toughly plated jazerant, following him through the Alpine passes of Mount Cenis. And at first his expedition was a triumphant progress. He was crowned at Milan with the iron crown of the kings of Lombardy. He rode from that city to Genoa, and from Genoa he sailed to Pisa. In each place he won allegiance and subsidies, and if later the plundering habits of his soldiers aroused enmity, and if also he left behind him both discontent and in some cases open rebellion, he was still able to proceed. Finally he marched across the whole of central Italy to Rome. It was there that his troubles began. For he reached Rome only to discover that he had stirred up the whole country like a nest of hornets, and that the longed-for city was occupied by the Florentine and Neapolitan troops of the Guelph allies. Six weeks of bloody, hand-to-hand fighting among the classic ruins followed. Then he was obliged to forgo his dream of being invested with the purple at St. Peter's. A substitute coronation at St. John Lateran—this confirmed him as emperor, but gave him no prestige—was arranged, doubtless to the secret satisfaction of the papal legates who accompanied him. Afterwards, he withdrew to Tivoli in shame.

From then on his fortunes went from bad to worse. His next step was against Florence. He had already thundered against this place. Although he had entered Italy with a soldier's scorn for battles fought with words, he had later succumbed to the inexpensive appeal of war by document, and in a document had proscribed the whole city. A cart was to pass over her walls. She was to be deprived of the right to coin money. The leading families of her new middle-class rulers were to be exiled. He now marched against her to put this decree into effect, but was stopped at her very walls when, although victorious, he was seized with indecision. He spent the winter that followed in the Florentine territory trying to repair the consequences of this mistake by what turned out to be a series of meaningless advances and retreats. Disease decimated his camp and he himself was taken sick, so that when in March, 1313, he "withdrew" to Pisa, it was really an escape. He did set out again—on the eighth of August—but he did not get far. On his new march toward Rome, he caught a severe cold, and as he was already in a run-down condition, the cold swiftly become a fever. He was obliged to halt at Buonconvento near Siena, and there on August 24th he expired. His doctors and his partisans insisted, as a matter of course, that he had been poisoned. A Dominican monk, they said, had offered him a poisoned host which for pious fear of sacrilege, he had refused to vomit. But the truth is that the venom which entered his veins was the bitter venom of disaster. His life ceased to continue because to his bodily fatigue had been added the fierce mental fatigue of failure. The poisoned sacrament which he had refused to vomit was the black sacrament of unsuccess.

And the hand that offered it to him was not the treacherous hand of a Dominican, but the trade-roughened hand of the place he had fulminated against. Namely Florence. The new Florence. The Florence of the wool merchants. The Florence of the hard, usurious money lenders. The Florence of the sturdy demagogic workingmen.

Her weapon had been obstinacy. Where the aristocratic

Guelphs, such as Robert of Naples, shilly-shallied this way and that, talked one thing and did another, "thought about" treating, the Florentines remained firmly obdurate. There was only one peace condition which appealed to them and that appealed to them greatly. That was that they be left alone. Money was much to them, but they would give freely their last *soldo* before they would be disturbed by an outsider. Fighting was distasteful—it unsettled economic conditions and took them away from their festivals—yet their last man would mount the walls, before they would allow a foreigner to misgovern them. That privilege they reserved for themselves.

The story of their resistance is one of the most thrilling in the whole history of Italy, or, for that matter, of the world. For in it, almost for the first time in modern days, strong for all its crudities, single of purpose for all its division, a rich democratic state meets success. It is likewise extremely important. For it was not the emperor's personal fortunes alone that were ridden into dust. At Florence at least,—though it was to some extent true of the rest of Italy—an idea was vanquished, and a new idea was crowned victor. The old ruling class—based on blood—was deprived of power, forever, and a new ruling class—based on commercial achievement—was substituted. It was henceforth so disadvantageous to be a noble that certain kinds of crime—notably offenses against the state—were punished by ennobling the persons who committed them. To hold office, to achieve any sort of success, for that matter, it was necessary to be a member of the middle classes. In consequence, since the Renaissance was very largely Florentine, was very largely middle-class Florentine, if there is such thing as evident fact in the whole long story of humanity's fortunes, it is plain and evident that the whole glittering period was made possible by Henry's defeat.

And nowhere is that made more apparent than in his bitter proscription of Florence, which we have already mentioned. For among those against whom the Cæsarian ire was directed was name after name which was shortly—and very resoundingly—to ring out. Corsini was one of these, as were Machiavelli, Albizzi, Guicciardini, and Ferucci. Unmentioned, but nevertheless implied and of great present importance were the great banking names of Bardi, Peruzzi, and Acciaiuoli. Unmentioned, but of future importance were the Medici.

Dante was, as we have seen, an aristocrat. Petrarch's father was a Ghibelline exile. But the men of the new day were to be of distinctly less illustrious lineage. They were not to be descendants of those haughty patricians like Dante's ancestor, Cacciaguida, whose mother, "drawing off the strong threads from the distaff, told to them old tales of the Trojans and Fiesole and Rome." That is, of their own distinguished forbears. The giants of the oncoming era were to be, rather, descendants of those stolid countrymen from Campi and Certaldo and Figghine, whose barnyard aroma, it appears, offended supercilious Ghibelline nostrils, who caused them such a snobbish dismay.

CHAPTER II

AND already the first one of these new men had been born, or if not would be very shortly; his low plebeian origin being made even more base by the smirch of bastardy, though it was, as far as we can determine, from his disgraced and unknown mother that he derived most of that distinction of character which made possible all that he was later to achieve. He would reserve subsequently somewhat of a place for himself in the hall of fame of men's lips, but considerable time was to elapse after Henry's demise in a Sienese monastery, before he would be anything but a squalling and presumably unwanted brat.

At about the time that Henry was chosen and crowned, a young Florentine merchant departed from Tuscany for Paris. He was from Certaldo, one of the very towns despised by Dante, a cluster of red brick houses on a windy hilltop overlooking the main road that runs south from Florence through the Val d'Elsa, whose product and whose symbol, as enshrined in a white field on its coat of arms—was the onion. But members of his family had been settled in the city by the Arno since the end of the last century, and he himself had probably done business nowhere else. Now, however, either times were bad or competition was too hard, so he became one of those Florentine financial adventurers who were swarming all over Europe like a plague of locusts, and some of whom like the famous "Monsieur Mouche"—the Musciatto Franzese of the first story

of the *Decameron,* who from penniless vagrant became coun-
selor to the King of France—were amassing much power and
gold.

The details of his voyage are not known. He was accompanied by his brother Vanni and presumably they took one
of the two or three conventional routes. By road to Pisa and
from there by boat to Porto Venere or Genoa. Along the
sharp jagged Ligurian Riviera. Along the French Riviera.
Past La Tourbie, that town set on a pinnacle which is so well
known to the modern tourist—Dante's Turbia, "that most deserted, most tumultuous ruin" which inspired one of that clear-
writing poet's more amazing descriptions. Along the white
Provençal seacoast to Marseilles, just as to-day crowded with
masts and shipping. Up to Avignon, "the western Babylon,"
home of exiled Papacy, "windy" and clangorous with bells.
Up the Rhône valley to Lyons, swelling and industrious, its
silk looms even then spinning busily. And so north.

With good weather and with good luck, the voyage could
be accomplished in some twenty-two days. That is, if there
were no undue gales, no undue hail storms and snow storms.
That is, if the poor roads, badly graded and tortuous, hardly
repaired, except in stretches, since the days of the Romans,
had not been carried away into a nearby ravine by floods and
torrents. That is, if the engaging strangers who from time
to time joined the little party with its fat mules, its bales
and its money bags, and who entertained them with merry
stories or with sad stories, did not, when a lonely place was
reached, turn out to be brigands who robbed them and stripped
them. That is, too, if the castled barons under whose strong-
holds they passed did not decide that their treasuries, their
store rooms needed replenshing. For not every Fourteenth

Century voyage, it is needless to point out, was brought to a successful close.

At Paris, this young merchant quickly established himself. He found an apartment in the quarter reserved for the Lombards and Caorsini—men of Cahors—as all money changers of whatever nationality were contemptuously denominated. He set up his bench and started out in business. And he must have succeeded, which is not strange, for it was a good business, if you did not overstep yourself, and more especially if you kept in the good graces—which meant not being too pressing—of those in authority. Money is always needed. It was a simple matter of handing over hard, ringing money to those who required it. Of handing it over cheerfully and willingly, merely asking in return some small usance for it. Not a great deal when you considered the risks taken. Thirty per cent, let us say.

He did one other thing too . . .

Love is never very far from the mind of a Florentine. It comes to him with the fragrance of the acacias and the overburdening melody of the nightingale. It comes to him with the swift spring that leaps almost overnight from wet, gusty March to an April that is really a May strewn with flowers.

The young Florentine merchant fell in love. He became involved in an affair with one of those dark-eyed, provocative, and thoroughly feminine women of Paris, with whom, graceful and slender as cats, the city by the Seine was as well supplied then as now.

And it was not a platonic affair.

Presently a son was born, and the son was named Giovanni. The father's name being Boccaccio, the lad after the Florentine fashion was Giovanni di Boccaccio. Giovanni di Boccaccio del fu Chellino—Chellino being the defunct countryman grandfather—da Certaldo. Fame has simplified it, however,—fame which is impatient of long names and of many syllables. It was, then, as Giovanni Boccaccio that the future author of the *Decameron* was to go sounding down the years.

CHAPTER III

THAT, at any rate, is how we read the story, supplying —not too boldly, I think—certain of its lacunæ by the known laws of greatest probability. For there is, it must be confessed, a certain paucity of documents relating to Boccaccio's early days. Not so many, however, as to prevent his saga being told.

That Boccaccio Sr. was in Paris at the time, is indicated by an entry in a French *livre de la Taille* or tax book of the period, where, under the year 1313, one *"Boccasin lombart et son frère, changeurs"* are set down as having made payment. Their residence is given as opposite the church of Saint-Jacques-la-Boucherie at the corner of the Rue Pierre-au-Let and the Rue des Arsis. The elder Boccaccio's nickname of Boccaccino was sufficiently established to appear in legal documents and of this *Boccasin* is but the French form. It is hardly likely that another Italian of the same name would be engaged in the same business, approximately at the same time, especially as there is no record of such a person. His Paris sojourn is also known from the later writings of Giovanni himself. Describing in one of his Latin books the burning of the Templars and of their Grand Master, Jacques Molay, he concluded: "These things were related to me by Boccaccio, a worthy man and my own father, who told me that he was present when they took place." The two executions were carried out on a square of the French capital in May, 1310, and in March, 1314, respectively.

That his mother was a Frenchwoman was set forth by two earliest biographers. "The father of this man," wrote Filippo Villani, son and nephew of the two great Florentine chroniclers, "was Boccaccio, of Certaldo, a town in the Florentine territory, a man renowned for the decorousness of his morals, who while he dwelt in Paris in pursuit of business, since he was free and easy-going of disposition and gay of spirit, fell readily in love. And by indulgence of this nature of his he began to burn violently for a certain young Paris woman, in rank midway between the nobles and the citizens, to whom, as the admirers of Boccaccio's work assert, he was joined in lawful matrimony, from which union was born Giovanni." His father, said Domenico Bandino, was Boccaccio, "a man shrewd and extremely skilled in affairs" who while he dwelt in Paris for the purpose of trade "loved vehemently" a young woman of that city. "And her, as the admirers of Boccaccio state—*although far more common is another opinion*—he later made his wife. She bore him Giovanni."

The year in which that event took place is established by a letter in the hand of Petrarch. It was written on that poet's sixty-second birthday. "If you do not lie," he tells Giovanni, "and if following the custom of the young you do not rob yourself of several years, in the order of birth I preceded you by nine of them." Laura's poet, moreover, as the same epistle informs us, was born at dawn on July 20, 1304. Simple arithmetic, then, gives us the information that Boccaccio was born in 1313.

But it is not in documents so much as in the man's own writings that we have the story in its entirety. The tragic interlude of his French mother whose name Gianna or Jeanne we know from an anagram in his first romance, the *Filocolo,* and who is believed to have been of the semi-noble family of

De la Roche, seems to have fascinated Giovanni. Again and again he referred to it. Sometimes in an allusion. Sometimes in an allegorical relation. Once at least he gave the account with something rather close to directness, although in that instance the names and places were changed very thoroughly. It was as if its mystery appealed to all the romantic elements in the character of this writer of such vivid realism. It is certain, too, that he liked to imagine that from this shadowy person who brought him into the world somehow a superior strain had been introduced into his blood. For democratic as he essentially was, he was never quite happy in his mind about his rustic Certaldese origin.

It is in the *Decameron* that the story is told most straightforwardly. There Fiordaliso, the Sicilian damsel "who was very handsome, but disposed for a small matter to do any man's pleasure" gives this account to her prospective victim, the young horse-trader Andreuccio da Perugia: "Pietro, my father and thine, as I doubt not thou knowest, abode long in Palermo, and there for his good humor was and yet is greatly beloved of all those who knew him; but among all his lovers, my mother who was a lady of gentle birth and then a widow, was she who most affected him, insomuch that laying aside the fear of her father and brethren, as well as the care of her own honor, she became so private with him that I was born thereof and grew up as thou seest me. Presently having occasion to depart Palermo and return to Perugia, he left me a little maid with my mother, nor ever after, for all I could ever hear, remembered him of me or her; whereof were he not my father I should blame him sore, having regard to the ingratitude shown by him to my mother (to say nothing of the love it behooved him to bear to me as his daughter, born to him of no serving wench or woman of mean extraction) who had, moved by very faithful love, without in anywise knowing who he might be, committed into his hands her possessions and herself no less. . . .

"*Ma Che!*" concludes the plausible prostitute philosophically. "Things ill done and long time passed are easier blamed than mended. However, so it was."

A similar account—more poetic in form, but also with a greater fidelity to what actually happened—is given by Idalagos in the latter part of the *Filocolo*. Idalagos, it may be pointed out, it is agreed to by virtually every student of the man, is one of the numerous names used by Boccaccio throughout his writings to designate himself.

Eucomos—Boccaccio, the elder—a shepherd dwelling in that part of "fruitful Italy" which the ancients, "and not undeservedly" called Tuscia, was watching over his flocks, when he was called to that country which is described as "near enough those waves toward which the horses of Apollo, having passed the meridian circle, with great eagerness hasten, both to quench their thirst and to find repose." Thither he went, and "the gentle herds of Franconarcos, king of the white country," having been placed in his charge, he watched over them "with greatest care."

But it so happened, says Idalagos, that Franconarcos had many fair daughters, and one of them Gannai—Gianna or Jeanne—Eucomos saw as he was sounding his flute in the woody grove. With her promptly he fell in love.

And to fall in love with her was to try to win her. Using his music as a lure he persuaded her to follow him to a part of the grove far away from her sisters.

"And seeing her there, it seemed to Eucomos time to discover her his long desire, so changing his music to true and sweet words, he laid bare his love to her; to which words he added deceits and promises, and he commenced to show her how gracious it would be in the sight of the gods if she should put his desire into effect, because he felt toward her the same sentiments that her father had felt toward her mother. Gannai at first wondered and then was afraid, fearing perhaps that he would serve himself by force if his fair words and his promises did not avail; but then, harkening to his wiles, simple-minded, she believed in him, and solely on his own pledge she put faith in the wretch; so that as to her mother had been her father so he was to her; and in the deep valley she consented to his pleasure; as a result of which two sons were born to her of which I was one. And the name which they gave me was Idalagos."

Another Boccaccio character to tell in different words the same story is Ibrida. His account, given in the *Ameto,* is a little more specific perhaps. For he describes his mother as a young and comely widow; he says that her home is by "the pleasant waves of the Seine."

And in her instance the seducer is quite as plainly recognizable as the young Certaldese merchant. This time he is described as the son of Tritolomeo, "a plebeian man of no renown," dedicated to the service of Saturn—possibly farming—and of "an unlettered nymph." His birthplace is half way between Fiesole and Siena. "Almost half way between Coritus and the land, home of the nurse of Romulus." His career is business. Like Eucomos he makes promise of marriage, and it is then and then only that his desires are yielded to.

Nor in either case did the marriage ever transpire.

"But no long time elapsed after we were born," said Idalagos, "before abandoning the foolish girl and the flocks too, he returned to his own country; and he took us with him; and not far from his natal site, the faith promised to Gannai, to another called Garamirta he promised and gave; from whom in a short time he received new offspring."

"But my father," said Ibrida, "as though, unworthy of such a consort, he were drawn thither by the fates, occupied himself in breaking the oaths sworn and the promises made; and the gods, not caring whether or not they lost the faith of so low a man, with loosened reins allowed him to do this, reserving their vengeance for another time; and that which my mother truly was, he made falsely of another in his native land."

It was thus, then, in the guise of fiction but none the less lucidly that the romancer informed us of those occurrences which brought him into being. For if Ibrida's narrative needs no interpretation whatsoever, that given by Idalagos is hardly less apparent. The "white country" near the setting sun is France; Franconarcos is, at least figuratively, the French monarch; Gannai, that elusive and probably pretty and vivacious Parisienne who happened to be his mother.

Yet for all that it is not safe to deduce therefore that this person was a French princess, or even further, as one modern Italian has ingeniously done, to "prove," that he was the missing Prince John, son of the Countess Jeanne, wife of the King's son Philip, then Count of Poitiers. After all the story is poetical and in real life Boccaccio's father was not a shepherd. It is enough that his French birth is established, or better yet confirmed. It is sufficient that it is indicated that his mother was of slightly better rank than he.

And beside being enough, it is, too, very singularly appropriate.

For in all Boccaccio ever wrote, there was a most evident fusion of these, his two mighty heritages. To the Ciceronian cadences of his almost Latin prose was added the robustious-

ness and the full-bloodedness of Rabelais. To a Vergilian
sensitiveness to the grave classic outlines of his fair country was
added the wisdom, sharp yet a little sententious, of Montaigne.
To the satire of Juvenal and the warmth and the color of Ovid,
the slightly sad humorousness of Molière. In respect to an
Italian, the latter quality was especially an exotic one. Humor,
more particularly humor of that suave, urbane sort that turns
its sharp edge against its own user, as did so much of Boccaccio's, has never, truly, been part of the Italian equipment.
The light, sword-bladed touch seems, in classic times, to have
come from Attica. And in more modern days—whether its
users be Boccaccio and Goldoni or the present-day Alfredo
Panzini—its inspiration has almost inevitably come from Gaul.

CHAPTER IV

THE exact date of Boccaccio Sr.'s return to Florence is a matter that has never yet been settled, and with it the corollary problem of the return of young Giovanni. Did the man of account books make a hasty, back-door exit when his irregularly born son appeared in the world? Did he take Giovanni with him? Or was the baby, black-eyed and swarthy of skin like the squirming *bambini* which you see even to-day on the backs of flat-footed and broad-hipped country-women in the city of the lilies, brought along later by Florentine friends of the father—perhaps when the abandoned mother had died miserably of loneliness and hurt pride? Or did Boccaccino himself remain in Paris for another four or five years? These questions have not yet been finally answered. There is little reason to suppose they ever will be.

Boccaccio's own comments on this subject are extremely limited. "Fair lady, and sole fire of my mind," Caleone tells Fiammetta in another episode of the *Ameto,* "I, born not far from the place where your mother had her origin, sought out the Etrurian lands while a boy, and from there, having reached a more mature age, came hither." "I will follow the order of the alphabet," wrote Boccaccio in his Latin dictionary *De fluminibus,* "and place at the head of this long line the Arno. And this not only because it merits the place by reason of the order of the letters, but also because it is the river of my fatherland and was known to me before all others, even from my very infancy."

19

Literal-minded scholars have shown a conflict between these two statements, each of which refers to a slightly different period of life, while their over-finicky brethren have piled document on top of document, illustrative of just when, according to the medieval mind, *infanzia* ended, *puerizia* began. But while definition is valuable, to carry either of these approaches too far is to show extreme and really damning lack of imagination. For neither passage is, after all, an excerpt from a diary. It is possible that Boccaccio himself did not know exactly when he had been taken to the Tuscany of his forebears; that he knew only that his memory did not extend to a time when his outlook had been other than the streets and bridges of Florence; that his whole connection with Paris was merely something that had been told to him; that he was Florentine from the beginning of his conscious life.

And this thesis is certainly borne out by the only clear document bearing on the subject. In the Florentine archives a petition still exists carrying the date of October, 1318. In it Boccaccio di Chellino and his brother Vanni claim exemption from certain assessments in the communes of Certaldo and Pulciano on the ground that they have been residents of Florence "for four years and more." By those who prefer to believe that Boccaccino reached Florence somewhat later, it is pointed out that it would have been perfectly legal for Vanni to have made this claim on behalf of the firm even if he alone were actually in Florence, and it has also been noted that while mentions of Boccaccino are frequent in Florentine records from 1317 on, none occur in 1314, 1315, or 1316. However, no firm of "the sons of Chellino da Certaldo" has as yet been shown to have existed, and as for the second point, it could be accounted for simply by the increasing prominence and importance of Giovanni's father.

The city to which he returned bore little resemblance to the Florence of the late Nineteenth and early Twentieth Centuries. Far from being a safe paradise for near-sighted and sentimental old lady tourists with their dangling eye-glasses and their always open guide books, far from being a sleepy museum of dead beauty, it throbbed with the nervous energy of the energetic commercial era which followed so swiftly on the slow heels of the Middle Ages. Like the England of a half century later which has been so vividly described in the spirited and pictorial narrative poetry of Geoffry Chaucer, it was characterized by movement and activity. Mysticism, and at least professed unworldliness were swept aside, or trampled aside by the strong onrush of worldly realism. And the Florentines rose thereby. For the quick, active Florentine spirit, never very much at home in the Cretan labyrinths of subtilizing theology, at last found its own.

The criterion was money. "He who to-day has none is rated as an animal," declared one of the early novel writers. "And he who has most is acknowledged the most worthy. Therefore it is wise for every man not only to save what he has but to add to it what he can." Pope Boniface VIII twenty years earlier already judged Florence the fountainhead of wealth. "I have sent you thither," he wrote Charles of Valois. "It is your fault if you have not quenched your thirst." There should be something rather familiar about these words to modern Americans, especially in these post-war days of treaty revisions and complicated debt settlements. Nor did the Florentines appear to resent their implication. Rather they took very great pride in them, and strove to make them incontestably true.

And with amazing success. The wars against the emperor had been extremely costly and the new wars that followed them were hardly less so. Furthermore it was at exactly this period in her history that Florence received two of her most crushing defeats. She had prisoners to ransom, mercenaries to hire, captains to salary. Worse than that, at the Florentines' own invitation, a series of dictators fastened themselves on the city. The first of these, Lando of Gubbio, "a man bloodthirsty and cruel," cost them less in money than in ferocity, but the civilized Duke of Calabria, only son of King Robert of Naples, consumed nearly half a million florins in the first year of his signory. And accomplished nothing.

Yet in spite of all these drains it was precisely at this time that Florence attained her prosperity. Marauding brigand-like soldiery imperiled but could not arrest the inward flow of raw materials, the outward flow of the finished products, the final inward return of the reward therefor. Her merchants—as the story of Boccaccio's father shows as well as any other—were everywhere. Her merchandise reached the Orkney Islands, reached Iceland, reached the Sea of China. Her florins could be seen in Muscovy, in Syria, in North Africa. Her letters of credit were known to the Grand Khan of the Tartars. And at home under the bright dazzling Italian sun, in the crooked, unpaved or roughly cobbled streets, under the brown somber spanning arches, there was continual activity Wheels were turning industriously. New shop after new shop was being opened. Glittering, golden money was being stamped. There is one further evidence of her ample wealth. The chroniclers of the period record little of the raw, almost Communistic discontent which was to break out in England under the leadership of John Ball and Wat Tyler, and although there is plenty of evidence that the city swarmed with beggars, cadgers, and other "poor wretches" it does not tell the whole story simply to put this down to Italian or at least Latin indifference to social misery as so many Nordic writers smugly do. Noting the hypocritical, pseudo-religious whining of these beggars, it is at least equally plausible to say that they lived by charity because they were too shiftless to do anything else, and to attribute the fact that in Florence all internal discord rose from a battle for power rather than from class unrest to the other fact that, for all who wished it, a livelihood could be obtained for work.

At the head of all this were the two great Woolen Guilds—the Arte di Calimala and the Arte di Lana. They controlled most of the wealth and nearly all of the political power. The constitution of the Arte di Calimala is still extant. It makes an interesting commentary on the temper of the times.

Leading off, were a series of pious professions. The members engaged not to blaspheme God or the saints. They promised to keep all the feast days, of which, Sunday excluded, there were forty every year. Every morning, at the members' expense, monks said masses for the Guild in the church of San Giovanni. On St. John's Day, every member of the guild offered a half pound candle to the city's patron saint. And besides this there was a series of strict rules of conduct, designed to prove the guild's altruistic and virtuous character. Usury was forbidden "because it displeased God," and fortunes and profits were at least theoretically limited. Gambling was not allowed in the booths of the merchants, only chess and checkers being permitted. No women were allowed in the shops. No persons living in buildings belonging to the guild were allowed to leave them after the third hour of the night.

Yet none of the above many provisions caused the hardheaded Florentine wool-merchants to lose sight of the essential purpose of their organizations, and by far the greater part of the constitution dealt with the rules of business procedure. The machinery for the government of the guild—the election of

consuls, priors, chamberlains and so forth—was carefully provided for, and it was arranged on the Florentine theory that
only by elaborate checks and counterchecks could official
honesty be made sure of. The very employees were governed
by an exacting code. No apprentice or artisan could loiter
around the shops looking for work, and the same persons were
compelled, if employed outside of Florence, to return to the
city to settle accounts with their master. No apprentice could
marry outside of the city without special permission, under
pain of being banished and having his goods sold. If an
apprentice, declared a curious section, entered a religious order
with money or property of his master, the order was obliged
to restore the same. The penalty was an effective one. Any
order failing to do so was cut off from a source of multitudi-
nous blessings. It was deprived of future charities.

This great guild, however, with its thriving adjuncts such as
the dyers, clippers, stretchers and dressers, each plying its trade
on a street bearing its own name, was strictly limited in its
business. Only foreign cloth could be handled. Far more
voluminous was the trade carried on by the second woolen
guild, the Arte di Lana, which lorded it over the other merchants of the town from its home—even to-day picturesquely
standing with its slant overhanging roof, barred windows, and
its device of a crowned sheep—in the *canonica* of the Or' San
Michele. Its business was to make rather than finish cloth,
and it was allowed to import only raw material. "Ultramon-
tane"—in other words, non-Italian—cloth could not be dealt in.
But the Arte di Lana did not suffer thereby, being rich enough
to import sacks of wool from England, Spain and "Algarvie"
or Portugal. And some idea of its immense size can be gained
from the pages of the elder Villani. In 1338, he says, twenty
shops of the Arte di Calimala, imported 10,000 pieces of cloth,

having a value of 300,000 florins. In the same year, the Arte di Lana maintained two hundred shops which manufactured 80,000 pieces of cloth, having a value of 1,200,000 florins, and gave employment to 30,000 of the city's approximately 100,000 inhabitants. This, he pointed out, was a hundred shops and 20,000 pieces of cloth less than thirty years previously. "But those," he added, "were coarser, and of only half the value, since in those days they did not know how to import and work with cloth from England."

It was around these two bodies—with a third, the Bankers' Guild, the Arte del Cambio, and perhaps a fourth, the Silk Guild—that the city's seething activity had its being. They it was who were responsible for the mighty influx of prosperity. And around them the lesser trades and the professions grew and flourished, having as their chief cause for existence their wealthy merchants and their well-off employees' desires and needs.

Many indeed were these latter. At their head were the doctors and lawyers stuffed with the pedantries of Pisa and Bologna and sometimes even Paris, though the latter's specialty was theology; proud and haughty in their robes trimmed with vair and their wide cowls; jealous of their right, shared with the knights, to head wedding processions. Then there were the notaries, the mercers, and the apothecaries. Then there were the barbers, in whose hands was such minor surgery as dentist work and bleeding. The butchers with their stalls in the Mercato Vecchio, and their proud boast when, as often, they were haled before the authorities for some disturbance, that "they fed the people." The inn-keepers with their sour wine and their dirty bed-linen. The second-hand dealers. The shoemakers. The wood and stone workers. The same chronicler we have just cited records three hundred shoemakers and one hundred and forty-six master wood and stone workers at about this time. Then too there were the rough, sturdy countrymen who drove their sheep and cattle into the city, clad in a gray jerkin drawn about the waist with a leather belt, without cloak and often without trousers. There were the millers, proverbial for their red faces. their white, dusty clothing, their dishonesty.

There were other groups of citizens too, less useful and in many cases actually demoralizing. The idle, foppishly dressed sons of hard-working fathers, whose pride it was that they did nothing useful, and who had only time to quarrel senselessly among themselves, play crude practical jokes, and set horns upon their more industrious neighbors. Sacchetti relates how one of these young men was fined 1000 *lire* for riding with spurred legs out-thrust through the narrow, crooked streets so as to block insolently all pedestrians. He also tells how a group of the same played a merry jest upon one Maccheruffo de' Maccheruffi of Padua. The latter came to Florence as *podestà*, "and since with his cowl and loose robes," he seemed more a doctor than a knight, they left outside his door a collection of a certain sort of lowly domestic vessel filled with that which even nowadays doctors are wont to analyze. Maccheruffo took his revenge in the same hearty fashion. He caused the offending vessels to be nailed up in the great hall of his palace, and then summoning the principal men of the city, told them coldly that they had judged him aright, and he would indeed be a doctor to their ills. He next made investigation as to who were the malefactors of the city, feeling that among their number would be his scoffers. "And he then commenced, now one as a thief, now two as murderers, now three or four as users of cogged dice to dispatch them to another world. And in short he hanged so many, and beheaded and otherwise

executed so many, that at the end of his office he left so healed
and cured a city that it rested very well for a very long time."
There were also the street singers, ballad writers, and jugglers.
Likewise the piazza priests, equivalent approximately to the
Holy Rollers and revivalists of to-day. Finally there were
those, sad sordid ladies of pleasure whom no pious law-making
can regulate out of existence. At about this time Florence by
city ordinance did away with them, only to find that they still
had their being as numerously and more of a menace than
ever, only to have enough wisdom to repeal an unwork-
able law.

It was, then, amid such surroundings, that Giovanni passed
his early and formative years. Florence it was that began the
slow shaping of his character, and however distasteful her mer-
cantile point of view was to be to the full-fledged man of letters,
she gave to him certain qualities which he was never to lose.
Not such bad qualities either, and to him extremely important
ones. Very Florentine for example was his direct way of looking at things, which was to control and to make convincing
and real even the most romantic of his writings. Florentine,
too, was the strong sense of independence which practically
no student of Boccaccio has failed to observe in him. Florentine was his resoluteness and obstinacy, that dogged single-
mindedness of purpose which enabled even a man of such
exaggerated modesty and unnecessary self-depreciation as he
turned out to be, to hold unswervingly to his elected vocation
in spite of all obstacles and all opposition.

And we know pretty well too just how Florence did her
work on him. Here, as often elsewhere, details are lacking.
But the broad, essential outlines we possess.

When his father came back from Paris, he was no longer an
obscure, if ambitious, young man. He must have made his

mark in the French capital, or at least acquired the name of
a man of some ability. For in 1318 we note him in partnership
with Simone Orlandini and with Cante and Jacopo di Amma-
nati in what appears to have been a paying business. And in
1322, so some would believe, he headed the *signoria,* although
it is more probable that he was simply one of the five consuls
of the Bankers' Guild. Either position had a certain prominence. Similar offices were held by the father of Boccaccio in
1324 and 1326, the indications all being that he was a man
heading rapidly for success.

As a result of this, he was, among other things, able to give
his son the best education that the period offered, and for a
time it appears that he did so. To study the *grammatica*
young Boccaccio was sent to Giovanni da Strada, father of the
poet Zanobi whose time-serving propensities were to annoy him
so in his later years. That, in the parlance of the time, designated Latin, and the text-books from which he tortured out the
conjugations and learned to decline nouns were the Psalter and
the *Metamorphoses* of Ovid. Shortly, however, the materialistic spirit of the money-minded banker rebelled at such time-
wasting nonsense, and his son's days of schooling were over.
Merchandising—the pursuit of business—was, after all, the only
career. It was not recorded that "Homer left any great fortune." The verb *amo* wrote no bills of exchange. So he took
the boy from his Latin and set him to the more useful study
of *arismetrica.* This was preparatory to employing him in
the bank.

But even this change made little difference, for it was not in
what he learned from books—though later, to be sure, he was
to be erudite indeed—that Giovanni was to find that from
which he would win renown. It was in what his eyes saw,
his ears heard, he noticed all about him. It was in the jostling

street life, with its haughty knights, its rude tradespeople, its vermin-covered lazars. Later on Boccaccino was to acquire a suburban house in the pleasant village of Corbignano, but at that time he occupied one of the bare, dark, drafty tenements, —such in those days were even the homes of the rich,—in the city quarter of San Pier Maggiore, which was located west of Santa Reparata, now the Duomo. Moving from there to the bank where the young boy was undoubtedly welcome, he would rub shoulders with the Florentine people high and low, with the "strange fish" he was later to make his stories of.

Giotto, "so excellent of genius that there was nothing of all which Nature, mother and mover of all things, presents to us by the ceaseless revolution of the heavens, but he with pencil and brush and pen depicted it," but who was often so shabby of appearance that he seemed a peasant, had not yet begun his campanile. He was in Florence from time to time, however, and the boy probably saw him. Bruno and Buffalmaco, the merry painters, who thought nothing at all of pitching a worthy, if simple-minded fellow citizen into the public sewers by way of jocularity, or of stealing and eating a pig belonging to a friend in the sheer spirit of merriment, were at the height of their glory. If he did not know them, they must, surely, have been pointed out to him. The medicines of Messer Simone da Villa, "richer in inherited wealth than in learning," with his house "in the street which we nowadays call Via del Cocomero"—Street of the Watermelon —may have aggravated some of his boyhood ailments. Monna Nonna da Pulci who confounded the *popolano* Bishop of Florence with her witty retort was still living. He would hear men talking who had known Guido Cavalcanti, that eloquent and morose friend of Dante, bitter and unsociable, whose only occupation, the common people firmly believed, was "seeking to prove God is not." To his father's bank came men from all over the world. They would tell him the story of Ser Ciapelletto, that prince of cozeners who was so dishonest that "he thought it very great shame when any of his documents was found other than false" yet who died true to his faith of trickery and was buried as a saint. Or of Bernabo of Genoa who was duped by Ambrogiuolo into believing in his wife's infidelity. From this he was to write a tale that would give Shakespeare the plot for "Cymbeline" and so win immortality in two tongues.

Nor was it only in Florence that he began to see and to observe.

There is no reason to suppose that his family lost touch completely with Certaldo. At a much later period his father still owned land there, some of which was inherited by Boccaccio. And the descriptions of the River Elsa, whose waters form a deposit of stone on any object immersed therein, and of Certaldo, with its fossilized sea shells, which occur in a number of his writings, seem to record an impression made in early childhood. Thither, then—to this country town which bred his forebears—it is not, surely, too bold to assume that at least holiday excursions were made.

So that it was then perhaps that he first saw his model for Fra Cipolla—Brother Onion—that gay fraud, "little of person, red-haired and merry of countenance, the jolliest rascal in the world" with his fine talk and his feathers of the Angel Gabriel. And the parish priest of Varlungo—"a worthy priest, and lusty of his person in the service of the ladies." And Mistress Belcolore, the "jolly, buxom country wench, brown-favored, and tight-made"—in the Boccaccian phrase "as apt at turning the mill as any woman alive." And if so, he noted them and remembered them, for like most men of literary ability, there was little he ever saw which he forgot. And added them without realizing it to that retentive storehouse from which later he was to fish out the *dramatis personæ* for an immense, full-blown human comedy which was possibly to surpass the divine.

It was at this time, too, that his whole future course was decided on. "For I plainly enough remember," he wrote in his later days, "that before I had reached the age of seven; before I had set my eyes on any of its created works; before I went to school, and when I hardly knew even the rudiments of the alphabet, my nature was urging me to invent, and although none of them were of any worth, yet did I begin to produce trifling poems." Nor is it entirely unaccountable when you consider that he lived in a city where it is recorded that Dante heard a blacksmith intoning some of his verses as his hammer clanged on his anvil, and later met a humble ass-driver who was singing words of his—interposing to be sure an irreverent *"Arri!,"* "Gee there!," but none the less singing them—as he drove along his ass.

None of these poems have survived for us, but it is of no moment, for Boccaccio's estimate of them was probably the correct one.

The impulse did survive, however. Poverty was to assault it. Parental disapproval was to assault it. Lack of self-confidence was to assault it. Yet it was to stand firm. Boccaccio said that "Nature drew him from his mother's womb" already a poet. Even against his own wish to reform himself which in middle age made the last attack against his career, he was to be a poet until the day he died.

CHAPTER V

THERE is one other episode relating to the youth of Boccaccio which must here be made note of. Possibly in the determination of his character it was more important than any other thing that happened to him. For early indeed it forced him on his own resources, and in consequence his childhood had none of those sheltered and idyllic qualities which we like to think should by right belong to that time when the young mind, like the young muscles, lacks steel and iron, is immature and sensitive. There is a well-held theory that genius is little more than the product of unhappiness working on a fine mind at just that critical period. If it is correct, the genius of Boccaccio was formed, certainly, in an orthodox manner. For unhappy that part of his life indisputably was.

The event referred to was his father's marriage which took place, as has already been implied, not long after Boccaccino's return from Paris. The exact date cannot be established. It is known only that the elder Boccaccio became a married man not later than 1320, and that between the woman he wedded and his already begotten son there was never anything but enmity. And since she was a grown woman and he but a boy it is easy to read what transpired.

Yet of her we know really very little. Her name was Margharita, whence the Garamirta of the allegory. She was the daughter of Gian Donata de' Martoli. She brought Boccaccino a good amount of money and was perhaps—no, almost prob-

ably—of a better family than he. Some, further, have supposed
she was the model for the bitter portrait of "Madame So-and-
So, daughter of the So-and-So's" drawn by Boccaccio in his
last work of Italian fiction, *Il Corbaccio*. There is no proof
of this, however, and there is much reason to believe that
another was intended. On the other hand there is little question that many of that lady's unattractive qualities must have
been suggested to him by his memories of his stepmother.
When he set down in vitriol those ladies "come like swift and
ravenous wolves to devour the substance of their husband," he
must surely have been thinking of Margharita. When he made
note of their "dashing hither and thither, in continual noisy
quarrels with the servants, the maids, the factors, the brothers,
the very sons of their husbands," his mind must have run back
to the days of his boyhood; his mind must have run back to
his father's first wife.

But it was not until the union bore fruit that the life of
Giovanni became really intolerable. Whenever the marriage
took place, this occurred in either 1320 or 1321, and the boy born
was named Francesco. Then Margharita's dislike of Giovanni
which was at first presumably merely instinctive and sentimental found something practical to augment it. He was no
longer merely an annoyance, but an actual menace. And it
was her son's well-being that Giovanni menaced. It was her
son's food that he was eating. Worse than that it was her
son's lawful inheritance that he would one day divide.

So she seems definitely to have set out to get rid of him,
using those feminine weapons of unswerving and aggressive
tenaciousness, and of utter indefatigable lack of reasonableness
that must have been, in the crowded medieval circumstances,
even more effective than they are to-day. On the one hand, as
we suppose, by a continuous and nagging attack on her hus-

band. On the other hand, as it is recorded, by making each
day of young Giovanni's life increasingly miserable, by
oppressing him in all the thousand ways available to her until
one day he could stand it no more.

This last phase he describes for us himself.

"I, trusting and ignorant," says the same Idalagos we have
already listened to, "following, as I have already said, the footsteps of my deceitful father, and wishing one day to enter the
paternal home, saw before me two fierce and savage bears who,
with eyes burning savagely, greatly did desire my death. And
fearing this, I turned back my footsteps, and from then on was
forever afraid to enter the place. And to tell the truth so great
was my fear that it was for that reason that I came to these
woods to carry on my learned trade."

As can be seen, of course, once again there is allegory. It
goes without saying that there has been, too, once again the
vast confusion of efforts to make it literal and to give exactness
to it. Who were the two bears? Margharita and Francesco?
Margharita and his father? Vast flood-gates of ink have been
unloosed on this subject; sharp critical shafts—not always without venomed tips—have been shot back and forth, and the
question has not yet been solved.

It is of little importance;—what is important being simply to
show that the childhood of Boccaccio was colored by this
thing, and to determine why it took place.

And to do even the latter is extremely simple. It is, as has
already been indicated, the old and very human story of the
mother who preferred her own child to the child of a stranger.

"And Sarah," runs the story in *Genesis*, "saw the son of
Hagar, the Egyptian, which she had borne unto Abraham,
mocking. Wherefore, she said unto Abraham, Cast out this
bondswoman and her son: for the son of this bondswoman

shall not be heir with my son, even with Isaac. And the thing was grievous in Abraham's sight because of his son."

Nor can we be too harsh on Margharita even if we admit all the recorded stridencies.

History may have been unjust to Boccaccino and certainly he was far kinder to his writer son that it has pleased most of the latter's biographers to make record of. But he was a man whose mind moved him toward a single objective, that of acquiring money, and such are not easy to live with.

And suppose she did ply him with her wrangling jealousies. "Well enough do I know how you love me! I would be blind if I did not realize that some one else was in your mind far more often than I am! I know who you go tagging after all day long! I have better spies than you think I have!"

After all, there was young Giovanni as a living evidence of the fact that his father's path had not always been the correct one. We are not to suppose that Margharita was a remarkable person, or even that she was maligned or badly treated by the vindictive pen of her stepson. Nevertheless, the life of a woman of the Middle Ages was hard and disappointing, and not one to develop great width and magnanimity of character.

And even to-day it is not always easy for a wife of however great tolerance to have before her continually a living reminder that her husband is liable to stray.

CHAPTER VI

IN the fall of 1327—some time, as has now been established, between the first of September and the latter part of November—Boccaccino, the father of Boccaccio, removed himself to Naples. It was not, however, as he had gone to Paris some seventeen years previously that he made the long journey southward. For although there is absolutely no evidence that he brought Margharita with him or in any way regarded his Neapolitan sojourn as likely to prove permanent, he was no longer a young opportunist, backed solely by his own daring and his own resources.

The shrewd man from Certaldo had made excellent use of the years which had elapsed since his return from the French capital. Among other things he had succeeded in ingratiating himself with the powerful Florentine house of Bardi, which like the Medici of a century and a half later, like the Fuggers and the Rothschilds, like the present-day Morgans, had grown too rapidly to be confined within the narrow limits of its own soil, and now straddled the world, a huge giant of international finance. The Bardi, it appears, were not wholly satisfied with the results shown by Bentivegna di Buonsostengno, their chief Neapolitan representative. Possibly they wanted younger and more energetic qualities. At any rate they appointed "Bulcatius de Certaldo," as he is termed in various Neapolitan documents, now a man in his middle forties, to be associated with the former as head of their big branch in the swollen southern city. Outside of an actual partnership in this or one of the other big banking houses in Florence, it was as important a position as existed in the Fourteenth Century financial world.

Giovanni, as we think, accompanied him. This cannot definitely be proven, and a literal interpretation of those allegorical passages in his own writings which throw greatest light on this period might lead to the conclusion that the boy did not leave Florence for another year. In that event, we can assume that the practical business man made up his mind that it was better to wait until he saw how his own affairs were going before having his son make such an extended and difficult trip. The boy came, as he himself relates to us, "by way of gracious mountains" which we take to be the green hills lifting up around Siena; under "peaks savage and alpine and cold"— those of the Abruzzi; across "wide and fertile plains"— Campania; through "many famous cities"—Perugia, Aquila, Sulmona, Capua; across "many streams"—the Tiber, "filled with gentle waves," the swift turbulent Volturnus which swept stones before it in rapid course "until almost calm, between Falerno and Vesuvius, wearily it sought the sea."

His frame of mind, it can be hazarded, was a joyous one. The journey was, to be sure, hard and dangerous, and indeed just about the time he made this trip one of the agents of the very company his father represented had been murdered by brigands in the Apennines. But that probably would have seemed merely romantic and thrilling to a boy of thirteen or fourteen. And on one hand he was leaving behind him Florence and his hated stepmother. While on the other he was seeing the varied panorama of a good half of Italy unspread itself before him like a crowded roll of tapestry.

Whether or not he accompanied his father, it was toward the latter part of the year—though certainly not much later than the first of December—that he passed finally the dark wall of the Castello Capuana, halting there for a short time as the *doganieri* or customs officials of King Robert, themselves undoubtedly Florentines, went through the baggage of the party and exchanged gossip and news with the merchants. Then he rode in along the Via Capuana, a wide noisy artery which was lined with majestic palaces and boiling over with people on foot and on horseback, seeing thus for the first time, drenched in a golden sunlight which must have contrasted thrillingly with the raw Florentine autumn he had left behind, the magnificent city that sat queenlike under her circle of ancient hills, and that was to dominate and give her quality to the next dozen years of his life.

It was a good time to have arrived, for at last Naples was rising to her old time splendor. In the classic days, the Greek-Roman city of Parthenope or Neapolis had been the pleasure center of the rich world-wide empire. Poet and emperor, wheat speculator and mere idle man of pleasure had known equally her dazzling extravagance, and the whole ample circle of her shores from Baiæ, as it was then called, to Surrientum was dotted with white villas. She was the *"dulcis, otiosa Neapolis"*—the "sweet, lazy Naples"—where Virgil distilled the fragrant honey of his eclogues. St. Peter himself converted her to Christianity, and the great Constantine called her the fairest part of the empire after marching up and down and tasting nearly the whole world.

But with the downfall of the Romans, Naples drooped into a decrepit slumber. She did, to be sure, as a more or less free city under the nominal suzerainty of the Greek emperors, maintain a certain amount of commercial standing. But even in that she was far less important than Amalfi. And later her case became truly dire. The Saracens raided her. The Nor-

NAPLES

FROM A FIFTEENTH CENTURY WOODCUT

mans neglected her. The great Swabian house of Hohenstaufen maltreated her. Finally she was reduced to a state of actual misery and, worse than that, impotence when Conrad, son of the almost legendary Frederick II under whom the mighty German dynasty reached its apogee, in punishment for a rebellion reduced a large part of its walls.

But now under the French house of Anjou she was once more a glittering capital. Charles I was a simple count of Provence when he received the Pope's invitation to wipe out the royal line that was at once too modern for the Papacy and too medieval for the logical development of Italy. His wife, the only one of Raymond Berenger's four daughters not married to a king, pawned her jewels so as to become equal in rank to her sisters. Charles was victorious and he made Naples his seat of government. His son Charles II set about to beautify the city. When his grandson Robert was crowned at Avignon, the new dynasty had completed nearly a half century of rule. The Duomo had been rebuilt. The rich churches of San Lorenzo and Santa Chiara were rising among half a dozen others equally resplendent. A university had been founded. On the steep slopes of Forcera above the main town, and in the prosperous and fashionable sections of Nido and Capuana, great palaces and mighty hotels were rising. These were occupied by the powerful French barons who had ridden southward to the conquest, and by the old houses such as Capece, Carracciolo and Brancacci, descendants of the ancient *primati* or first men of the kingdom, none of whom had ever yielded to the Teuton "intruders," most of whom had gone into foreign exile after vainly helping the Normans defend their kingdom against invincible Germanic foes.

Of course the whole city had not risen above medieval squalor. *"La Napoli onorata finiva a li pendini,"* ran the saying. Honorable, or better still, respectable Naples does not reach below the hillsides. The lower city was a cesspool of actual and of human offal. There were narrow and tortuous alleyways, dark passageways, courts packed with ill-seeming and evil-doing inhabitants almost any one of which might have been the inspiration of Scarabone Buttafuoco, that almost stock-company stage villain, "a very masterful fellow with big, black bushy beard on his face" who would apparently quite cheerfully have "knocked" Andreuccio da Perugia "on the head," and "taken his life as well as his purse." Even the main streets were muddied with rain water and well water, while the piazzas near the main gates and even the principal churches "reeked of manure."

Moreover, disorders and crimes of violence were of daily occurrence. Not only were there annual riots at Christmas and during Carnival on the part of the students, whose throwing of stones and "other insolences" are noted in more than one Latin document. The sultry climate seemed to produce a fiery unreflective type of human animal that preferred to express its emotions, whether of love or hate, by direct action. Murders and rapes, therefore, were very frequent. Indeed so common were the latter that even the sage Ugo di Sanseverino, Count of Chiaramonte, a man "of vast intellect," scholar, lover of letters and philosophy, and would-be patron of Boccaccio in his old age, having become enamored of Lauretta, wife of Enrico della Marra, assailed the latter's castle of Trecchina by night, and having beaten and driven off the husband, carried her away. In fact so intolerable had grown this situation that the king was obliged to take cognizance of it, and in October, 1332, with the collaboration of the city's leading jurists, he drew up a series of stringent ordinances "against those Neapolitan malefactors who force virgins under the pretext of matrimony." It must, however, deplorably enough, be admitted, that of this earnest endeavor, there has been recorded no salutary effect.

That, however, was but one side of the multifarious Neapolitan life. As has been pointed out, the French dynasty which held sway was actually Provençal in origin. From that country of the troubadors came, then, all those gay highly colored diversions which the romantic-minded like to imagine were the only occupations of what we now call the age of chivalry. They hardly needed acclimatizing at all.

Chief among these were the tournaments and the jousting held at Carbonera, Castello Capuana, and Correge; and so popular were they that not only the barons of the realm took part in them but "in the year 1337, between January and May" King Robert himself six times *equitavit ad justras.* Through the lips of the heroine of his *Elegia di Madonna Fiammetta* which was Englished in the Elizabethan age under the more expressive title of "Amorous Fiammetta," Boccaccio describes these displays.

It was, says that lady, the ancient custom, at that time of the year "when the destructive blasts of winter were over, and the springtime with her flowers and new grass" had brought back to earth "all her vanished beauties" for the young men and the young ladies to meet together. The young ladies were decked out in their brightest jewels. The young men were mounted on fiery chargers "so passing swift in running" that "any other beast, yea the very winds themselves" in coursing, they would leave behind. On these they came prancing in, "clad in purple and in cloth woven by Indian hands out of various colors intermingled with gold, and embroidered over that with pearls and precious stones." Their horses were similarly caparisoned. "The blond locks hanging down over their shoulders" were bound "with a fine filament of gold" or gathered about their heads "with a little garland of green laurel." Each one carried on his left arm a light shield and in his right arm a mighty lance. At the "swift sound of the trumpets" each one "rode against the other" in a sort of maneuver, the purpose of which was to display their horsemanship. He was adjudged the most skillful "who keeping the point of his lance closest to the ground, and its shaft close to his shield" kept his seat without any awkward or ungraceful movements. After that there was actual encounter, with the victor crowned by the ladies. Memory of these tournaments must, however, have recalled to Boccaccio the sad ends of some of their participants. In the first ones that Giovanni witnessed, Charles, Duke of Calabria, King Robert's only son, carried off the honors. He died, hardly thirty, on a hunting trip in the mountains. In the later jousts, Charles, Duke of Durazzo, was the plumed knight. He was to be murdered by his cousin, Louis of Hungary, and his body cast into a ditch.

Seaside excursions to Baia were another popular diversion. There were, as the *Fiammetta* also points out, "a little beyond the pleasant hillside of Falerno, in the midst of old Cuma and of Pozzuoli, delightful bays set against the seashore," the situation of which was "so sweet and pleasing that their equal will not be found under heaven." These were surrounded "with fair hills all covered with trees of various sorts, in the valleys of which there are no kinds of wild beasts which can with pleasure be hunted that may not there be found." Not far distant was "a great plain filled with all sorts of game" such as could be taken by the kingly sport of falconry. Near at hand were "the islands of Pitacuse and Nitida, abounding in conies" and "the tomb of the great Mæcenas, leading to the kingdom of Pluto." There too were "the oracles of the

Cumæan Sybil, the Lake of Avernus, the theater where the ancients held their games, the hill Barbarus, and the vain works of the emperor Nero," all of which "although very ancient are new to the eyes of modern men and give great pleasure." And besides that there were "a multitude of health giving and refreshing baths," and the air "being very temperate and pleasant" afforded good opportunity for using them. There were—when the weather was hot—many idle excursions onto the limpid and pellucid waters in "swift boats winged with many oars" when "ploughing the marine undulations, sometimes singing, and sometimes playing various instruments," the gay Neapolitans went rowing up and down "seeking remote reefs" and "caverns hollowed out into the face of cliffs" which "because of the shadows and the winds were very cool." There were fishing expeditions when with "nets and with all manner of new devices" they sought to entrap the ocean's hidden inhabitants. There were suppers spread "on cloths of tapestry and arras" or set on tables on the sand. And after they had "with great feasts banqueted themselves," and after "the cloths being removed they had danced in their usual manner many gay-hearted rounds" often they reëmbarked and going hither and thither sought out secret places where sights "very dear to the eyes of young men" were discovered to them. "That is, many fair young ladies, stripped to their sleeveless underdresses of white satin, swimming in the cool water," or bending over "to gather shellfish from the hard rocks," and thus showing "the hidden delightsomeness of their swelling breasts."

The courts of love were another occupation of the noble part of Naples. They were held under the cool trees of the spacious gardens belonging to the royal palaces. One of these places has been vividly described. In the midst of it was a wide meadow "very fair with grass, and replete with sweet soft perfumes, around which were many enough handsome young trees, by the green and abundant leaves of which the whole place was protected from the rays of the great planet." In the midst of the meadow rose handsomely from the sward a fountain made of blood-red porphyry. It was decorated with feminine figures carved of common stone, of white marble, of black marble, and of green serpentine. Here, as in the other gardens of the city, were held receptions to the foreign ambassadors and other state affairs. Here jongleurs sang their songs and performed their amusing tricks. Here *istrioni* or mimes gave their comic performances. Here too were propounded and answered the questions of love which had been adopted from the Provençal *jeux partis* and made famous by Boccaccio in his *Filocolo:*

"Who is the more unhappy, a man who having tasted the pleasures of love, afterwards loses them, or one who deeply loving never attains to them?"

"Who is the better off, a lover who is not loved in return, or one who being loved in return is nevertheless jealous?"

"For a man's good which is better, that he fall in love or that he never fall in love?"

"Of two ladies which should be preferred, one more or one less noble than her lover?"

"Which is it better to fall in love with, a maid, a married woman, or a widow?"

But it was not only in such things—which did indeed show a city fully a hundred and fifty years ahead of Florence on the gay, pagan road to the Renaissance—that the lavish and expansive temper of the town was made manifest. Every detail of the Neapolitan life seemed to be carried out on the same colorful, extravagant scale, and the account books of the worthy merchants showed a series of advances both to the great nobles and the royal household. Boccaccio's father, for instance, in the short space of a few months paid over fifteen thousand dollars to the Duke of Calabria "for the expense of his household and the maintenance of his rooms." There is no reason, either, to suppose that this was the only money the Duke used. The wedding feasts were like Roman saturnalia, and indeed a list of the hens, lambs, capons, ducks, pigeons and other foodstuffs supplied for the marriage of Marie of Valois to the heir to the throne, and later when the future Queen Giovanna wedded Andrew of Hungary, read like the supplies for an army. Nor was personal expenditure less lavish, as was indicated by the great number of rings set with rubies, diamonds, and sapphires, gold garlands and crowns, golden cups, pearl-studded crystal vases, "small plates, ewers, salt-cellars, and perfume bottles" of silver, crosses and reliquaries of gem-studded gold, and unset pearls, diamonds, Samarcand rubies and sapphires left by King Robert's mother.

"So great was the luxury that Florentine, Lucchese and Genovese merchants furnished the court with scarlet cloth-of-Ghent, samite, damask broidered in the Oriental fashion, objects of gold and silver. There was a special merchant whose one function was to purchase gems and precious stones for the use of the royal household."

And this at a period when the so-called Dark Ages had not yet come to a close!

It was not, however, with this phase of the Neapolitan life that Giovanni made his first contacts. In that well-known autobiographical passage in the last book of the "Genealogy of the Gods" from which we have already quoted and which gives us, even if only in outline, a story of his early experiences, he tells us that before "he had even entered the period of youth" and when he "had acquired but some small knowledge of arithmetic," his father put him "as apprentice to a merchant of great consequence" with whom he did nothing "but waste irrecoverable time" for "nearly six years."

Who this merchant was is not known and the guesses plausibly hazarded include most of the business men of the kingdom. It is, however, very certain that the time spent in this unappealing calling coincided with his first years at Naples. Since we know that the Florentine men of affairs then occupied a whole quarter of the city—it was near the sea in the neighborhood of the Porta Nuova, and not far from where, below the noisy modern city, the vari-colored stacks of lean transatlantic liners and squat freighters from the Mediterranean islands are huddled together behind moles and breakwaters—and since we know also that Charles II had given "one of his exchanges" in the Ruga Cambinorum "near the Pietro del Pesce" in the same quarter of Naples to the house of Bardi, we can say pretty well how and where he passed that part of his life.

His duties were simple if exacting. On the one hand he was to stay at the bank, receive the clients, weigh gold and silver money on scales approved by the Master of the Zecca, or Mint, give change—bright *carlini* and handsome *gigliati* of silver; copper *tornesi*—take care of the correspondence, keep the books recording the purchases and sales. On the other hand he was to run errands and execute commissions which took him all over the city from the harbor to the heights, from Castel Nuovo where the king lived via the Rua Catalana to the foul hole of Malpertugio. According to the Florentine custom his father had pledged him to do faithfully and accurately whatever his master should require of him. The latter, on his part, promised to take care of the boy's ordinary needs; to furnish

him, as articles invariably stated, with those four indis-
pensables: namely, "food, clothing, shoes, and bed."

And for all that his position was modest rather than humble.
The son of a rich banker was not, then any more than now,
an ordinary beginner. "In case you do not know it, my
friend," he wrote Francesco Nelli many years later, "I lived
from boyhood until I was a grown man in Naples, and among
youths of noble blood who were of a suitable age. And they,
however noble, were not ashamed to enter my house or to pay
me visits. They saw me living in the manner of a man, not a
beast: well enough, as we Florentines have the manner of
living. They saw my house and my goods which, according
to my means, were very excellent indeed."

This passage, incidentally, is extremely important, not only
for the light that it throws on Boccaccio and on his way of
living, but for the light that it throws upon his father. It has
become the fashion to dwell scornfully on the latter, and to
point out how he both misunderstood and maltreated the son
he had begotten, on the one hand failing to recognize his
genius, on the other forcing him away from his natural line
of development into hateful and uncongenial tasks.

The first of these two opinions may be true, and if so it is not
surprising, for there is little that is less inspiring—and for that
matter less convincing—than a young writer who has yet his
work to do. His combination of arrogance and uncertainty
make a particularly unattractive form of adolescent awkward-
ness, and it is difficult to see just how such a person could
possibly impress a hard-headed and unimaginative man of
business—as Giovanni apparently tried to do—that if he were
"indulgent" to his son's "wishes," while yet the latter's mind
"was of an age to learn these things," the said son "would turn
out one of the world's famous poets."

Or for that matter that it would make any difference if he did so turn out.

The second, however, does the elder Boccaccio a distinct injustice. For although perhaps severe, and although certainly unsympathetic, Boccaccino never maltreated his son. During the early Neapolitan days, he kept the boy plentifully supplied with money, and even when, somewhat later, he himself was no longer well-off, one of his conspicuous cares was to see that Giovanni was provided for. Certainly these were not the actions of a man "very low and miserly of spirit," as commentators from the High Renaissance on liked to call him, especially when you realize that he did not approve of what his son wanted to do, and could not conceive of it as anything but an utter waste of time.

CHAPTER VII

BUT it was not only with worldly goods that the young man was well-provided. As one of the most important bankers of the kingdom, Boccaccino, the father, was not confined to the business quarters of the city. He was "friend and familiar" to King Robert, and had ready access to the royal household. He knew, thus, all the leaders of the realm, and through him his son came to know them. Barons who wrote poetry, and poets who became barons, seafarers who became philosophers, and philosophers who went seafaring, they represented the first beginnings of that new activity, both mental and physical, that was about to spring suddenly to life on the rich, traditional soil, after nearly a dozen centuries of deep slumber. Presumably they liked to talk to that reticent and clever young man who was so avid in noting every detail of what they said. Presumably, too, he listened to them attentively, for his later works were to refer frequently to their conversations. From them—as he had already done from those into contact with whom he came at Florence and Certaldo—he was filling in, point by point, the gaps of his experience, making further ready to paint a complete three-dimensional picture of a many-sided world.

A list of these men is, if you know the time, most impressive. There was Marino Bulgaro, "a man of advanced age and long memory, a skillful sailor from the days of his youth," whose daughter Restituta was the heroine of one of the more romantic *Decameron* stories. This old sea dog had fought

under three kings of Naples, and at one time, established off
Crete with a single galley, had interrupted all traffic between
Venice and Alexandria, yet with "the Calabrian Constantino
da Rocca" who was treasurer to Queen Sancia, he found time
to tell young Giovanni of the "low beginnings and extraordinary fortunes" of Philippa of Catania who from humble
washerwoman rose to a high position and great influence as
governess to the two royal princesses.

There was Giacomo di Sanseverino, Count of Tricarico and
Chiaramonte, "captain" of Rieti, and father of Ugo di Sanseverino. He it was who informed Boccaccio, with a nobleman's privilege of indiscretion, how his father used to relate
to him that King Robert "the wisest of kings since Solomon"
had been so backward a student that he could not be taught
to read at all, until one day one of his preceptors had recited
to him a fable from Æsop whereat he had become so interested that he had learned immediately.

There were Giovanni Barilli and Barbato of Sulmona, both
poets, both men of affairs, both friends of the great Petrarch
who was put in their charge when in 1341 he came to Naples
to be examined as to his qualifications to be crowned laureate.
One of these certainly first showed Petrarch's work to
Boccaccio.

There was Paolino of Venice, elected Bishop of Pozzuoli in
1324, who used to discuss the origins of poetry with Giovanni
and advanced the theory that it was invented by Nimrod and
the Babylonians.

There was Dionigi Roberti of Borgo San Sepolcro, astronomer, theologian, commentator on Valerius Maximus and
other ancient writers, and possibly poet. He had lived at Avignon and it was by means of him that Petrarch informed King
Robert of his desire for the laurel. His influence at the court

was great and his death in 1340 or 1341 deprived Boccaccio of great hopes for favor and advancement.

There was Niccolo Acciaiuoli, like Boccaccio the son of a Florentine banker, unlike him, cynical, worldly, unscrupulous, and practical. He was progressing upward step by step and although he was only a few years older than Giovanni and had started with no more advantage he had already reached a position of some importance. More was to be heard of him later.

Also there was Paul of Perugia, "a man of proven age, serious, learned in many things, entirely occupied, in his capacity of royal librarian, in hunting up everywhere, at the command of the king, rare books of all sorts, both histories and the works of the poets." Paul was a great scholar according to the standards of the time, and his huge shapeless collections were a storehouse of all the then known fragments which had escaped the ruin of the ancient world. They were ill-sorted and undigested, and the critical faculties displayed in them were often naïve enough to have unconscious humor. Africa, for instance, was derived in one of his books, from *a,* away, and *frigore,* cold; while *asinus,* or donkey, was derived from *a,* without, and *senos,* sense. However, they were about the earliest attempts at classical study to be made, and they represented an enormous amount of energy which, if misdirected, was misdirected in a good cause. His own defects, too, his own many limitations were compensated for by patient tirelessness. What, for instance, he could not discover himself, he learned carefully from the conversations of others, and indeed all that he wrote concerning Greece, came from his talks with the Calabrian monk Barlaam, "that little man great in knowledge" who was, in one sense at least, rather than either Boccaccio or Petrarch, the father of the revival of

learning, inasmuch as he was actually the first Greek scholar
in the whole modern western world.

Paul does not, however, close the list, for there was one
other great man of the court with whom Giovanni came into
contact. Possibly he was the greatest, and certainly his influence on Boccaccio was most clear. The person referred to
was he whom the same Idalagos we have already pointed out
represented Boccaccio designated as Calmeta "that learned
shepherd to whom almost every known thing was made manifest" who showed the former the wonders of astronomy. In
real life he appears to have been Andolo de' Negri, "one of
those truly extraordinary intellects who after the downfall of
the ennobling arts drew back, from the muddy lagoons of
the Arabs to the pure founts of Italy, the imperial and almost
unfathomable science of the stars."

Little enough is known of Andolo other than that he was
born in Genoa in the neighborhood of 1260, perhaps earlier,
and that he wrote many books, including a treatise on the
spheres of the heavens. This is still in existence. It was
copied out patiently by the hand of the pupil who made his
great teacher famous, and exists now as part of a Boccaccio
manuscript within the brown walls of the Laurentian library
in Florence. Another thing we know about him is that in
1314 the signory of his Ligurian city sent him as ambassador
to Alexius Comnenus, emperor of Trebizond. In this mission
which took him almost to the extremity of the far Black Sea
he visited almost all of the eastern end of the Mediterranean,
for he was a man prematurely endowed with that great restless curiosity which was soon to sweep every part of Europe.
"He voyaged," Boccaccio pointed out, "almost all over the
whole world, in nearly every climate, within almost every
horizon." In consequence, in everything he knew, "he was

made more certain by the teaching of experience." "What we learned," was another conclusion of the man who studied with him, "by hearsay, he saw with his own eyes."

In his old age, however, Andolo felt inclined to settle down. King Robert offered him the position of court astronomer and court physician and he accepted the same with alacrity. He received for his duties "six golden ounces" of salary. This office he held until his death in 1334. His duties were various. His works show that he was, for the age he lived in, a profound student of the science of the heavens. But as court physician he was expected to be something, too, of an astrologer. In the confused mental state of the time, even a sage philosopher-king was not above what would now be regarded as childish superstitions. When Robert was ill, therefore, Andolo was supposed to humor these superstitions. He was supposed to consult the stars and from their conjunctions diagnose the royal ailments. He was also, by the same methods, expected to prognosticate the course and duration of the illness, and to suggest its infallible cure.

And yet while he was trying to do all this, so sincere was his devotion to true learning, that he found time to gather about him the young enthusiasts of the city and to them impart at least some small part of his vast knowledge. Boccaccio attended his classes, and from his description it is not hard to reconstruct a picture of this kindly, sharp-eyed man of learning, as wise in human ways as he was in mathematical formulæ, as aware of the poetry as he was of the science of his calling, whose eloquence and enthusiasm as, "sounding his flute," as the words of Idalagos put it, "he began to tell about the new movements and incredible courses of the ensilvered moon," first "disposed" his later to be distinguished listener, who had "already given over the pastoral life," that is, the pursuit of commerce, "to follow Pallas Athene," that is, learning, "with all his heart."

It was then, we learn, Andolo's custom to invite such young men as were eager for instruction to his house, and there, having seated them around them, to give one of them a text to read aloud. This he would interrupt from time to time to make his comments and his explanations, thus giving them all the matter that it had to offer.

But it was not only the crude astronomy of the time that he was accustomed to teach them. Sometimes the text would suggest to him some story or some experience he had gathered in his years of wandering. Sometimes it would suggest some myth or ancient fable. He would pause to tell it to them, thus making his course on the science of the heavens more a lesson of the whole wide world as it then existed to an eager and retentive mind.

One of these stories has remained famous. The text was that the stars are not to be blamed when a man meets with misfortune. Andolo said that it reminded him of an ancient fable. His pupils begged him to tell it, and he went on.

Fortune, it seems, met Poverty one day as she was seated at a crossroad, and guyed her without mercy. Poverty answered by challenging Fortune to a combat. Since neither had arms they were to fight with bare hands. After a long discussion the battle began and shortly Fortune lay stretched on the ground. Victorious Poverty placed her knee on Fortune's chest and obliged her to confess herself vanquished. As punishment she imposed the following conditions: Fortune must chain Misery to a stake, and from thenceforward he could only cross the doorstep of one who sets him free, while she must let Happiness move about at will.

"It was a marvelous thing, never before seen, never to be

seen again," said this wise man with a quiet flash of humor. "Fortune promised this to Poverty. She chained Misery to a stake at the disposition only of those who would free her. And so, my good friends, you can consider proven by this fable that which you rightly said above."

In other words, calamity can only come to those who by their actions invite it. At least thirty years later, Boccaccio was to recall this tale and to pause to tell it in his writing of the *De Casibus virorum illustrium*—"sad stories of the death of kings," for Shakespeare's phrase can be applied to this Latin book. It was not surprising, for it appealed both to his growing love of moralizing, and his inherent common sense. It was a tribute to the vividness of Andolo's teaching just the same.

CHAPTER VIII

SO far, however, we have not even touched upon the most important and the most dramatic episode of his whole crowded life at Naples. It was to be the crown of all the others, and indeed, apparently, of everything that was ever to happen to him in a long, not uneventful life. Its vibrant overflowing exaltation was to turn him from a gauche, boyish maker of crude, if well-intended, rhymes to a mature, full-blown, and at times actually great poet. Later its disappointment, reacting in a nature, the deep and inherent sensitiveness of which is only too apt to be disregarded, was to steady that poetry into prose. Yet, because of the initial quickening fire it had aroused, that prose was to be about the first which was truly warm and human since Greek feeling went down before the onslaught of barbarous and uncivilized monkish Christianity. What we are alluding to is that transforming happening which commentators on the author glibly set aside and pigeon-hole as the "enamorment." Just as if the sudden burst of passion on the part of this warm-hearted great man—just as if any sudden burst of swelling and expansive human emotion for that matter—could be relegated to the card-index of technical terms.

In the proem to the *Decameron*, which is in a certain way a sort of *apologia*, Boccaccio makes reference to this: "For having from my first youth up to the present time been inflamed by a high and noble passion—perhaps higher and nobler it would seem to you, were I to relate it, than was fitting to my low estate, although I must tell you that by many discreet persons who knew about it, I was praised therefore—this love became a passing sore travail to me; not so much, certainly, because the lady was cruel to me as because of my own overweening appetite which, inasmuch as it would not permit me to stand content at any reasonable bounds, caused me frequently to feel more chagrin than there was any need for."

Thus in the self-control of his more philosophical years was he able to refer to his young love for that glowing person whom he always meticulously designated as Fiammetta. In real life, the name of this more living and more passionate counterpart of Dante's Beatrice and Petrarch's Laura was Maria d'Aquino. She passed in the court of Naples as a daughter of a nobleman of that princely line whose other contribution to the world's list of remembered names was Thomas Aquinas, and of his wife, a Provençal lady whose name one modern writer guesses, without much authority, to have been Sibilla Sabran. Actually, however, it seems exceedingly unlikely that the lord of Aquino played very much of a part in her begetting, for like her famous lover, her birth had, as you chose, the stigma or the glamor of illegitimacy. Sibilla was indeed her mother. But her father was King Robert, the Wise.

It was hardly to be expected that a young man of Giovanni's known temperament would long allow himself to be confined entirely to the dusty tedious columns of his account books, and indeed we have already recounted how he had been led astray by Andolo and others toward the Castalian springs of poetry and learning. But it was not only the muses that tempted him. Naples with her sparkling violet bay and her warm fragrance of mimosa and of orange blossoms that blew in from Castellamare di Stabia and Sorrento, Naples with her cropped lawns and the hot, almost aphrodisiac nights of her languid, miraculous springtime, had another distraction to offer.

Ten years later or thereabouts, Boccaccio wrote a facetious letter in the Neapolitan dialect to a young Florentine merchant. He signed it "Janetto da Parisi of the grotto."

"We want you to know, dear brother, that the first day of this month of December, Machinta went to bed and gave birth to a strapping son, may God protect him and give him a long and prosperous life! And from what the midwife who assisted at the birth told me, he resembles his father in every way. I assure you that I believe it, for the child's godfather who knows him says that he is a very fine fellow. Oh blessed God, if madame our Queen would only have one too! What a festival we would then have, for the love we bear her. God's bodikins, we wish, too, that you had been with us! What a celebration we would have had with you too!

"And know this, that no sooner had Machinta brought forth the brat than his sponsors sent her the finest octopus you ever saw. She ate it all herself, though it was big enough to have given her the itch, not a piece of it did she send to us. And after several days we had him baptized, and the midwife carried him wrapped up in the long robe of Machinta, in the velvet one trimmed with miniver: I don't know whether you remember just the one I want to say. And Giannetto Squarcione carried the lighted torch which was chock full of silver *carlini,* and the sponsors were Giannetto Corsario, Cola Scrignario, Franceschino Schizzapreti, and Baldasserino Sconzaioco, and Martuccello Vulcano too, by gosh, and I don't know how many more of the *crême de la crême* of Naples.

"And along with them went Mariella Cacciapulci, Catella Saccone, Zita Cubitosa and Rodetella di Porta Nuova, and all the other baby dolls of the piazza. And they gave him the

name of Antoniello in honor of St. Anthony, may he always
protect him for us. And if you had only seen how many fair
ladies even from Nido and Capuana and from the other piazzas who came to visit her, I am sure you would have marveled
just as I did. More than a hundred, I think, that there were
with their pleated bodices, and with their long sleeves broidered with pearls and likewise gold, may God be praised who
made them! Oh, how beautiful they were! Our square
seemed exactly like heaven!

"As for Machinta, she is very well and is tickled to death
with her child. She won't even stay in bed as a woman of her
condition should. . . .

"And now we want to tease you a little if you will let us.
What kind of work did you do to Machinta with your ——!
that we now have such a fine-looking boy?"

The same lovely apparitions that he notes so enthusiastically
in this vivid painting of the Neapolitan street-life moved
through the streets of Parthenope when he first reached the gay
southern metropolis. Nor—with his father's connections—
could he have had any trouble in meeting even the noblest of
them. The fascinating game of love was, therefore, added to
his occupations. His first affair was at the age of sixteen when
he had hardly been in Naples two years, and it was, as far
as we can determine, entirely platonic. It was soon followed,
however, by other affairs. In them, before he had reached the
technical and legal age of manhood, he who was later to be
regarded as love's expert, was able to carry the pleasant passion
to what he regarded as its logical conclusion, namely physical
fulfillment. It was, however, later to transpire, that while his
emotions and his emotional nature had been stimulated, his
heart and his true inner feelings had not yet really been touched
even in these.

Of these young triflings with fire we have, sad to relate, neither exact nor comprehensive information. Idalagos gives us a passing account of how in that same springtime in which he gave himself, under the tutelage of Calmeta, to the study of astronomy, he came upon a group of fair women wandering in the grove. Seeing them, at first he was disposed to flee, fearing that he would be wounded by the arrows of Cupid. Later, however, because of them, he first dedicated himself to Orpheus. In other words, wrote poetry. And next he too became an archer. In other words, a servant of love. And with his shafts he pursued first "a white dove"; then "a dark blackbird"; and finally "a green parrot." Caleone describes briefly his love first for "a young nymph, Pampinea by name."

"And from her sight another, hight Abrotonia, drew me and made me hers. She certainly surpassed Pampinea in comeliness and nobility, and by her gracious acts gave me good reason to love her."

Just how these various affairs were related to each other is lost, presumably forever. Was each a separate incident, and so were there five in all? Or did they overlap and were there then but three affairs? The latter seems likeliest. It seems, for instance, probable that the white dove represented the early platonic affair we have already indicated and which was not mentioned by Caleone. "Nor," says Idalagos, "did my not being able to wound her fill my heart with great grief, which was moved to pursue more for her worth than for any other reason." It seems probable also that the blackbird "who, making with her red beak pleasant manners of song" did cause him "to desire her greatly" was the same as Pampinea, and that the parrot who "flying away" from him "fluttering green feathers" disappeared "among leaves of the same color" was Abrotonia. Yet to say that this is probable is as far as we can go, and our guess may be many miles wide of the mark.

Which, too, of the alluring Neapolitan ladies, now long since red poppies, and purple clambering mesembryanthemum, and the white incandescence of peach and of pear blossoms, were hidden in these names is equally a mystery.

Nor does it seem likely that Boccaccio intended we should solve it.

For if our Giovanni occasionally "kissed and told," as the current understatement puts it, and as men of his calling generally feel they have a right to do, his telling was so discreetly veiled that only those concerned had the least chance of comprehending it. Even in the case of his principal affair it has been largely accidental that we have been able to pierce through the labyrith of changed names and of circumlocution to reach to the actual person of Maria. Fiammetta was to have been protected as thoroughly as any of the others but he loved her so long and so deeply that he forgot much of his cautiousness. The masks that he used were more transparent. Also, certain of his writings—notably the prefaces to two of his narrative poems—have reached us, which seemingly were intended only for her.

But if we do not know these things we have not lost anything that is of any great moment. What does it matter, after all, who these young persons were since at best they would be only names. Five or three, with one exception they left no great impress on his character. He went to them much as a young he-puppy seeks out the she of his species. To sniff and satisfy his curiosity. Afterwards to seek out something new.

One of them, had a larger effect, however. "But then," says Caleone of the second of the ladies he loved, "having made me content with her embraces, she gave me these for no long time. For moved by I know not what reason she suddenly became angered at me and denied me entirely. Which caused me to lead a very wretched life." Not only from what is set down here, however, but from countless other allusions, we know that before Boccaccio had ever even dreamed of Fiammetta he had encountered what to his young mind had seemed to be disillusion. He had loved sincerely, as he thought, and his love had come to dust and ashes.

She to whom he gave the melodious name of Abrotonia was the person responsible for this, and for that reason it is regrettable that she too has been lost with the others. What was she like? Was she one of those blue-eyed xanthochroous princesses which, to judge from his many descriptions of fair women, seem to have exercised such a spell over him? Or was she, on the contrary, dark-eyed and dark-haired with olive skin, one of those intriguing bits of femininity such as we nowadays see with a camellia in her hair selling flowers at the entrance to one of the narrow, steep side streets that run into the noise and bustling of the Via Roma? *Una bella Napoletana?* Noble, yes, but with the dark spontaneity of the common Neapolitan? Graceful of body, and with slow hidden fires as profound and as potent as those deeply buried under the round vine-covered slopes of Vesuvius? As keen and as stirring to the taste as the brown wine of Lachrymæ Christi? Some one to move swiftly and unforgettably a young poet and a young Florentine?

There is no answer.

We know only that once before his great love he thought or he imagined or he dreamed that he loved greatly.

And that after he had been rejected he drew away from love, and knew that he would never love again.

Sixteen months later the handsome and susceptible young man walked into the Church of San Lorenzo. "A gracious and fair temple in Parthenope, named after him who to become a god suffered that he should be burned alive on a grill." It was—Andolo's astronomical lessons have permitted us to know with amazing exactitude even after nearly six centuries—on March 30. The year was 1336. Giovanni was 23 years old. It was Holy Saturday. Spring was on the land. The Franciscan friars "with song filled with sweet melody" were celebrating the holy offices "which on that day they sing."

"And I standing there, and according to what my mind computed, the fourth hour of the day having already passed the eastern horizon, there appeared before my eyes the marvelous beauty of this person, come to this place to hear that which I heard: and as soon as I saw her my heart commenced to beat so fiercely that I could truly feel it beating violently in the smallest pulses of my body."

Thus then did he first see her from whom he would never extricate his heart, and seeing her, he loved her instantly.

She too would disillusion him and betray him. Because of her too, he would say that he would never love again.

But this time it would be without conviction.

Even the suave sophisticate we have already indicated he would later turn out to be, and who regarded—and who seems to have had some reason for regarding—nearly every other woman simply as some one you could have a successful intrigue with, would still love her. Even the old man, turned religious, would still reverence her. In a sonnet written to Petrarch after the latter's death, he would place her in the highest circle of heaven—in the very sight of God.

CHAPTER IX

THE affair into which Giovanni thus found himself plunged was, however, to be of a much less idyllic nature than the poetic language in which his idealizing worship and later his idealizing memory was to enfold it, would seem to indicate. Fiammetta was no fair, inaccessible princess to be adored from a safe distance. This attractive-looking person with her waved hair "of fine gold," her "black eyebrows," her complexion of "white lilies and vermeil roses commingled," her lips "like twin rubies" whose comely, yet placidly selfish face, is known to us from a fresco in the Spanish Chapel of the Santa Maria Novella, was rather what we would nowadays call a fairly hard-boiled and fairly worldly young lady.

"And although I pleased all," Boccaccio makes her say in one of those rare moments when intense bitterness seems to have made him able to write about her realistically, "all did not please me. But that does not mean that I refused anybody, but with kind looks gave vain hopes to each one. And by this means I drew them all into my nets. I laughed at them all, choosing, however, those who took my fancy, and who were judged apt to give me pleasure. But no sooner was the fire spent than I broke the vase and flung away the pieces."

In other words, she was one of those not uncommon, clear-headed women, who realize that physical loveliness has a definite, merchantable value, whether the price received be in money, pleasure, or power, and who would no more think of not demanding and receiving the same, than a stock-broker, say, would deliver valuable securities without receiving his commission for the transaction, or that—to use a comparison more in keeping with the subject matter—Boccaccio Sr. would have lent a thousand florins without accepting his due usance.

We already have the circumstances of her birth. And since we know likewise, both that she was born at that time of the year "when the revestured earth shows itself more fair than at any other time" and that she was "not quite as old" as Boccaccio, this event can be assumed to have taken place in March or April, 1314. In that case "the great festival," during the course of which, Fiammetta says, King Robert carried on his intrigue with her mother, must have been held in the summer of 1313. It is known that this monarch convened his first parliament on February 12 of that year, and it is, therefore, probable that this body was adjourned either the end of May or the beginning of June. Presumably, then, it was during the celebrations held in connection with this adjournment, that the lady of Aquino, having some petition to make to her king, fell while she was making the same into "his set snares," and "not following the example of Lucrece" complied with the royal desires.

The outcome of this indiscretion was not, however, brought up as King Robert's offspring. "Knowing the matter hidden," Fiammetta tells Giovanni, "she kept silent about the received outrage." And having—with a cynicalness that was typical of the French court—enjoyed relations on the same day with her husband, she was able to pass off the child on him as his own. It was only when she was dying that she told her daughter the true story. The lord of Aquino died shortly after his wife did, and the young girl was sent to a convent to be educated. At first she was extremely happy there. She found the life of a religious thoroughly congenial. Indeed, as she later told her lover, all that she needed were the vestments to become actually a nun.

But she was too good-looking to be able to carry out any such wasteful intentions. The reception room of a convent was in those days a center for social gatherings and too many of the young men were attracted by her beauty for her not to receive many offers of marriage. Fiammetta refused these with a steadiness that must have wrought great devastation. Then she encountered a suitor with a determination equal to her own. This "young man of great fortune and noble blood" went, when he was refused by her, to the man who was reputed to be her father and made formal demand for her hand. King Robert consented, and there was nothing she could do.

Even in this pass, she did not, though, marry willingly, and before she would finally agree to the ceremony, insisted that she be allowed to continue her religious activities. This was agreed to, and for some time after her marriage, she returned frequently to her convent. Then suddenly she lost all interest in things spiritual. Another side of her nature, for which probably her pious activities had been but an unconscious outlet, was awakened. Never having loved her husband, her first contact with the emotional possibilities of passion came in one of those extra-matrimonial entanglements, into which, in view of the way the Neapolitan life of the day was lived, she could have drifted without any effort. And one experience must have led to desire for another. She had not, either, inherited any tendency to continence. So presently the would-be devotee of the Virgin Mary was a worshiper of the goddess Venus. Among all those who were involved in the complicated plot and counter-plot of love-making in a certainly not cold-blooded court, she played about the most important part.

It was with this person that our poet, for all his early entanglements still an inexperienced amateur, became involved. He was unable to take Fiammetta in the one way she could successfully be taken, namely, cynically. Instead of matching his wits and skill against hers in this amorous warfare; instead of striving to obtain the better part of the bargain in this trafficking of emotions, he lost his heart to her. It is not, then, very surprising that his feelings received numerous hard knocks in the days that followed. It is not surprising, but to him it was extremely painful. Like a small craft when the waters of the sea are suddenly disturbed he was tossed hither and thither. Now lifted up toward heaven on a mountain top of hope. Now plunged very deep into the dark trough of despair.

The first incident of his love was—unfortunately for him— of the former nature. Unfortunately, because if he had been discouraged in the beginning he might have lost the heart to continue. It shows, incidentally, just how he was regarded by his chosen lady; why she liked to have him around her; why she was never likely really to take him seriously as she did people of her own sort.

A few days after Boccaccio first saw Fiammetta, he followed her to the convent of Sant' Arcangelo at Baiano. As she sat there with a group of young people the conversation ran from one thing to another until finally it fell on the story of Florio and Biancofiore—the Fleur and Blanchefleure of French romance—one of those sets of lovers like the better known Aucassin and Nicolette, in whose sad, complicated fortunes the lords and ladies of the Middle Ages were so interested. Their adventures were talked about. The "great constancy of their spirits which by amorous power kept faith through all difficulties" was praised. Next the actual stories were discussed.

"Certainly," was Fiammetta's emphatic contribution to this subject, "the memory of those lovers receives great injury in not being preserved by some poet, but being recorded only in crude fables told by the ignorant."

Then she saw Giovanni, and realized that he called himself a writer. She also realized the way he now felt about her, and it pleased her vanity to have some mark of the same.

So she turned to him.

"I beg of you," she asked him, " by the light that was in my eyes when you first saw me and also by the love you bear me to write a little book in the vulgar tongue in which the birth, love, and fortune of these two are related to the very end."

He was only too glad to.

"Lovely lady," he answered somewhat stiltedly, "the kindness of your request—to me a firm command—compels me so that I could not refuse to undertake either this or any other great task that you should set me."

After which he paused, his ingrained modesty embarrassing him.

"Even though I do not feel that I have enough skill for such a work," he added.

He was now no longer in business, his father having given up as hopeless the task of making a banker of him, and his new occupation, namely the study of canon law, in which he wasted a second six years, if equally distasteful, took less of his time. He was already a poet, to be sure. Aside from his lost juvenile efforts, we have numerous sonnets of the Naples period that apparently refer rather to Pampinea and Abrotonia than Fiammetta. Moreover, the *Caccia di Diana*—"Dian's Hunt"—a *serventese* or poem in honor of women, in which

aside from Diana, the huntresses are all actual Neapolitan
ladies appearing under their own names, had, as far as we can
determine, already been written. But now for the first time
he was to try composition on a large scale. The "little book"
which Fiammetta demanded was, when it was completed, to
be that two volume accumulation of verbosity to which he
gave the name of the *Filocolo,* or—as he misunderstood Greek
—the *love-weary.* It was perhaps the first novel of modern
Europe. With all its faults it was certainly the first novel of
modern Europe written by a distinguished hand.

To discuss this work critically would not contribute greatly
to our understanding of the man we are considering. Whether
Boccaccio drew his story from one of the two early French
versions still extant, or from a rhymed ballad in Italian now
in manuscript, or from a vanished version in the bastard *lingua
franca* known as Franco-Venetian are matters that are of little
interest save to technical students of the language and literature. For those concerned more with the person who wrote
it it is enough simply to know that there was no question of
his having made it up himself. As with a majority of great
writers, invention of this sort was a detail with which he
troubled himself only when it suited his convenience. He
could not be bothered exerting himself to be original. Origi-
nality was, however, as with all great writers, inevitable, since
it was absolutely and congenitally impossible for him to look
at anything or write about anything like any one else.

The plot is as follows: Quintus Lelius Africanus, a noble
Roman, a Christian, and a descendant of the great Scipio, and
Julia Topazia, a descendant of Julius Cæsar, have been married five years yet they have no children. Lelius, therefore—
it is by this one of his names that he is designated—makes a
vow to St. James, promising the saint that if he is given

progeny he will make a pilgrimage to the latter's holy shrine in Compostella in Spain. Only a few days later Julia tells her husband that she is pregnant. Lelius then informs her of his vow. She begs to accompany him. Together they set out.

But their journey is not to be completed in safety. The enemy of the human race, namely Satan, enraged to see another party of pilgrims on their way to Galicia, takes on himself the guise of the governor of Marmorina—Verona—and hastening to King Felix, pagan monarch of Spain, tells him that the Romans have attacked, pillaged, and burned this city which is one of his possessions, and have also massacred the inhabitants. Felix immediately puts himself at the head of an expedition to avenge this. En route, he encounters Lelius and his party. He imagines him to be the wicked marauder and attacks him. Lelius and his party are virtually all slain, Julia and some of the women alone surviving. It is only after this battle that King Felix discovers his error. Then he is overwhelmed with grief and brings Julia back to his court at Seville. She is received there by the queen, and treated kindly but does not live long. She dies bringing into the world a daughter who is named Biancofiore, and on the very same day the queen bears a son who is named Florio. The queen adopts the little girl. The two children are brought up together in the royal household almost as brother and sister.

And of course the inevitable happens. As they are studying together in "the book of Ovid," the young god of love visits Florio. In consequence he becames enamored of Biancofiore. She returns his love. One of their tutors notices the same and reports it to the king. He in turn tells the queen. Both are in consternation. This daughter of an unknown captive in love with our son and heir! Immediately they take steps to end such nonsense. First Florio is taken to the nearby city of

Montorio to study, and next he is tempted with other women. First Biancofiore is offered another husband, and this failing, she is tricked into seeming to have tried to poison the king. For this last offense, she is sentenced to be burned to death, but Florio, in disguise, rides up in the true knightly fashion and rescues her. She is then sold into slavery. The merchants who buy her are so impressed by her beauty that they tell King Felix to take in exchange for her what part of their treasures he desires.

It is in consequence of this happening that the last and, by a great deal, the more exciting part of the story takes place. Florio discovers that Biancofiore had been sold and against the prayers of his father and mother who display—now that it is too late—a most thorough and most useless repentance, he sets out in search of her. Ascalione, his fathful tutor, one of those loyal elder knights the early romancers so liked to include in their tales, accompanies him. They rove the whole Mediterranean world. Finally in Alexandria, they discover that she is imprisoned by the admiral of the place in a tower where he kept women destined for his overlord, the Sultan of Babylon. By playing chess with the guardian of this place, Florio succeeds in gaining admittance to her. He is raised to Biancofiore in a basket of flowers, and would have spent the night in her chamber successfully but for the unfortunate fact that the admiral, vexed by her unbending purity, had the same idea. The two lovers were discovered by the angry Mahometan. Once again Biancofiore—this time accompanied by her Florio—was sentenced to be burned at the stake.

But naturally this is not to be the end of the book. Venus and Mars see the plight of their devotees, and hurry to their assistance. Descending on the field just as the lovers are about to be burned, they raise up such a huge cloud of smoke that

the executioners cannot see to reach them. Then, more practically, Ascalione and his men-at-arms ride up, and complete
the rescue. There is nothing left to tell except to note rather
wordily their long voyage home again. To describe their passage through Rome, and observe there how Biancofiore discovers her noble origin. To report—for such, according to
the taste of the day was necessary—their conversion to Christianity. To record their final return to Spain, and the conversion of King Felix and his wife. To show lastly how,
Felix dead, King Florio and Queen Biancofiore ruled Spain
in what became a truly golden age.

It was around this simple scheme that Giovanni, to please
his lady-love, piled up such an overwhelming mass of verbiage
as to make one wish we knew what she really thought of it,
if indeed she ever read it at all. Digression follows digression in weariless procession, and long speech leads to additional
long speech. In its essentials, the story was a good one, yet
the essentials are nearly impossible to reach through the welter
of "alases" and of invocations. The book has life, color, vividness, and, strange as it may seem, even a certain amount of
narrative pace. What the writer lacked more than anything
was experience. Like so many other beginners, Boccaccio,
later master of bare statement, was then woefully afraid of
the same. The result is that the novelist's first sustained piece
of writing—although it may indeed have satisfied the age in
which it was written—is something that nowadays even Italians
can hardly read.

Yet it cannot, on that account, be disregarded. For one
thing it is one of the most important sources in regard to the
younger days of Boccaccio that we possess. We have already
quoted again and again from the story told by Idalagos. Idalagos told his tale to Florio, when the latter, returning from

Alexandria, halted for a while at Naples. It is from the introduction of this book that we derive most of our information regarding the beginning of his love for Maria. The episode of Fileno—Biancofiore's unsuccessful lover—and more especially Fileno's conversation with a man from Certaldo tells us a good deal about the subsequent course of that affair. In the incident of the Questions of Love, to which we have already referred, we learn much about the life of Fiammetta's city. This takes place during Florio's first visit to Naples. On his way to Alexandria in quest of Biancofiore, Florio halts there. He is persuaded by Galeone—again Boccaccio—and by Fiammetta to take part in their amorous games.

And besides that the *Filocolo* contains in embryo almost all of the qualities which Boccaccio was later to display more successfully. We have already named quite a list of them. Another could be added and that is his striving for reality. Many of the characters which were given to him by the story were quite impossible, yet even with this limitation we can see him striving for psychological correctness, and more than once achieving it.

Boccaccio's reputation being what it is, there is a last point of interest to the *Filocolo*. It is in this book—both in the account of Florio's meeting with Biancofiore in the tower and more especially in the account of the two young ladies who are placed in his way to distract him from his love—that for the first time occur passages of that sort of writing which certain of his critics call pornographic. But which were better named warmly sensuous, as there is nothing either smutty or furtive in their phrases, and the rich cadenced beauty of their prose is far too ornately complicated to reward even the most persistently prurient of the vice-suppressors with his favorite kind of secret delight.

CHAPTER X

THIS enormous romance was not, however, to be brought to a conclusion. Not, at least, while Giovanni was still at Naples, though later, he was, indeed, to pick up and indite to the very end the fortunes of the two lovers. But now—it happened—the pace of his attempt to win Fiammetta was such as to make it impossible for him to retain interest in so cumbersome and meandering a piece of work. Moreover, another bit of writing occupied his attention.

It was, then, as we think, in the spring of 1337, or just about a year after the episode in San Lorenzo, that Boccaccio broke off the *Filocolo* at the end of the third book—just where Fileno, rejected by Biancofiore, departs dejectedly from Marmorina— to start work on his long poem, the *Filostrato*. The preface to this first telling of the story of Troilus and Cressida throws so much light on the progress he had made with Fiammetta, that it is regrettable that it cannot be dated with exactitude. It also throws considerable light on the interior development of Giovanni. If the awkward prosateur had become a skillful poet,—and indeed the *Filostrato* ranks high among all narrative poems ever written—so the crude enthusiast for love was acquiring technique as an amorist. Beneath his words we can hear a heart fluttering, which should not be so. Yet in spite of that, these same words are used with expertness to achieve a purpose. And the purpose is not entirely unachieved.

A while ago, he wrote, it happened that "I who almost

74

from my boyhood up to this time had been in the service of
love," finding himself in a court of love, heard this question
debated: A young man is enamored of a fair lady, and only one
boon is to be granted; he can see her on one or two occasions;
or he can talk about her; or communing with himself he can
sweetly think about her. Good arguments were offered on
all sides of the question, but he, because his loves had been
"more ardent than fortunate," insisted that it was better to
think about her, giving as one of his reasons that no small
part of a lover's happiness lay in being able to make the beloved one be toward you just as you wished her to be. This
you could not be sure about either when seeing her or when
talking about her with another.

But now, he said, the reality of separation had changed this
opinion, and he cried out against his former stupidity.

"I swear then, my fairest lady, that it is true that since you,
by departing from the delightsome city of Naples and going
to Samnium in the finest season of the year, took suddenly
from my eyes—more enraptured by your angelic face than
by any other thing—that which they were accustomed to seeing, I knew by its absence that which I had not known before.
That is, the deprivation of seeing you has made me so far beyond all reason sorrowful, that I now plainly know—which
was little before known to me—how great was the happiness
which came from your fair and gracious sight."

He next described his feelings. Whenever he thought of
how she had gone where he had no honorable excuse for following, his eyes filled with tears. But it was not only that.
How often had he turned away from looking at the church
where he became enamored of her, the *loggie* where they used
to talk together, the piazzas where he used to see her, to cry
with the prophet Jeremiah: "How doth the city sit sorrowful,

that was full of people! How is she become a widow, she that was great among nations!" His sadness was only mitigated when he looked toward "that countryside, those mountains, that part of the sky, in which and under which I believe surely you are. Then every breath of air, every soft breeze that is wafted thence, just as I feel it on my face so certainly it must have touched you." He could not even write love poems any longer, he said. In this way he lived distant from her and realized what delight it was when there was no such thing as distance. Just thinking of her was not unmixed with pleasure, to be sure. "Yet this pleasure comes mixed with such an ardent desire, which kindles all my other desires into so great a burning to see you, that I can hardly control myself from casting aside all honorable and reasonable ideas, and going thither where you dwell." It was, he said, only by thinking more of her reputation than of his happiness, that he held himself in check.

But at last realizing that it was impossible to contain his grief, he thought of a way of releasing his emotions. It was a highly modern way. He would do the same by making a poem of his sufferings. He chose the story of Troilus and Cressida, after revolving in his mind various other ancient tales, because this seemed best adapted to his case.

"And so, excellent lady," he explained, "I have written these worthless rhymes in the form of a little book to bear perpetual witness to whoever may read them both of your wonder and of my melancholy. In which if you happen to read them, as often as you find Troilus weeping and lamenting for the departure of Cressida, so frequent may you understand and know were my complainings, my tears, my sighs, and my anguishes. And as often as you find the beauty of Cressida, her winsome ways and other things laudable in a woman set down, that often may you think I wished to speak of you."

He next made a bid for the future.

"Of the other things, of which there are many enough, none, except those of which I have already spoken, have to do either with me or with you, but are there because the story of this noble young person requires them, and yet even there, if you are as clever as I think, you will be able to understand what and how many my desires are, where they end, what they ask for more than any other thing, and whether or not they deserve any pity."

He followed this by saying that he does not know whether or not these words would have sufficient skill to "touch with compassion her chaste mind."

He affected to doubt the same.

"Yet I have prayed love to lend this strength to them."

He concluded by saying tactfully that he did not think that it would be a fair thing for these writings to come into the hands of any other person before they reached the hands of her "who was the true and only inspiration of them."

Therefore he sent them to her "as a little gift."

The state of affairs here referred to is not hard to interpret. It is considerably easier, however, if you have clearly in mind the story of the fair, fickle Greek lady and her mooning, romantic lover, in the telling of which the twenty-four-year-old Florentine displayed such skill and such eloquence, and out of which he made his swift-moving four thousand line poem.

Troilus, a young Trojan and one of the sons of King Priam, scorns love but this does not prevent him from amusing himself with his friends by looking upon and considering the young beauties of the city. He passes them in review, compares their various charms, discusses them with an utter lack of discretion. Particularly during those religious ceremonies which give an especial opportunity of observing them as they come in all decked in the finery of their best clothes.

But one day, so doing, he meets his downfall. A comely widow, clad in black weeds which only enhance her loveliness, enters the temple and turns up a pert nose at the insolence of his regard. This is Cressida—Griseida, as Boccaccio somewhat more correctly calls her—daughter of the high priest Calchas, who, leaving her behind him, has fled to the Greeks. Troilus hardly has seen her when he falls in love with her. The scorner becomes the smitten, and his new feelings are made all the more complicated by a keen sense of humiliation that he should have succumbed to the despised emotion. Furthermore, he is helpless.

For no really good reason, except, apparently, to add to the complication of the story, he does not know how to win her. He wanders about the city in a state of unhappiness. Then he meets Pandarus, who is his friend and her cousin. Pandarus notes his gloom and presses him for the cause of it. At first he will not tell. Then he yields to the latter's insistence. I love Cressida, he says. Instead of being angered, Pandarus is immensely pleased. His medieval sense of loyalty impels him, too, to aid his friend even in this situation. It is only Cressida that Troilus wants? Should he desire Polyxena or even Helen herself, he can have them! "As long as you will promise to protect her honor you can have her!" Troilus promises. Pandarus then goes to his cousin, and tells her that young Prince Troilus is in love with her. He urges her to yield to him. At first she demurs. Then she gives in too.

The next part of the narrative deals with their realized love. There is little action, only a series of incidents, but biographically it is as important as anything Boccaccio ever wrote. In the sharp, nervous lines of his *ottava rima*—a meter which he did not invent, but which he does use for the first time in a poem of this sort—he describes the first, and then the subsequent amorous encounters of the two lovers. He minces no words, but dwells lovingly and sensuously on each detail. But he does more than describe. Impelled by his own beating hopes, what he writes is sheer propaganda. It is propaganda for the physical consummation he so ardently burned for. Quite evidently he wanted his book to play the exact part of Pandarus, and that is perhaps why this man who, in Chaucer's version of the story seems contemptible enough, and, in Shakespeare's, so utterly despicable that his name has become a synonym for a vile calling, here shines with a certain sort of glory.

For if Troilus represents young Boccaccio, Pandarus is likewise unconsciously the same man. Another phase of him, however. A maturing and persuasive Boccaccio. "Secret water," he makes Cressida say, "is sweeter far than wine drunk in abundance." But he was thinking of Fiammetta. Jejunely retaining enough illusion about this person to believe still that she required this sort of argument, he wanted her at once to be her high inaccessible angel, and at the same time to come down to him. The *Filostrato*—which means ironically enough in the lame Boccaccian Greek, man beaten or vanquished by love—was written and sent to the lady to accomplish this wellnigh impossible, yet often sought after end.

For that reason, the rest of its cantos tell a story that is only of relative interest. How Calchas persuades the Trojans to exchange Cressida for one of the prisoners the Greeks had taken; how Cressida promises Troilus to be faithful; how instead she becomes enamored of Diomede, and is made his mistress; how Troilus learns thereof; and how, finally, after wreaking his vengeance upon the bodies of Greek soldiers, the young Trojan prince is slain by the great Achilles, have little or nothing to do with the fortunes of Giovanni. Boccaccio took these events fairly directly from the monk Benoit de Saint-Maure's *Roman de Troie,* which was unquestionably the principal source for all the uninvented parts of the poem. He wrote about them well because by now he was interested in the tale he was telling, and because by now he was a good writer. The coincidence between the way Troilus' affair turned out, and the way Boccaccio's was to, makes us pause for a moment, while the matter-of-fact manner in which Cressida went from the old love to the new, causes us to think one or two thoughts about the women of Naples, or at least such of them as Giovanni seems to have known. But the principal reason for writing the poem lay in what we have found in the earlier stanzas. They written, its principle motive was satisfied. They successful, its principal purpose was achieved.

And it seems that it was.

But not immediately, however. Considerable water was to run under Boccaccio's bridges before he was to become to Maria, as Troilus was to his lady-love. For one thing he had to go through a long period as her accepted servitor, a sort of always hopeful, if still platonic *cavaliere servante.* Constantly at her side. Constantly doing what she wished for her. Constantly devoted to her. In the second place, he had to surprise her into giving some sort of evidence that she felt toward him as he did toward her. In the third place, having arrived at this state, it was necessary to persuade her to forget discretion. That was to be the hardest task. Even with the loose moral sense of the court of King Robert it was one thing to persuade a woman to love you, another to have her in your arms.

The exact chronology of all this is hard to come at. Naturally there are no documents, and worse than that there is no series of conveniently dated letters. We have discovered already, however, that the *Filostrato* was written in the springtime. Elsewhere Boccaccio tells us explicitly that he was her servitor for one hundred and thirty-five days. We have a whole series of ecstatic sonnets that indicate a bathing season spent at Baia with her. And at least one of these seems to show that it was here that he first knew that she had strong feelings for him. Such a momentous happening could not have taken place later than September. Since Boccaccio fell in love in 1336 this, then, is what almost certainly happened:

The *Filostrato* was written in April, 1337, and its sweep of emotion had sufficient effect on the young lady to induce her to withdraw her ban on his being near her. Perhaps the envy of her friends made her, for the moment, place a higher value on the devotion of a poet than she would herself have been likely to. Perhaps the warm-hearted words actually did find their mark; actually did make her visualize him in a way that was physical. He had no ties. He was a law student and his university was having its vacation. He followed her to Baia. There he took part in the various diversions of the place; went boating, fishing, swimming, hunting and hawking with her. And showered her with a veritable deluge of sonnets in such of which as still survive we can still feel the warm laziness of the Baian summer. The oars splashing. The lutes twanging. The hot mirror of the waveless water. And plied her with his insistent request of her, growing more and more convincing. Until finally propinquity did, as it must always do, its work.

Just what she first granted him on the late September day
that it must have been, there is no way of knowing. This is
evident: that it was not all that he desired, and yet that it
showed him indisputably that at last he had reached her. Perhaps it was one of those swift cycles of emotions in which she
almost yielded to him, only to change her mind. Perhaps as
she ran away she called back to him: "But I do love you,
Giovanni! But I do love you!" Perhaps they were simply
interrupted.

Whatever it was his heart was exalted, and his hopes lifted
too. Now he would never despair again!

Nor did he very long have need to. That very autumn,—
only a few months later, indeed,—most unexpectedly and in
an extremely dramatic fashion, he got him his great desire.

The bold stroke by which he won to this, is, fortunately,
one of the episodes of his exciting life, of which he gave all
the details. We may assume he exaggerated if we wish. We
may even assume that he lied utterly. But at least three times
he told identically the same story. And since he harped on it
so often, and since also it is in no way inconsistent either with
the morals of the time, or with what we know of the character
of Fiammetta or, for that matter, with what an audacious
young lover would be likely to do, there is no reason for not
believing it to be substantially true.

It was, then, as follows: Some time toward the end of
October, or the beginning of November, Maria's young husband went to Capua. He was a land-holding noble and one
of his three principal estates was located there. Word of
this reached Giovanni, and feeling in his heart that a sense
of cautiousness was all that kept his fair lady from yielding
to him, he decided that it was now or never. That he must
win her, in other words, immediately, or relinquish her for

always. Since he had no intention of doing the latter, he proceeded to act.

He went to her maid and found, it seems, no difficulty in bribing her. She conducted him to Fiammetta's bedchamber. There he disrobed himself and hid himself in the great bed curtains. In that place, quietly, but no doubt with heart beating ten times as violently as it did on that day in San Lorenzo, he waited patiently for what was to come.

And he did not wait long, for presently Fiammetta, too, was in the room. Aided by the same maid who was betraying her, she prepared for her night's slumbers. She let down her long hair and undressed herself. Shortly she climbed into her large sleeping place. Her maid extinguished the light and then left her. Very soon she was asleep.

And then, with great caution, Giovanni moved forward. He climbed into the bed beside her, and just as if he had been her husband, laid his hand upon her body.

She stirred.

"Who is it?"

No answer.

"Who *is* it?"

Still there was complete silence.

Then she became alarmed.

"Help!" she cried out. "Who is it? Help! The servants!"

With his firm hand he quieted her.

"Be still, dear. There is no danger. It is Giovanni."

She was awake now.

"Giovanni? Go away! Go away! Do not be a fool! Can't you see the risk you are taking?"

He did not move.

"Please!"

He guessed what she feared, and made haste to reassure her.

"I come not, dear lady," he told her, "to violate your chaste bed—"

"Go away!"

"—but as a lover to obtain what I long for."

"Oh please, Giovanni!"

She was not angry, however.

"Very well," he said.

Now he had a speech to make. He drew from his breast a sharp dagger.

"You alone can satisfy me," he began, "and if not I die."

"Giovanni!"

"Surely I will leave you either satisfied or dead."

What could she say to him?

"Not that I wish to gratify my passions or force any to raise cruel hands against me."

Certainly he was completely mad, he was a raving lunatic.

"But if you are deaf to my entreaties, with this dagger I shall pierce my heart."

"But no, Giovanni!"

"What shall I do?"

A pause.

"Plunge this cold steel into my heart?"

A second pause.

"Or joyful, let it be warmed by yours?"

It was theatrical. It was not at all the correct way to make love to a young lady. Still it had its points.

For one thing, Giovanni knew fairly well that his Fiammetta was not really averse to yielding to him. Perhaps, even, she was eager to. For another thing, where would she be if his dead body were found in her bedroom?

There must have been a long momentous interval during which the short strip of steel twinkled and sparkled.

Then she threw herself into his arms, dashing the evil blade out of his hands.

"I will be always yours, Giovanni," she cried. "I don't believe there is any need to beg you to be mine. But if there is need, I beg you many, many times."

CHAPTER XI

THUS then did our poet win to her he sought, and had he been able to continue playing his hand in the same reckless manner, he might thus have been able to keep her. But such was not to be the case. Boccaccio was not yet —if indeed he was ever to be—a decisive, self-assured man of action, and his daring on this occasion was rather one of those sudden moves into which even the most unaggressive persons are sometimes hounded by the stinging whips of desperation, than it was something truly belonging to his character. It was not, therefore, to be followed by other acts of daring. This, perhaps, was fortunate. For by losing Fiammetta he was, ultimately, able to recover his idealized picture of her. And by this fact, it seems, we have been spared another poetizing courtier to add to the world's oversupply of writers of trifling, unread verses, and given instead—as we have already indicated—a great man.

But this was not to transpire immediately. Though certainly it seems utterly unlikely that Fiammetta ever felt even a fraction of the regard for Boccaccio that he felt for her, it is quite evident that she got a measureable thrill from him, and with him she may even, as far as she was capable, have been in love. He was so different from the brainless, if well-built barons who thought only of drinking, hunting, and fighting, and who regarded love-making as but an incident. He was so intense. He was thoroughly devoted to her. So for a while she was quite glad to accept him as, at any rate, one of her many admirers, and to give him at least the impression that he was the only one whose feelings were reciprocated. In this status, apparently, he went through the glorious winter of his twenty-fourth year,—the winter of 1337-38, as we would to-day put it.

Then she began to tire of him, and it would not require much boldness in the regions of psychological guesswork to hazard the reasons therefor. They must have been the same reasons that in the beginning caused her to have a liking for him. A single-minded, idealizing lover is all right as a novelty, especially when he contrasts as much as Boccaccio must have, with your other lovers. But his charm soon becomes a nuisance. For one thing he expects you to live up to his ideals of you. He expects you to be as pure and constant and devoted as he dreams you are. He expects you to be faithful to him in every thought, as well as every action, and when he discovers you acting as you had always intended to act, there are ghastly scenes about it. Perhaps, too—if you happen also to be married—there are embarrassing, and even compromising, scenes. At any rate, your style is cramped.

It seems safe to say that Fiammetta found her style considerably cramped by the white-faced, intense adoration of Giovanni, and also that before long he wearied her not a little. She did not waste much time, either, in letting him know this fact. First she was cold to him, we assume: and then, we know, she was no longer accessible to him. At about this time, he had, for some reason or other, to make an extended trip. When he came back—we take it this was in the spring of 1338 —she indicated very plainly that she no longer loved him, and his misery knew no bounds.

The story of all this is told here and there throughout the writings of Giovanni, and it is only by piecing various fragments together that we can read it in its entirety. The particular phase we are now dealing with is discussed at least implicitly in the preface to his next work, the *Teseide*. This somewhat lengthy poem—it contains nine thousand lines—relates to us the loves of Palamon and Arcite for the fair Amazon Emilia. Like the *Filostrato* it was sent and dedicated to Fiammetta. And the dedication rang with his new woe.

"Although the memory of my vanished happiness is to me in my present misery a cause of great sorrow," he there said.

"Love who knows all my sighs," he added.

"Alas, it is true that I who was once very fortunate am now most hapless," he lamented.

"My loving you, you consider more annoyance than pleasure," he complained.

It breathed also with his still overburdening feeling for her.

Your face more divine than human," was a phrase.

"This is that Fiammetta," was another, "the light of whose fair eyes first inflamed our own."

"Neither adversity," was a third, "nor your unfriendly regards can, nor ever will, be able to extinguish in my heart that flame which, by means of your beauty, you lighted therein. I am, then, as I have always been, one of your subjects."

The very book was written for the purpose of pleasing her.

"I remember that in those days which were more long than happy, I knew that you were always anxious to hear and sometimes to read one story or another, and especially those dealing with love; so having found a very ancient tale, and one not known to many, which was very beautiful not only for the material of which it speaks, namely, love, but because those, of which it speaks, are noble young people and of royal blood descended, I have written the same in the Italian tongue and likewise in rhyme, desiring only to cause you pleasure."

As in the *Filostrato,* too, she figured in it as a character. The story was so composed, he said, that in one of the two men he can be read and in the young woman she. "Which of the two I will not tell you since I know you will be able to guess it."

It was written, lastly, in the vain hope of rewinning her.

He prayed, he said, that when it had been read, "relighting" in Fiammetta "the snuffed flame," it would bring her back to him, whom "hostile fortune" had taken away—"he knew not for what reason."

The poem which followed these almost vibrantly sincere observations was not, however, one of Boccaccio's most successful pieces of writing. Indeed, his attempt to manufacture a large epic in the classic twelve books, out of what was material for little more than a romantic narrative, failed so signally, that even for those who know Italian, it would be better to turn to the first narrative of "The Canterbury Tales" if they wish to familiarize themselves with the story. There at least it is succinctly told in not over a thousand sprightly couplets. For the moment, at least, Giovanni's ambition appears to have outstripped his ability. In spite of some excellent bursts of poetry here and there, it is about the poorest thing he ever did. Not even excluding the unwieldy *Filocolo* it is the least readable of all his works.

The argument is as follows: Theseus "Duke of Athens" makes war on the Amazons, and at its conclusion, victor in all senses, brings back as his wife Hippolyta, their warlike queen. With her comes her young sister Emilia. Then Theseus makes war on Creon, the tyrant of Thebes, slays him, and brings back as prisoners Palamon and Arcite, two young Theban nobles. He imprisons them in his castle. From their window they see Emilia as she is walking in the garden. Each falls in love with her, and thus the stage is set.

But this period of harmless rapture is not to last long. First the fair weather ends, and Emilia can be no longer seen from their window. Then Pirithöus, a friend of Arcite, ransoms him. He is freed on condition that he will leave Athenian territory. Naturally this is like being condemned to death for him. He accepts the conditions, however, and wanders gloomily through the various cities of Greece. Finally he can stay away no longer. He changes his name and adopts a disguise, returning in this manner to the city. In this guise he enrolls as a squire in the service of Duke Theseus. So he is able to see his fair lady every day.

And now Palamon reënters the story. While Arcite was away, he could love, if distant and alone, at least without a rival. But now he sees his former friend even closer to Emilia than he is. Arcite may be able to speak to fair Emily, whereas he can only look at her. He is overcome with jealousy. Risking everything, he escapes from prison, and meets Arcite in a nearby forest. They begin to battle with each other. Suddenly Theseus appears on the scene, stops them, and recognizes them. Apparently they are both lost.

But this is not to be, it happens, and the reason is that their combat appeals to the Duke's love of chivalry. He decrees a tournament with Emilia's hand as the prize of it. The two champions arrange for conflict, summoning the various warriors of ancient Greece to take sides with them, and thus transforming Agamemnon, Peleus, Castor, Pollux, Evander, Lycurgus and the rest of them into knights of the Middle Ages. Arcite prays to Mars for assistance, asking that he be granted victory. Palamon prays to Venus, asking that he win the lady. The battle commences and each, naturally, gets his prayer. Arcite is victor but is slain when his horse falls at the end and,

dying, bequeathes Emilia to Palamon. After Arcite's truly Neapolitan funeral, Palamon and Emilia are wed.

Like the *Filostrato*, this poem was, apparently, written in
the springtime. It seems certain, too, that it was written before
Boccaccio was aware that he had lost Fiammetta completely.
In that case it was undoubtedly memory of the success of his
story of Troilus and Cressida which led him to take the last step
toward disaster. Once again he followed Fiammetta to Baia.
This time, however, he was destroyed. For this great over-
grown mass of words was not the clear enticing persuasiveness
that its predecessor had been. Besides, the young lady had by
now known Giovanni. He was not an exciting romance whose
uncut pages whetted her eagerness to examine it, but a book she
had read and been bored by. It is therefore perhaps just as well
that there remains no full chronicle of that second unhappy
summer when one bitterness was followed by another bitterness,
one disappointment by another disappointment. How often
must he have remembered that other summer only a year before when his only annoyance—an irritated impatience at not
being able to have Fiammetta entirely—was at least lightened
by not too fantastic hope! How often must he have remembered how she sought his company, how she wished for his
verses. Now, apparently, he was but a nuisance, and he walked
sorrowfully and alone on those very beaches, through those
very woods that had brought his love to him.

Then all at once he realized that he was more than a
nuisance, that he had been replaced by another. It was not
a pleasant way, either, in which he found this out.

He had already suspected that all was not well, and his feelings against Baia—which only the year before he had praised
with the best meters at his service—crept in the same way into
his poetry. Here, said one of his sonnets, all they do is make

merry. Here all they do is talk of love's conquests. Here Venus has such power that many a one who came hither a Lucrece returns a Cleopatra. It is true that these words are lifted almost directly from Martial, where, speaking of the same place, the Roman poet says that a woman went there Penelope, and returned a Helen. But that does not destroy their value. The fact that a youthful poet is imitative does not make him any less sincere.

One day—as we reconstruct the story—he was walking alone. Suddenly—and our sense of irony would like to think that it was at that very place where only a summer before she had given him to know that his feelings were reciprocated—he heard a voice that was familiar to him. A voice that could still wring his heart. A voice that would always—if we can trust his report—have, and have alone that effect on him, even after all the bedchambers that we suspect he would like to have us think he visited en route to the *Decameron*. We imagine he strode forward. Then it was, we assume, that he heard the other voice, and halted, only to advance again cautiously. There he saw his Fiammetta—in the arms of his successor!

We suppose he ran. We hope and, wanting any record to the contrary, we believe that he made no foolish and ineffectual scene.

Some time—possibly as much as a week later—he had recovered enough equilibrium to express what was seething inside of him, and out came the stinging words:

"May thy name perish, Baia, and thy place!
May thy fair beach become a savage wold!
May poison corrupt thy splashing fountains cold,
And lightsome bathers give thee a wide space!
May seafarers avoid thy once fair face,

And every joy of thine meet an ill end!
In thee may fire and smoke and sulphur rend
Thy clear clouds and thy sky's serene clear grace!
Who hath corrupted the most chaste, pure mind
That ever woman had with thy ill ways,
If mine eyes saw the truth not long ago!
There where in grief I shall now live always,
Deceived by foolish faith as if made blind:
Oh that I had been blind not long ago!"

It is to be noted that it was the place he inveighed against, it was the dust of Baia that he shook off from his feet, Fiammetta herself still gleaming like a goddess through his bitterness and anger.

It was considerably later that he was to inveigh against the emotion. When at Florence, in the resumed *Filocolo,* he did take up the question of whether or not love itself might not be responsible, it was the lady he had loved whom he made do the speaking.

"This love then is evil," he made her say, "and since it is evil it should be avoided, for he who flees evil things by the same token follows the good, and is good and virtuous. Its beginning is no other thing than fear, its middle sin, and its ending sorrow and grief. It is without doubt the destroyer of the spirit, and shame, and anguish, and passion, and grief, and bewailing of the same. And it never consents that a heart shall hold it without bitterness."

Parenthetically, it might be observed that the love she is talking about is illicit love.

The only obvious comment on which is that it seems to have been extraordinarily easy for Boccaccio to be highly moral after he had been unsuccessful.

CHAPTER XII

AND on top of this disaster, came another disaster. Boccaccino, who had so far been able to temper his querulous complainings of his son's supposedly profitless and ne'er-do-well ways, with what must have been at least a reasonably generous allowance, suddenly found himself floundering about amid financial shoals and reefs. For him, and in consequence for his son also, the days of golden plenty were ended. Now there came a close, cramping time when every detail of expenditure must be watched with great care. News of this, reaching Giovanni just at that critical point in his career, when his groundless hopes of regaining a lost paradisiacal haven made him more anxious than ever to play the part of the gilded and extravagant youth, undoubtedly was a final crushing blow.

The exact causes of this devastating calamity have not yet been definitely established. Certain facts, however, having important bearing on the subject have persisted through the obliterating dust of the centuries, and by correlating various of these we can come moderately close to the truth.

There is proof, for example, that the elder Boccaccio left Naples sometime before 1332, for it is recorded that he was then again in Paris; and we also know that he was at that time still connected with the Bardi: his resignation is inscribed in the company's books as taking place on July 1, 1338. Furthermore documents even to-day extant show him transacting personal business, with at least the outward appearance of solvency, as late as October, 1337. However, by November, 1339, the change had occurred. For on the fifth day of that month, he and his second son Francesco sold some property to Bartolomeo del fu Coppo de' Canigiani, and to a certain Lapa, lay devotee of the Order of San Domenico, and to a certain Giovanni, lay devotee of the Order of San Francesco, for three hundred gold florins. As a result of this sale, Bartolomeo declared himself satisfied in regard to a debt of one hundred florins to one Betto da Certaldo for which he stood guarantor. He also declared that he and the above-named two were now satisfied in regard to all debts owing to them as heirs to the late Simona del fu Coppo de' Canigiani. Sometimes, then, in the two-year period that elapsed between those two points, the catastrophe took place.

And just at that moment there was a financial earthquake at Florence, the tremors of which would go a long way toward accounting for it. In 1339, the two houses of Bardi and Peruzzi failed sensationally. Two causes have been assigned for this. First of all, speculation in England, where, plunged into the wool business, they had been, like present-day stock-buyers, discounting future rises of value beyond all but the wildest hopes, and had bought privilege after privilege from the restless and ambitious Edward III, at the price of enormous loans to him. To do this not only the strongboxes of the London offices were drained: all the reserves of the home companies were poured out, as were also the fiduciary deposits. The default of the English monarch, after his French and Scottish wars failed to turn out just as he had expected, left him owing the Florentine bankers more than a million florins, which they would never be able to collect. Second, the war against Mastino della Scala, lord of Padua, Verona, Vicenza, Brescia, Feltre, Belluno, Parma, Modena and Lucca, over the possession of this last city, which the warrior son of Can Grande had filched from the Florentines under the pretext of conquering it for them. Into this, they poured another fortune, and when Florence's principal ally Venice made a separate peace, they were still further in deep water. One of two things, therefore, must have happened. Either Boccaccino lost his job in the general paring down of expenses, which took place in the companies' vain efforts to stave off the inevitable. Or else he was actually involved in their ruin, and went down with the rest.

The first thing that Giovanni did when he received these tidings was to flee from Naples. It is not to be supposed, however, that he was compelled to do this by any actual and pressing neediness. Indeed, we know definitely that it was some time later before he was actually penniless. If—as far as that goes—he ever was. But the new state of his personal affairs humiliated him deeply, and he did not wish those who had seen him in his glory to witness him in his present condition. He went, therefore, to Piedigrotta, which is located above Posilipo, in the craggy, fire-shaped hills that form the north end of the Bay of Naples. Not far from Baia, it happens, so that in his woe he could almost look down upon the scene of his days of joyousness. There near the tomb of Vergil, he took up his residence in a rude country house, being glad, apparently, to flaunt his misery. It was this phase of his life, incidentally, that gave rise to the legend that it was while brooding over the final resting-place of the mellifluous Roman that he first commenced his career of writing. The urn resting in that igneous, subterranean-seeming country—made only the more solemn by its wide, umbrella-shaped pine trees—that is so appropriate to him who first took us down the steep slope to Avernus, the legend is a pretty one. It is a pity, in a way, that it is not true.

The life that he lived there—we know from four of his Latin epistles that survive to tell us of it—was a great and unpleasant contrast to the dozen-odd years he had so unexpectedly left behind him. Even if you make allowance for exaggeration— and their intense, bitter vehemence makes it difficult to believe that they were merely literary exercises as some seem to imagine—they paint the picture of a dreary anti-climax that was sorrowful indeed.

In the first place, his state of mind was not such as to make him pleasant company either to himself or to anybody else. Three goddesses, he said, tormented him. Venus, Juno, and Ramnusia. Love, money, and vengeance. In other words, he had been plunged into the depths by the shipwreck of his affair with Fiammetta; and his money difficulties had deprived him of all opportunity of making any sort of a readjustment. He could not, for example, show a pretended indifference, and thus salve his hurt pride by a series of other amorous engagements. What his idea of vengeance was, is not so clear. Did he wish to even his score with Fiammetta, and if so, how? Or was his rage directed against his father, whose very straitened circumstances he would have been capable—especially at that moment in his hypersensitive frame of mind—of believing to have been part of some ingenious scheme directed against his independence? Or was, finally—and this would not have been inconsistent with the temperament of an as yet unmatured poet—his vindictive mood directed against the very pattern of destiny and the very way of life itself?

In the second place the actual manner in which he was obliged to live was quite thoroughly distasteful to him. The Florentine does not rusticate easily, and although later Giovanni was glad enough to retire to the calm of Certaldo, first of all that was a place every inch of whose ground was familiar to him, and secondly he was then older and wearier. Now he was young and active, so, like Machiavelli in the latter's involuntary retirement, he cried out against the rural life that brought him ineffable monotony and ineffable boredom. He was miserably clad, he said. He was living on vile herbs that turned his stomach. All that he could hear were the crude disputes of the rough countrymen with their uncultured voices like the barking of dogs. Their Stygian breath was the only odor which reached his nostrils.

Two other happenings further contributed to his unhappiness. In October, 1338, Niccolo Acciaiuoli set sail for the Morea in Greece to aid his royal protectors and his royal protégés, in recovering their princedom there. Niccolo had risen fast, yet had still maintained his friendship for his compatriot. His expedition, therefore, deprived Giovanni of his last hope for court favor and court advancement. "The departure of Æneas was not more melancholy to Dido, nor did Penelope long more eagerly for the return of Ulysses," was his comment. He was also forced back into business, at least to a certain extent. Out of his own ruin, Boccaccino had saved at least something for his son. But he had saved it in such a way that Giovanni had to take the responsibility of getting it. On the sixteenth of November, 1339, he leased for a year the income of the church of San Lorenzo in Capua, and the next autumn this was renewed for a second year. It amounted to twenty-six florins and this Giovanni had to collect himself. It was as if—as Hauvette points out—Boccaccino had said to the young man: "You do not care to go into banking or really to become a canon lawyer. Well, that's up to you. As far as I am concerned, all that I can now afford to give you is this small amount of money. But I have given it to you in such a way that if you choose to you can probably make it amount to a great deal more. Now let's see you take care of yourself!"

Insult, thus,—as Giovanni saw it—being added to injury, his misery was well-nigh complete.

His only refuge was to plunge furiously into intellectual activity. First of all he resumed his legal studies which presumably seemed more attractive to him now that he had been given another taste of business. Second, he started writing once more.

"Here," he jested in his witty letter in the Neapolitan dialect to which we have already referred, and which shows that this melancholy period had at least an occasional lighter moment, "lives Abbot Gio. Boccaccio and night and day he does nothing but scribble. Often enough have I told him so, and have wanted to commiserate with him. At this he laughs, and says: 'My lad, beat it, skedaddle! Go to school and play with children of your own age. I do this to keep myself busy.' Old Judge Barilli tells me that he knows the devil of a lot more than even Scaccinopoli of Sorrento. I don't know why he does this, and by the Madonna of Piedigrotta it worries me."

What the products of his pen were at this time can only be guessed. A request for the *Thebiad* of Statius has led some to think that it was then that he composed the *Teseide* which we have referred to an earlier period but which was obviously based on that Latin poem. But this does not follow, for in asking his friend to send him the same he stated plainly that he wished simply to copy the notes in his own copy. Thus, clearly, he already possessed the book.

He was, finally, immersed deeply in the study of classic authors. Vergil, Ovid, Statius, and Apuleius were among those he read. He lifted to his lips their wine-filled chalices, seeking therein forgetfulness, and not finding it; finding instead, and by way of compensation, wisdom which he had not sought.

In this way he lived for two years. Then there was a third catastrophe. He was obliged to return to Florence. Of all, it was the most crushing, for as long as he lived near Naples, he could entertain, however fantastically, the hope that things would be once again as they had been. But now even hope was taken.

The circumstances are exactly those related, among other places, in the "Amorous Fiammetta."

"Inevitable death, the final end of all things," Panfilo there tells that lady who bears the name of her Giovanni loved, "of many other sons has left me sole to survive with my aged and reverend father. He, burdened with many years, and living without the sweet company of his deceased wife and loving brothers, who might in his old age have comforted him, and remaining now without any hope of more issue, being determined not to remarry, doth recall me home to see him, as the chiefest part of his consolation, whom he hath not seen these many years."

In actual life, Margharita had died and Francesco had died, and the old man was left alone.

So Giovanni was obliged to go back to him.

We assume that as Panfilo does, he delayed and delayed, but finally he could delay no longer.

A Florentine document shows him to have been in that city on January 11, 1341, and as various references in his works make it probable that he was still in the kingdom of Naples until late the year before, and as the journey from Naples to the city by the Arno took twelve days, it is assumed that it was in December, 1340, that he left the southern metropolis. He went, as an English commentator has put it, "into the strong and delicate Florentine country, along the bad roads, through the short days."

Yet though it was his own city toward which he journeyed, he was going, in a sense, into exile. Not as Dante might have done, though certainly he came later to love Florence, but bitterly, sorrowfully, did he ride in between the brown houses with their slant red-tiled roofs.

For where your treasure is, it has been observed, there will your heart be also. His treasure had been left by the magnificent lapis lazuli waters of that curved bay that faces violet Capri and the rugged magnificence of the blue Sorrentine peninsula. It was no mean treasure either. In one sense, it was the dream of a woman who, although she still lived, had never really existed. In another, it was his own gleaming youth.

CHAPTER XIII

IN the shaping of Boccaccio, the next seven or eight years were to be extremely critical. In that they put the final touches to his character and equipment, they were, in a certain sense, to be the most critical of all.

He had already, as we can see, assimilated almost all of that intimate and sympathetic knowledge of the variegated Italian life, expression of which was to call forth from his heart and brain that great masterwork of eloquent and living prose by which—except by students—he is alone remembered. Circumstance—to him it seemed bitter and unpleasant circumstance, though all who have read and been delighted must judge differently—had blocked him off from the pleasant byways of mediocrity. The only qualities that he still needed were maturity and detachment—the impersonal point of view—the latter being, perhaps, an adjunct of the former. These he now proceeded to acquire.

And he acquired them, as we judge him to have acquired all of his strong qualities, through the chastening of personal unhappiness.

In the first place, the life that he was obliged to live in his father's joyless house contrasted even more sadly with the gorgeous days at Naples than had his self-imposed exile at Piedigrotta. He himself describes this plainly, and although the words come from a work of fiction, they are written explicitly in the first person, and have the exact value of autobiography:

"There, there was beauty, noble blood, and worth,
Gay words, and good example, pleasure, love.
There strong desire moved men to salvation.
There just as much of good and happiness
As man could have, there was. There you enjoyed
All of the world's delights, and their sweet savor,
You tasted and you knew. But here, alas,
Is melancholy and eternal woe.
For here one never laughs, or laughs but rarely,
And a dark, silent, very mournful house
Keeps me and sadly knows my unhappy step.
Here the most dour and most horrible sight
Of a rude, cold, and miserly old man
Every hour—to my loathing—grieves me more.
So that to have seen the dear day reach its end
And to return to such a cheerless inn
Turns every joy of mine to bitterness."

Boccaccino, in a word, was growing old. He was now sixty, perhaps a little more than that, and sixty in the hard life of the Fourteenth Century brought a man close to decrepitude. Besides that, the elder Boccaccio was close to ruin. All his hopes and schemes had shattered, and he was now too full of years to rebuild them. You are to visualize, therefore, a sordid and complaining old man. Bitter against life. Bitter against luck. Bitter, particularly, against this useless, wasting son of his, whose help he now felt convinced—if only Giovanni had done something more practical than scratch worthless trash on good paper—would have stayed off disaster, would have shored up the timbers of the falling house.

In the second place, Florence itself had fallen into woeful and heart-rending times. "Thy city," Boccaccio made Fiammetta tell Panfilo, "is full of haughty and boasting words, but even more so with pusillanimous deeds. It is a slave not only to a thousand laws, but to as many different opinions as there are men. All of whom—citizens as well as foreigners—being naturally contentious do stir up continual civil war. And as it is full of proud, covetous, and malicious people, so, too, is it filled with innumerable cares." These strictures could have been applied to the town by the Arno at almost any time during the Fourteenth Century: never, however, with any more aptness than at the exact moment when Giovanni returned from the south.

Then, indeed, the "gluttons, innkeepers, whoremongers, and other similar filth" which, according to his later judgment, ruled the city, had brought her very close to ruin. Then, indeed, her free government came close to being wiped out.

It transpired in this way. The series of unsuccessful wars in which Florence had been engaged, and the confusion and even actual tumult which followed the failure of her banking houses, had stirred up a bitter contest of factions, and rather than let any one of these triumph at the expense of the others, the city fathers chose to deliver her to an outsider. Walter of Brienne was the man selected, and although he assumed the high-sounding title of Duke of Athens, he was neither a Duke nor an Athenian. He was, rather, a cheap, vulgar adventurer; a cold-blooded and unscrupulous Frenchman who thought that the Neapolitan success of the house of Anjou—to which he was connected by marriage—gave him a splendid and compelling example. Just as the Angevines had taken over Naples, so he would acquire Florence. And he almost did. By intrigue—he conspired with both the nobles and the proletariat against the reigning middle classes—and by wholesale executions, step by step he extended his power, succeeding finally in having himself made lord of the city for life. It was only when his terrorism touched so many persons that four or five con-

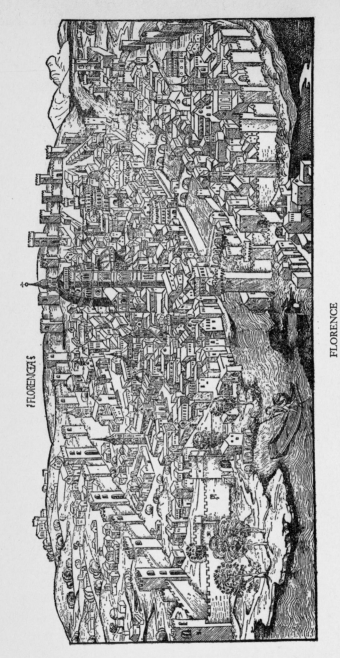

FLORENCE

FROM A FIFTEENTH CENTURY ENGRAVING

spiracies came into being independently and yet simultaneously, and were then fused, that he was removed from power by the application of the same methods by which he had established himself. He was thrown out—that is—by armed force.

And yet even this removal was accomplished at a price. So universally had Walter become hated that nobles, middle class, and that same proletariat—*popolo minuto*—which had shouted for his election, combined in the dramatic insurrections of St. Anne's Day, 1343, by which the French tyrant was driven from the city. In consequence, these three classes for a short while forgot their animosities and were associated in ruling the city. But such halcyon days did not last for long. The *popolo minuto,* thus given their first taste of power, found that they liked it exceedingly. They wanted more of it. New turmoil, therefore, broke out in October of the same year. Ostensibly it was directed against the Bardi, half noble, half burgher, who in spite of their recent disasters were still firmly entrenched in the Oltr'arno quarter of the city, but its real purpose was to end the truce between the classes. At the end of it the nobles once again had lost their right to a share in the government, and the rich middle class found itself in the minority on the governing bodies of the city.

For one thing, all this danger and disturbance was extremely distasteful to peace-loving Giovanni—Giovanni *delle tranquilità,* as his friend Acciaiuoli ironically called him. For another, it was his friends who had suffered the most under Walter, and who had been either disenfranchized or greatly reduced in power in the disturbances which followed his rule. Finally, however democratic he was in theory, Giovanni had the intellectual's utter contempt for the seething mob. Like Henri Brulard he seems to have hated the rabble at the same

time that under the name of the people he longed passionately
for its well-being. It is not hard to imagine, therefore, and it
is utterly impossible to exaggerate the bitterness of this part of
his life.

Two occurrences did, however, in some way mitigate its
unhappiness. One was the arrival of his old friends, Niccolo
Acciaiuoli and Giovanni Barilli, who came to Florence in 1341
as ambassadors from King Robert when the Florentines asked
the Neapolitan ruler to assist them in their war against Pisa for
the recovery of Lucca. It was at this time that Acciaiuoli, by
his generous donation, established the Certosa at Galuzzo.
Boccaccio, in the capacity of lawyer, was one of those who
helped the magnate draw up the deeds by which he endowed
his native city with that magnificent monastery which, sprawl-
ing over a breathless hillside, still overlooks the whole
panorama of Florence and her valley. We know, therefore,
that he must have had an opportunity of seeing these two men
and of renewing in conversation his old days in the south.

The second was his father's remarriage. Sometime before
May, 1343—the probabilities are, at least a year earlier—
the elder Boccaccio took a second wife. Her name was Bice
di Ubaldino de' Bostichi, and like his first wife she seems to
have brought him a fat dowry. Unlike his first wife, however,
she was responsible for a betterment in her stepson's condition,
for with his improved finances and with his renewal of youth,
Boccaccino's disposition improved also. In December, 1342,
he bought part of a house in the Sant' Ambrogio quarter.
This, it appears, was for Giovanni, who was thus allowed to
have an establishment of his own.

CHAPTER XIV

DURING these years, Boccaccio was, as always,—was, as especially during periods of personal stress—plunged deeply in creativeness. Judged by certain modern writers, perhaps, he did not produce any amazing quantity. But in those days the fabrication of a work of art went with extraordinary slowness. Before the edifice was constructed, the very stone had to be quarried. You had, almost, to form the actual language you were using, and if you compare Giovanni's collected works, each unit a completed book, with, say, the accumulation of fragments left by Chaucer, you will see plainly the magnitude of his achievements. It was as if he wrote in a sort of wild disordered fever, knowing that the scratch of his stylus upon parchment made the only music that would drive out of his mind crowding thoughts, any one of which might lead him to annihilation. He finished the *Filocolo*—such of it, that is, that he had not already done at Naples or during the eighteen months at Piedigrotta—and at the same time indited four new long books. Three of these pointed back with a fiery and regretful poetry to the days that he had left behind him. The fourth one looked resolutely ahead.

First in order was, it seems probable, the *Ameto,* set on paper almost certainly in the summer of 1341. Known also as "The Comedy of the Florentine Nymphs," it was cast into a form modeled after Dante's *Vita Nuova.* That is to say, it was made up of prose narrative alternated with passages in poetry.

The imitation was intentional. Boccaccio was an intense and self-effacing hero-worshiper of his great predecessor—*"il Maestro,"* he calls him, *"del quale io tengo ogni ben"*—and he unquestionably meant the whole book to be a Dantesque performance. But it was as impossible for this candid and affable lover of the flower-starred meadows of the five senses to follow his austere preceptor into the paths of even verbal asceticism, as it would have been for him to don wings and fly, so with form, the resemblance ends.

The story of this book is extremely simple. Ameto, a young hunter, is wandering through the woods near Florence, when suddenly he encounters Lia, a nymph of well-nigh heavenly beauty. He falls in love with her, and thereby his rude spirit is filled with sentiments of heretofore even unimagined tenderness. He, therefore, follows her, and to her declares his feelings. If she will but favor him, he says, henceforth he will give over his cruel occupation. He will civilize himself. He will become a peaceful shepherd. His suit is partially accepted, and he is allowed to associate with the nymphs and take part in their pastoral diversions. He sees them reclining in woody glades and hears Theocritan shepherds sing of love or hold poetic contest as to the manner of tending their flocks.

Then one day he is fully accepted. Lia and six of her companions are seated in a circle, and they make him the president of their gathering. Each nymph tells the story of her life. At the end, a flame descends from heaven, and out of the flame comes a voice:

> "I am the light of heaven, threefold and one,
> The beginning and the end of everything."

It is Venus. Not that Venus, however, "whose name the ignorant have taken to designate their disordered passions, but she from whom all true, lawful and holy love comes down to earth." Ameto is then stripped of his rude garments, and plunged into a fountain. From this, clear-sighted and with the mist blown from his eyes, he rises joyously to embrace the service of the goddess. And as he rises, the meaning is plain to us.

The whole thing is an allegory. Venus is God. Ameto is untaught and primitive humanity. It is love that teaches him. It is love that civilizes him. Divine love, doing its ennobling work on him through the four cardinal and the three theological virtues, which are represented by the seven nymphs. The fountain is baptism into which Ameto, man, is plunged by Lia, faith. Thus, in this symbolical story written by the man whose vehement strictures against certain priests have led to the mistaken opinion that he was irreligious, humanity achieves salvation in the orthodox way.

And it is, really, this double reading that gives to the *Ameto* its principal present interest—the interest of revealing its writer's complicated nature. On the one hand, his heart believes and his head is skeptical. On the other—it seems almost a contradiction—all that he has learned makes him Christian and moral, all that he feels makes him a pagan. Nowhere is this brought out more clearly than in this book.

For it must be confessed that although in conception and intention the *Ameto* is highly moral and religious, in actuality it is just the opposite. With the exception of Fiammetta whose identity we already know, each one of the nymphs, besides representing a virtue, was a portrait of an actual Florentine lady. Some of them can be identified, and the names, thus, of Monna Lottiera della Tosa, Monna Emilia Tornaquinci, Monna Sismonda di Francesco Baroncelli, have acquired the modified immortality of at least being known to scholars.

They conducted themselves like Florentine ladies. At any rate, more like Florentine ladies than like the virtues of wisdom, justice, temperance, courage, hope, faith, and charity which they were supposed to represent. Each one had loved greatly, and each one's great love was both illicit and unchaste. Six of them were married, and therefore to love greatly were obliged to betray their husbands. The story of one of these betrayals has already been recounted, since it is in the account of Fiammetta and Caleone that Boccaccio tells with most detail the tale of his own nocturnal surprise of Maria. The other nymphs and their young lovers carried on their intrigues with a similar lack of principle, if not of audacity.

And there is one thing further. The intimate aspects of these amours are dwelt on with a frankness that causes even one accustomed to the outspokenness of the times some astonishment. For instance, Agapes, one of the nymphs, is married to an old husband. In justification of her infidelity, she discusses his biological limitations, dwelling on his senile impotence with the clammy and the unemotional coolness of a treatise on medicine.

Remember, too, that this was not a tale from a collection of merry stories—though it must be pointed out that in the *Ameto* with the compressed narrative of its seven stories we have the real forerunner of the *Decameron*—but a moral allegory. Agapes was not a buxom goodwife waiting for her priest paramour. She represented a cardinal theological virtue —Charity, called "the greatest of these three."

The next work to which Boccaccio set his hand was the *Amorosa Visione*. A long poem in *terza rima*—the meter of "The Divine Comedy"—it, too, was an allegory of divine love, expressed in the terms of that physical love which was the only kind of love that Giovanni could really understand. Far more complicated and artificial than its predecessor, it had, in addition to its meaning, one extremely important aspect.

It definitely confirmed the identity of Fiammetta.

The initial letters of every third line, strung together make two sonnets dedicating the poem to this lady, and a third addressed to the readers. The first of these refers explicitly to "Madama Maria" whom the poet declares to be his lady love, and whom he says he desires to serve always. It concludes with these words:

> "Cara Fiamma, per cui il cor ò caldo,
> Que' chi vi manda questa visione,
> Giovanni è di Boccaccio da Certaldo."

Translated:

> "Dear Fiammetta, for whom my heart still
>   burns,
> The one who sends this vision unto you
> Is Giovanni di Boccaccio of Certaldo."

Under this mask that he must, surely, have regarded as absolutely impenetrable, he spoke out.

The poem itself is written in the first person. Boccaccio, absorbed in contemplation of the woman of his heart, falls asleep and finds himself on a deserted beach. All at once a fair lady appears before him and offers to conduct him to supreme happiness. The poet accepts and follows her to a large and imposing castle to which there are two entrances. One of these, straight and narrow, leads to a steep stairway, up which, if you cast aside all the joys of this earth, you can climb to bliss eternal. The other opens on a fair garden. Over it is written:

> "Riches and dignities and every treasure,
> All worldly glory in abundancy,
> I give to him who steps across my sill."

It is not difficult to imagine which one of these entrances Boccaccio decides to choose.

He meets the objections of his guide by saying that it is no sin to know about the things of this world, but only to follow that which is evil, leave that which is good. Besides, one can always repent at the last moment, thus having all the joys of the earth and gaining heavenly joys also. Her last cautions—that it is easy to be tempted, hard to avoid temptation—lose their force when two damsels, one in white, the other in red, appear and offer to conduct him. He follows them and they lead him into a large room the walls of which are painted—with more skill than could be done by any painter "except Giotto"—with scenes representing the triumphs of Learning, Glory, Riches, and Love. These are the prizes that the world has to offer, and to prove their worth we here have a long, monotonous catalogue of all the names, from Homer to Dante, from Æneas to Charles of Anjou, that were held in esteem at that time. If you follow the world you may become one of these, is the implication. Living persons are not exempted, and in the triumph of Riches, both King Robert of Naples, and the elder Boccaccio figure. Unfortunately, however, in no creditable rôle. They are among the avaricious.

But that is not the whole story of worldly glory. Boccaccio next enters a small room in which the fickleness of fortune, and the insecurity of human affairs, are illustrated by a long series of famous examples. This gives his guide a second chance of urging him to turn back. Let him follow her. There is still time to mount the steep stairs to salvation. This almost convinces him but fails owing to the fact that he sees before him a fair garden that is, with its cropped sward and its marble fountains, extremely reminiscent of those at Mergellina and at Castel Nuovo. There, among many fair ladies, either directly named or readily recognizable as those of the court of Naples, he sees Fiammetta. He loves her, but the difference of their ranks makes him afraid for his success. She tells him to disregard this, and he enters her service for a while. The exact duration of this is given:

> "Five times three times nine days, I found myself
> Under the sweetness of her signory."

It is the very length of time that he had waited patiently but with rising hopes at Baia.

Finally she yields to him in a vision.

And it is then, strangely enough, that his guide is able to persuade him to go the way she wants him to. For Fiammetta bids him to return to the fair lady, and when he does, it is to Fiammetta that the fair lady unites him. She commands him to serve Fiammetta always and to carry out her every desire. She then tells the two lovers to repose awhile amid the flowers before ascending to beatitude. They do this and the book abruptly ends.

But not unfittingly, however. For since, as far as Boccaccio was concerned, they had already reached heaven, any further writing would have been superfluous. This is extremely illuminating. Like the *Ameto,* the *Amorosa Visione* was a deliberate Dantesque imitation, but Giovanni's "Vision of Love" turned out to be just the reverse of Dante's journey through heaven and hell. It was the negative to Dante's positive, black and white being exactly interchanged. This was not because Boccaccio wished to flout or even parody his forerunner. Quite the contrary, indeed. Just, however, as he was so far unable to understand Dante's transcendental passion as to explain—when he came later to write the latter's life— the poet's falling in love with Bice at the tender age of nine

by "the custom of the times," by "the sweet music and general
gayety" of the festival at which he met her, by "the influence of
the spring weather" and by "the delicate foods and wines,"
so also did the Alighieri's spiritual geography lie beyond his
comprehension. As is the case of the Mohammedan's houri-
filled paradise, Boccaccio's heaven had to be a mirror of the
earth he knew and loved. He placed it, therefore, in a garden
of this world.

His third book of the Florentine period was concerned
also with the great love that he had found in Naples. It was
the expression, however, of quite a different mood.

As we have seen, the *Ameto* was the product of the fierce
ache of physical longing. It was a book of the body. The
flesh cried for assuagement, and out of this cry was wrung a
work that for all its allegorical and poetic form, dwells on the
flesh with an insistence that seems almost the product of a
mad obsession. Indeed, the vehemence of the *Ameto* is
such, that it has caused some to conclude that each one of its
ladies represented some one with whom Giovanni carried on
an intrigue. *I have been faithful to thee, Cynara, in my
fashion,* as it were. The *Amorosa Visione* shows him, as we
have seen, less acutely in anguish. Though his nature would
not permit him to separate himself entirely from the flesh, he at
least essayed some sort of a sublimation. He had now reached
another stage, that in which he could regard his own experiences dispassionately. Though it concerns itself with emotion,
out of the intellect he spun this third book.

The *Elegia di Madonna Fiammetta*, was written in 1343 or
1344, and though as Boccaccio conceived it, it was but a prose
imitation of those poems of Ovid wherein an abandoned and
generally a seduced maiden pours forth her woes, it turned
out to be an acute analysis of a jilted woman. For all its

elaborate periods and its wordy circumlocutions, and for all
its classic comparisons—Fiammetta is, for instance, paralleled,
among nearly a hundred others, with Dido, Phaedra, Medea,
Œnone, and Ariadne, with a glib facility that should give the
lie direct to Boccaccio's supposed lack of education—it is, above
everything else, an extraordinarily clever study in psychology.
It is, indeed, really the first psychological novel ever written.
It is also—to judge anyway from the matter of reprints—
the only one of Boccaccio's works excepting the *Decameron*
which is still entirely readable. In this case, public taste
seems to be correct.

Its plot hardly need be dwelt upon. For one thing, there is
very little of it. For another it is, virtually, Boccaccio's own
story. This he plainly indicates in the text, but even if he had
not we could have guessed it from what we know of him. One
divergence is, however, to be noted. In real life Boccaccio was
discarded by his lady love. In this novel it is he who, under
the name of Panfilo, does the jilting. The reason for this
cannot really be any puerile idea of revenge on the part of
Giovanni. Such is the explanation commonly given, but
childish as Boccaccio may at times have been, it is hard to
believe that he was ever quite so childish as that. A more
plausible explanation lies in the very nature of his subject.
He wished to analyze a person rejected in love, and his instinct
told him correctly that for such a purpose a woman would be
far better than a man. The only woman he knew well enough
so to analyze was Maria d'Aquino. Nor was he in any way
obligated to tell the exact truth. He was, after all, writing
fiction.

And certainly the result he achieved more than justified any
such tampering with what actually happened. It is a great
book, and it will be long indeed before the subtle variations on

the theme of a lovely woman who has stooped to folly will be rendered with more skill.

Fiammetta sees Panfilo in the Church of San Lorenzo. She falls in love with him. He becomes her suitor. The scene of the nocturnal surprise is told by implication. He becomes her lover, and day follows day in delirious happiness. Then suddenly catastrophe. He is obliged to return to Florence. She cannot detain him, but she does exact a promise that he will return again. This he makes gladly, but the time elapses and he does not appear. A little later she learns that he is married. Then it turns out that it was not he, but his father who had married. A little later she learns that although he has not married he is in love with another lady. Finally she hears that he is coming to Naples once more. She once essayed suicide, her eyes were "depainted round about with blue and purple circles" but now the scale of her emotions rises, almost soars to joyousness. The day comes in a madness of expectation. The hour, and she is almost beside herself. It passes. Panfilo does not arrive. Then suddenly she learns a last crushing truth. He who was coming was not Panfilo but another of the same name. This is the note on which the book ends. Fiammetta's disillusion is complete.

It is not possible to give in brief outline any idea of the consummate skill with which Boccaccio dealt with this theme. A master of objective writing, he here left the exterior, dealing with which he was so expert, to penetrate to the interior. His success, it must be said, was complete. Fiammetta's passion was not a simple one. No woman's passion ever is. When first she fell in love she was aware of wrongdoing, and after she had been betrayed she realized that she had been gravely disloyal to her husband. This is noted. Yet, even so, she could not change from her love. This is noted, too.

But there are two incidents which show more than anything else Boccaccio's command of his subject. The first is the manner in which he dealt with Fiammetta's learning of Panfilo's supposed marriage. In Fiammetta's hearing, a young lady asks a Florentine merchant for tidings of Panfilo, and when she hears of his marriage she turns first red, then white. Instantly Fiammetta's jealous suspicions are aroused. Did Panfilo leave some one else heartbroken in Naples? Was he a sailor who had more than one wife in every port? Her jealousy next becomes anger, yet even her anger cannot last long, being swept—here Boccaccio's skill is shown—by the very incident into a resurgence of longing and of passion. The second is when he relates how Fiammetta reacts to news of Panfilo's imminent return. She has come to hate her love, and almost to hate him who is the cause of it. Yet when she learns that he will come again she can hardly wait for each hour, each minute that brings him nearer, to slip into the notch left vacant by its predecessor. It is so true that it is astonishing. It is superb and it is magnificent. Here we have writing by one who has become a great and very subtle connoisseur of love.

So great and so subtle, indeed, that in considering this, we are apt, as we read this account of poor amorous Fiammetta, to forget all the other aspects of the book. The description of Naples and Baia with their warmth and color to which we have already referred. The amazing characterizations. Two characters in this book have almost Shakespearean grandeur. One is the old nurse who warns Fiammetta against love, yet aids her in obtaining the same, and consoles her when she has lost it. She is so clearly drawn as to suggest an actual model. The other is Fiammetta's husband. His consideration, his kindness, his toleration and his concern make him no typical

Neapolitan baron. Such could not have been the husband of the real Fiammetta. Boccaccio when he wrote the *Fiammetta* was no longer a boy poet. He was a full-blown magician in the realm of the written word.

CHAPTER XV

IT was with this excellent novel that Boccaccio at last wrote *finis* to the dramatic episode which had occupied him for so long. He did not forget the lady, to be sure. We have already indicated his attitude to her as expressed in the prologue to his renowned collection of short stories, and it was only when his ardors had been chilled by the actual touch of age that he could strike the pose of grouping her with his other love affairs as nothing more than "certain juvenile indiscretions." Even then, as we have already noted, he wrote one or two sonnets. But from now on she was no longer an obsession. The Provençal tradition of the troubadors was still strong enough for a poet to feel that he ought to have an ideal lady, and as such Maria d'Aquino would do very well. The world, however, was too much with this clear-sighted materialist, late and soon, for him to moon forever about any one who was entirely inaccessible. Nowhere is this more clearly indicated than in the last book he wrote during these years in Florence. In it his mood had completely changed.

The *Ninfale Fiesolano* has nothing whatsoever to do with Naples. Outside of a few perfunctory lines of dedication, it has nothing to do with his princess. It has nothing to do, even, with unsuccessful love. This short narrative in rhymed octaves is purely Florentine. It is entirely local and entirely rural. Every line of it is redolent of the fine, rugged country that lies between the winding Arno, yellow close at hand, pewter-colored as you look down on it from an eminence, and the

tall, blue, crowned forehead of Fiesole. As you read it, you can
almost see the clustered white farmhouses, standing amid military cypresses, each one's littered back yard guarded by a
noisy, ferocious watchdog, badly in need of a bath. And the
fields, with their rows of gnarled olive trees, indescribably
weathered and old, often split into two parts, just as if a hama-
dryad dwelling therein had emerged, casting her tree shell
aside as does a butterfly its outworn chrysalis. And the trailing
vines suspended between them. And the tall, graceful wheat.
And the red, scattered poppies. And the white, gentle oxen
guided by sturdy olive-skinned *contadini* in blue smocks. And
the calm eventides so aglitter with flashing fireflies that the
very meadows seem like segments of the Galaxy that have
been flung down extravagantly. And the throaty sorrow of the
nightingales. And the wide river carded into straight lines of
cottonwool by the linear waterfalls of its many mills. And
the harsh, tremulous *rispetti,* quavered by its boatmen, endlessly
sifting and loading gravel for some mysterious purpose of their
own. Warm days and sleepy nights above Candeli and near
Rovezzano! Though hardly any of these things are specifically
described in this poem, so clearly does it evoke the atmosphere
and feeling of the Florentine *contrada,* that they flash before
your eyes.

The tale that it tells is extremely simple. Affrico, a young
shepherd, sees and falls in love with Mensola, a nymph dedicated to the service of Diana. He later surprises her with a
group of other nymphs and tries to declare to her his feelings,
but she is frightened and flees. He then disguises himself as a
nymph and is thus able to join her. An invitation to bathe
discloses his identity and once again all the nymphs flee. Affrico is, however, able to detain Mensola, and this time he tells
his love so effectively that she yields to him. She is now in

love herself, and another rendezvous is arranged. In the interim, unfortunately, she is overcome with shame and fails to keep it. Heartbroken, Affrico drowns himself and the small rivulet flowing into the Arno which now bears his name is stained red with his blood. A little later Mensola discovers that she is pregnant. She is aided by Sinedecchia, an older nymph, to give birth to her child in secret, but the babe's crying after it is born discloses it to Diana. The goddess flies into a rage at Mensola's broken vow and changes her into a stream. It, too, now bears her name and like the Affrico flows into the Arno. Sinedecchia then takes Pruneo, the baby, to the parents of Affrico. They gladly bring him up, seeing in him a reminder of their dead son. He lives with them until the arrival of Atalantus, legendary founder of Fiesole. Then he becomes one of the foremost members of that hero's illustrious band.

It was around this framework that Boccaccio composed his shortest, yet his most exquisite work. Of all his poems, it is the most perfect one. The *Filostrato* is a great narrative, and some of his sonnets express adequately feeling that appears sincere. But in the first case the verse is matter of fact, written on the level of prose, while in the second it is often truly crude. Now at last he had written something, the actual poetry of which is of the first order. Now at last he had written something which would win for him, not only in his own day, but from posterity, the title of poet which he craved.

The *Ninfale Fiesolano* is a true pastoral in that it employs both the vocabulary and the images of the country. Mensola "More fresh and joyous is than a white rose, And far more gleaming than the brightest star," which lines might have come from an improvised rustic love song sung by a country lover. The nymphs fleeing in affright before Affrico are compared to sheep left by their shepherd, who bleat in panic, as they scatter

in all directions before a ravening wolf. Affrico himself, when
he cannot find Mensola, is a hunter who has spent the whole
day in the chase and has not brought back even a single hare.
But this vocabulary and these images are used, it happens, not
by a country lover but by a great artist. Thus this precursor of
the Renaissance anticipates another one of its many aspects. For
both the writings of Lorenzo de' Medici and the painting of
Botticelli are foreshadowed in this slender idyll, and there is in
it, besides, a fragile and very heart-wringing sincerity that
neither of those two distinguished persons could ever quite
command.

Yet for all that, it is not the artistic merit of this poem that
alone causes us to dwell on it. Except for the *Decameron,* every
single one of Boccaccio's Italian writings reflects directly something of his personal life. The *Ninfale Fiesolano* is no exception. Quite the contrary, in fact, for the incidents upon which
it casts illumination are two.

Of the first one we have but a hint. The life of a nymph, as
discussed in this poem, closely parallels the life of a nun in
the Middle Ages. Was Mensola, then, a nun, and in the
Ninfale Fiesolano was Boccaccio narrating the story of an intrigue that he himself carried on with a member of a religious
order? This has been solemnly stated as so, but appropriate as
such an episode would be in the life of a man holding Boccaccio's somewhat skeptical opinions as to the morals of the church,
there is absolutely no proof of it. We must, therefore, leave
it at that.

The second we are more prepared to believe. In no part of
the poem is Boccaccio's sincerity of feeling more apparent than
when he deals with the tenderness of parenthood. The concern of Affrico's father and mother in their son's unhappiness
during his badly-masked love affair, their anguish at his death,

their fond interest in his son Pruneo have an extremely moving reality. They must have been derived from actual experience, and they could hardly have come from anything that Giovanni had observed in his own father. We know further that, although Boccaccio was never married, he begot more than one child.

Writing to Petrarch in his old age about the kind welcome given him in Venice by that poet's daughter Francesca, he added this apropos of Petrarch's granddaughter:

"Then after we had talked of various things, we sat down in your garden with some friends of mine. There Francesca graciously offered me your house, your books, and everything that was in it—yet not for a moment did she forget the modest demeanor of a perfect wife. And while we were thus engaged, who should appear but your Electra, who is a perfect joy! She walked in with a grave step that hardly belonged to her baby years, and before she even knew who I was she looked at me, and laughed. What delight I had when I saw her! How eagerly I took her in my arms! At first I almost thought she was my own baby, the little girl that I once had.

"What shall I say to you? If you do not believe me, ask William of Ravenna, the doctor, or our old friend Donato, both of whom knew her. Your little Electra is the very image of mine. She has the same laugh, the same dancing eyes, the same walk and gestures, the same way of carrying her dear little body. Perhaps my girl was a little taller, but then she was older. She was five and a half the last time that I saw her. Had they spoken the same dialect, they would have used the same words, and with the same lovely simplicity. But why all this talking? I could see no difference between them except that your Electra has golden hair whereas my baby's hair was chestnut. Ah me! How often when I petted your little one and listened to her childish prattle, did the memory of the small daughter taken away from me, fill my eyes with tears! How often did I turn aside sighing so that no one would see them! How sad I was as I wept over your Electra, you certainly must know!"

This passage, which certainly shows us an unexpected Boccaccio, is supplemented by his fourteenth eclogue, where under the name of Olympia he mentions her again, and also refers to four other children.

"By Olympia," he explained in a letter to Fra Martino da Signa, "I mean my little daughter, who died at that age at which, so we believe, those who die become the citizens of heaven. And so instead of Violante as she was named when living, I call her Olympia—that is, the angelic one."

The poem says that she died when he was in Naples, the probabilities being sometime during his second trip.

In that case, she was born at about the time he was writing the *Ninfale Fiesolano,* her mother being unknown to us. Fusca —for so in the eclogue this woman is called—may have been the mysterious nun, or she may have been Emilia Tornaquinci —the Emilia of the *Ameto.* Or she may have been neither of these.

And that, therefore, is the explanation of the poem's note of paternal tenderness. As Boccaccio wrote the story of Affrico and Mensola he was being given personal cause to know that unreasonable and yet overwhelming fondness a father can be capable of. Especially a father whose supposedly worldy self-assurance sets him above and makes him aloof from such foolish emotions. Nor—if we can judge from the lines in which he gave expression to these feelings—was he in any way ashamed.

CHAPTER XVI

WITH these four works, Boccaccio at last brought to a conclusion his exacting period of preparation. In spite of his many distractions, he had been able, during a period of approximately ten years, to produce no less than seven highly original books. Each one was of great literary importance, for each one either invented or made popular a type that would be used over and over again in the full flood of the Renaissance. Each one was, however, of far greater importance in Giovanni's own development. Step by step he had been making sound progress in the mastery of his medium. That mastery was now virtually complete. He was now ready for the greatest work of all.

But he was not to write it yet, and this seems to have been extremely fortunate. The time was not quite ripe for the *Decameron,* and Boccaccio who was to have the good luck to bring out this gathering and fusion of all his powers at exactly the right instant, could not, for the moment, turn his hand to it. The reason was that he was diverted from his literary career at this point by the pressure of necessity.

After an interlude of generosity, once again his father either tired of supporting him, or was no longer able to, and he was obliged to earn his own living. But in those days—as indeed, even, until some time after the invention of printing—there were only two ways by which a man of letters could do this. He could enter the service of some prince, half as private secretary, half as personal praise writer, and by flattering the latter's

self-esteem, wheedle enough money and leisure out of him to
be able to indulge his own tastes in study and in composition.
He could sell his knowledge of reading and writing, and of
Latin, to some republic, either serving in one of her numerous
secretariats, or acting as her ambassador—and spending, incidentally, much of his time in trying to collect at least part of
the money that was due him.

At this time either Boccaccio did not have the prestige for the
latter method, or perhaps he had already half guessed the conclusion he was to reach later, that it was better to have one
master than many masters. We do know, however, that he
essayed the former method at least twice.

The first lord whom he served was none other than Ostasio
da Polenta, successor to that Guido who ensured long life for
his name by sheltering Dante during the last gloomy days of
his exile. Petrarch tells us of this service in a letter written
some years later in which he reminds Boccaccio, then in
Ravenna, that he had been there once before "at the time when
the grandfather of the present ruler held sway." Giovanni himself implies it in the preface to his translation of the fourth book
of Livy. "If any honor or praise is deserved by this translation,"
he writes, "it should not be given to me but to that noble knight
Messer Ostasio da Polenta, my very special lord, at whose instances this crude work was undertaken." Ostasio died on
November 14, 1346, and we know that the *Ninfale Fiesolano,*
which was written at Florence, could not have been composed
earlier than 1344, was probably written a year later. We thus
have a date for this episode. We are given, too, some idea of
the triviality of the tasks to which these small rulers set their
talented servitors. Sforza, making use of Leonardo da Vinci
to design trick mechanical devices for his tinsel shows when

he might have been painting other "Last Suppers" was only following an established precedent.

The second lord to whom Boccaccio saw fit to offer his pen was Francesco degli Ordelaffi, captain of Forlì and tyrant of a half dozen or so small cities of the Romagna. Knowing Giovanni's genealogical antecedents, this was not without its aspects of amusing irony. For Francesco was, it happens, nearly the last, and certainly the most recalcitrant of that type of Ghibelline petty despot who had gathered around the standard of the emperor Henry when he marched into Italy. The son, therefore, of one of those stinking countrymen who were now rulers of Florence was taking money from the heir to one of those who would have gladly aided the Florentine Ghibellines in chasing his forebears back to their onion patches. Moreover, the Ghibelline despot was glad to pay out this money. Thus, just as to-day, personal advantage had a bad effect on memory. Thus, lucrative employment or the hope of glory led men to forgive and forget.

We know very little about this phase of Boccaccio's life. He had formed a literary acquaintance with Cecco da Mileto, an early humanist or student of classic letters, with whom he had exchanged Latin and Italian poems. Cecco, who was Francesco's secretary, secured him his position. We do know, however, that Boccaccio's connection with Francesco was responsible for the last event of importance in the first half of his life. This was his second trip to Naples.

"I have not received the Varro that you sent me," he wrote Zanobi da Strada in 1347, "but I would have received it, if I had not been on the point of going to the King of Hungary in the Abruzzi or in farthest Campania where he now is. For since my illustrious lord is preparing to follow the just arms of the latter thither, I am about to go there at his command. Not as a soldier, however, but rather, as you might almost say, as an onlooker, as an arbiter of what takes place."

Probably, then,—since Cecco remained behind—he went as Francesco's historian. In that case, he was a sort of Fourteenth Century war correspondent, obligated like his present-day successors to write an account of what transpired that was favorable to his employer. It may have been for this specific purpose that he was given his post.

The kingdom to which he journeyed was not, however, any longer that dream country, home of poetry and love, that he liked to imagine he had left behind him. Since his departure half a dozen years before, its lazy calm had been blown to pieces by blasts reeking of sulphur. Jealousy, hatred, and lust had caused it to seethe and bubble like the crater of the round, smoking mountain that loomed above its capital. Now, scattering brimstone and destruction, it burst forth.

The origins of all this lay in the fairly distant past. When Robert mounted the throne of Naples, he did not do so as the eldest son of King Charles II. Actually he was the third son. The eldest son was Charles Martel, King of Hungary, and although Robert's coronation was perfectly legal and indeed sponsored by the Pope, the Hungarians, for political reasons, never quite dropped the idea that the Neapolitan monarch was a usurper. Consequently there was considerable friction between the two branches of the house of Anjou. Robert, conscious of his surname "the Wise," felt that it was incumbent on him to end all this. How better could he do it than by uniting the two branches? His only son having died, his granddaughter, Princess Giovanna, was heir to his throne. He would wed her to Andrew of Hungary, youngest son of Charles Martel's successor, Carobert. Thus, with the marriage of these cousins, the two houses would be joined.

And joined they were, only to have their conjunction make for ruin. The wedding took place in 1333, when Giovanna was nine years old, and Andrew barely seven. Ten years later Robert died. Immediately turmoil broke out. Was Andrew to be crowned as joint ruler, or was the royal diadem to be worn only by Giovanna? The Neapolitans said the latter. The Hungarians said the former. They were stirred up by Andrew's confessor, Fra Roberto, described by Petrarch as "some kind of a three-legged animal, barefoot, hoodless, proud of his poverty, soft, bald, and florid, his cheeks swollen, his body hardly covered by his scant mantle" who "stalks with a dark silence through the royal chambers." Feelings reached such a point the Pope was appealed to. First he appeared to support Giovanna, but shortly he turned to Andrew. The Hungarian was to be crowned. That settled Andrew's fate. At midnight on September 18, 1345, just as the papal legates were on the point of arriving for the coronation, he was awakened as he slept by the side of the queen in the convent of Murrone in Aversa, coaxed into the hall, and strangled. His body was pitched over the balcony into the garden below.

Naturally there was a terrific outcry, and a sensation of horror went through most of Europe. Giovanna was then with child—indeed her son Carlo Martello was born less than three months later—but this did not prevent her from acting with decisiveness. The Moor, Raymond Cabani, once a cook, and his wife, Philippa of Catania, the laundress who had become a royal governess, were implicated. They were forthwith sentenced to death. So were Philippa's granddaughter, Sancia, countess of Morcone, Philippa's son Robert, and Philippa's son-in-law. Even this was not enough. Andrew's brother Louis, now King of Hungary, had convinced himself, in his sorrow and rage, that Giovanna was guilty of complicity in the crime, or at least had pre-knowledge of the same. He determined, therefore, to invade the kingdom of Naples. He was at war in Dalmatia, but he detached part of his army, and placing it in command of his natural brother, the Bishop of Fünfkirchen, sent it toward the south. Giovanna was in desperation. Not knowing which way to turn, she hastily married another cousin, Prince Luigi of Taranto, her principal object being, seemingly, to secure a protector.

Then Louis had no doubts at all. This comely, yellow-haired queen was indeed what she has been termed: "a great harlot that sitteth by many waters, and ruleth over Naples." Prince Luigi had been her paramour all along, and the baby Carlo Martello was not even his brother's son. So, at any rate, the Hungarian monarch firmly believed. In December, 1347, therefore, he passed through Foligno, and shortly afterward entered the Neapolitan territory in spite of a papal interdict. He would not halt until he had punished every guilty person, he said. He would not turn northward until he had avenged his brother's death.

But this, it happened, he was never able to accomplish. At his advent, both Giovanna and Luigi fled the kingdom. They left separately. Accompanied by Niccolo Acciaiuoli, Luigi made his way to Tuscany, where a vain attempt to secure Florentine assistance resulted only in their not being allowed to enter the city. Giovanna departed by water. Husband and wife rejoined each other in Provence, where the queen's pose of a beautiful woman in distress, and their wise act of selling Avignon to Pope Clement at a bargain price, secured papal intervention in their favor. Giovanna was pronounced innocent. Thus balked of his purpose, Louis turned what he had begun by regarding as a righteous crusade into a mere brigand's holiday. He vented his anger by causing Charles of Durazzo—

Boccaccio's friend, and one of the few Neapolitan barons who could hardly in any way be suspected of the murder—to be slain and cast from the same balcony Andrew had been. For the rest, he contented himself with pillaging the country, it being impossible, apparently, for any foreign invader of the peninsula to keep either himself or his army above the moral level of a present-day gunman. At any rate, for any length of time. When finally he was obliged to patch up some sort of a peace with Giovanna, all that he had accomplished was to disrupt Neapolitan tranquillity; was to sow a wind that would long shake the stormy south of Italy, that would be reaped as whirlwind for many, many years.

It was such an expedition, then, that took Boccaccio back to that part of the world toward which he would always be impelled by his longing. And we have fortunately the pattern of his reactions to it: four of the sixteen Latin eclogues, or poemdialogues, in which he discussed allegorically those political and personal happenings which he did not wish or dare to deal with plainly and openly, concern themselves with this attempted vendetta. They are interesting, as the comments of a great man on the events of his day must always be interesting. They are also extremely important: they are the only documents whatsoever that we possess that have bearing on this part of Boccaccio's life.

In the first one he was sympathetic to Louis. The writer-idealist aroused by an act that was unspeakable. Peace had reigned in Naples under the rule of Argus—King Robert— the good shepherd, but now all was confusion. For, dying, Argus had confided his kingdom to Alexis—Andrew of Hungary—and that poor young shepherd had been torn down and slain by a pregnant she-wolf—Giovanna. In consequence, fierce lions and bears—the turbulent Neapolitan barons—marauded the forest. At last, however, Tityrus—Louis of Hungary—heard, in his distant caverns by the Ister and the Danube, of the disorders. He hastened to march Naples-ward to put an end to them. The implication is, he *rightly* hastened. The Italian shepherds crowded to his standards. Among them was Faunus—Francesco degli Ordelaffi, Boccaccio's patron.

The second of this series—actually the fourth eclogue—shows a slight change in Boccaccio's feelings. Dorus—Luigi of Taranto—accompanied by Pythias—Niccolo Acciaiuoli—has fled to Volterra. There he is greeted by Montanus—a native of the place—who receives him hospitably. Dorus airs his sorrows. He describes the happiness of the Neapolitan lands under the reign of Argus. He next tells how, with Argus and Alexis dead, he married the beautiful Lycoris—Queen Giovanna—and how, suddenly, Polyphemus—Louis of Hungary—marched over the fields of Parthenope, laying waste all before him. Montanus, weeping, begs him to continue and Dorus goes on with the story, bringing it up to the point where he had reached Volterra. And by now Boccaccio's sympathies are with King Luigi. Although, therefore, the death of Alexis is deplored, and the vindictiveness of Polyphemus is still termed "just anger," Montanus, who represents, certainly, the Boccaccian point of view, tries to comfort Dorus. His troubles are not over, he says, and he has new and sorrowful trials to go through with. But the truth-telling raven has made a prophecy. In the end Dorus will return to power.

And by the time that he has written the last two of the group his change has been complete. In the fifth eclogue Calliopus tell Panphilus—a Neapolitan gentleman who loves his country greatly—the sad story of the woes of Naples that was related to him in Sicilian fields by Calcidia—apparently Naples herself. "Just anger" is forgotten, and the main interest is to relate the horrible fate that descended upon the city. In the sixth eclogue Melibæus narrates to Amynta the direful straights of his land. Amynta consoles him. All has changed, he says. Alcestus—Luigi of Taranto—has returned. They both break into a pæan of rejoicing that has the monotony of a Hebrew psalm. "Rejoice ye mountains, and ye hills, rejoice, For our Alcestus has returned again!" Over and over again the lines are recited, as the benefits thus acquired by Naples are enumerated. Yet this poem could not have been composed more than a couple of years later than the eclogue *Faunus,* which hailed the arrival of Tityrus, who had come to restore order in the woods.

For that reason a question naturally arises. How far was Boccaccio entirely sincere? Did he commence by believing that Giovanna was actually guilty, and that an effective intervention was badly needed? And was his attitude then changed when he saw Louis' supposed high purpose turn out to be merely a pretext for rapine? Or were all of these poems entirely studied? The first written to commend himself to his patron Ordelaffi? The others written when a taste of Naples made him anxious to reëstablish himself there, made him anxious to gain favor with Giovanna? Was he a time-server or an outspoken, honest man?

The probability is that no one answer would be entirely accurate. In the court of Forlì, Boccaccio would have heard nothing but talk of the queen's guilt, the queen's cruelty, the queen's lust. He would come to believe what he heard. At Naples he would have heard something of the other side of the story. He would come to doubt.

Nor would the fact that each of these points of view was the one that was the most advantageous in the place where he happened to hold it, be at all likely to keep him from accepting it. Boccaccio was not entirely above poetic fawning when its result was to be his own improved position. As a rule he was very independent, and certainly he set himself definite standards along this line, but he was humanly fallible enough not always to live up to his theories. We shall later see what efforts he made to gain the patronage of Niccolo Acciaiuoli, and how far he was willing to abase himself. The trouble was, however, that the position of genuflection was so unnatural to him that he could never long continue in it. Sooner or later, his independence flared out, and all that he was working for was lost.

CHAPTER XVII

BETWEEN the years 1346 and 1350, the whole civilized world was shaken to its very foundations by a great and terrifying calamity. An epidemic disease—comparable in its destructiveness only to the plague described by Thucydides which swept Athens in the Fifth Century before Christ or to that which ravaged the falling Roman world in the age of Justinian—appeared suddenly and without any known cause. It was of a fierce and well-nigh insatiable malevolence and it spread disaster like an advancing horde of Mongols. Known as the Great Plague, it probably came closer to annihilating the human race than anything that has happened before or since. In Europe, three out of every five persons perished, while its total toll has been placed at 25,000,000, or more than the complete list of casualties in the recent World War. Small wonder, then, that the superstitious saw in it a scourge wielded by the hand of God, a punishment visited upon mankind for the sins of an evil generation. Small wonder that the credulous were willing to believe the reports of "certain Genovese merchants, men worthy of faith" who related that in the East just before the beginning of its decimations, a great fire rose from the earth or descended from the heavens which burned the whole country, and that it was from this fire that the corrupting germs that bred the pestilence were generated. Small wonder that even the skeptical would not entirely reject the tale of a Franciscan monk of Florence who was a missionary in Asia Minor. At Lamech, recounted this weaver of wonders, for three days and nights, "it rained blood and serpents." And then the mortality began.

Its course can be traced with exactitude. There appeared— the chroniclers relate—"in the neighborhood of Cathay and upper India, and in the other lands bordering the shores of that ocean, a fierce pestilence which attacked men and women of all ages. They straightway began to spit blood, and thereafter they died, some at once, some in two or three days, some after an interval." From Cathay and India, it spread rapidly to all the other countries "in that third part of the world which is known as Asia." It next reached the shores of the Mediterranean, sweeping Syria, Turkey, Egypt, Greece, Russia, and Armenia. "And in that time certain Genovese and Catalan galleys departed from the Great Sea and from Syria and Romania to flee the death and to bring back their merchandise from Italy. But they did not escape swiftly enough to prevent a great part of their company from dying of that sickness on the high seas. And having reached Sicily, they held converse with the people of that country and left some of their sick there, for which reason the pestilence broke out incontinently in Sicily. And the said galleys visiting Pisa and Genoa, through contact with those men the death began in the said cities, but it was not yet general." Shortly, however, it was general. Following Sicily, it struck at North Africa and Sardinia. Then all of Italy "except Milan and certain sections in that part of the Alps near the German frontier." Then Provence, Savoy, "the Riviera of Marseilles and Aquamorta," Catalonia, Majorca, Spain and Granada. Then the western shores of Africa. Then "Ireland, the isle of England and Scotland, and the other islands of the west." It was not until four years after it came into being by the Sea of China, that it reached Germany, Hungary, Frisia, and Denmark, and finally spent itself "amid the Goths and Vandals and the other northern peoples" by the icy ocean of the north.

It was midway on this mighty sweep that it first reached "the notable city of Florence, fair above every other in Italy." The earliest deaths were reported toward the end of March in 1348, and by May the disease was in full swing. It lasted until the end of July, when it spent itself, possibly from lack of fuel. Various estimates place the Florentine mortality at from 50,000 to 100,000 persons. This was more than most people had heretofore realized the entire city held.

Boccaccio describes it for us.

Its symptoms were appalling:

"On men and women alike, there appeared, at the beginning of the malady, certain swellings either on the groin or under the armpit, some of which grew large as a common apple, some larger and some smaller, and these the people called plague-boils. From these two parts the above mentioned plague-boils proceeded, until in a short time they had appeared on every part of the body, and these after a while, the course of the contagion changed into black or livid blotches, which showed themselves first on the arms and about the thighs, and later on every part of the body; in some cases large and few in number, in others small and thickly-strewn."

It was virtually incurable:

"Whether it was that the nature of the disease did not permit it, or the ignorance of physicians, not only did few recover, but very nearly all died within the third day from the appearance of the above symptoms, some sooner and some later, but generally without fever or other complication."

It was highly contagious:

"No, the mischief was even greater. For not only did talking or contact with the sick give the well infection, but the

mere touching of the clothes or of anything that had been
touched or used by the sick was enough to communicate the
malady to the user."

Even animals were not immune:

"Of this my own eyes had experience one day. The rags
of a poor man who had died of the plague being cast into the
public way, two hogs came up to them, and having first, after
their fashion, rooted among them with their snouts, took them
in their mouths and tossed them about in their jaws. Then in
a little while, after turning around and around, they both, as
if they had taken poison, fell down dead upon the rags in
which they had, in an ill hour, intermeddled."

As a result of this, so much fear was bred that all amenities
were cast aside and almost all people devoted themselves to
one purpose, that of self-preservation.

Some felt that they could accomplish this best by living
moderately:

"They dwelt removed from every other person, and shut
themselves up in those houses where none had been sick.
There, using very temperately the most delicate viands and
the finest wines, and avoiding all incontinence, they lived with
music and with such other diversions as they might have, never
suffering themselves to speak with anybody, nor choosing to
hear from without any news of death or of sick folk."

Others took the exact opposite course:

"They maintained that to carouse and make merry, and go
about singing and frolicking, and to satisfy the appetite in
everything possible, and to laugh and scoff at whatsoever
befell, was a very certain remedy for such an ill. That which
they said, they put in practice as best they might, going about
night and day, now to this tavern, now to that, drinking without stint or measure."

The morals of the city went to pieces.

The wiser folk fled to the country, yet even all these did not escape, any more than did all those who remained perish.

"Brother abandoned brother, uncle nephew, and oftentimes wife husband. No, what is yet more extraordinary and indeed almost incredible, fathers and mothers refused to visit or to tend their very children, just as if they had not been theirs."

The abandonment of the sick by neighbors and relatives, and the scarcity of servants was such, that there arose a custom which before was practically unheard of:

"That is, that no woman, however fair or lovely or well-born she were, once fallen sick, thought anything of having a man tend her, whatever he was, either young or old; and without shame she discovered to him every part of her body, no differently than she would have done to a woman, if only the necessities of her illness required it. And it was this, perhaps, that was the cause of lesser modesty in time to come on the part of those who recovered."

The condition of the poor people and even of many of the middle class was almost unspeakable:

"The most part, retained by fear and poverty in their own houses, sickened by the thousand daily, and being altogether untended, died almost without help. Many breathed their last in the open street, while others, even though they died in their houses, made it known to their neighbors that they were dead rather by the stench of their bodies than in any other way."

Funeral processions were not matters of sorrow for the dead. In them, "with laughter, jests and jibes, and with merrymaking in company," the survivors, instead, rejoiced that they were still living. The bodies were carried to the graves, not by fond friends, but by "a sort of blood-sucker, sprung from the dregs of the people, who styled themselves pickmen and did such offices for hire."

So many were those who perished that the consecrated ground would not hold them. In consequence, trenches were hollowed in the various churchyards.

"In these, those who came after were laid by the hundred, and being heaped up in layers as goods are stowed aboard a ship, were covered with a little earth, until such time as they reached the top of the trench."

It was in this catastrophe that Boccaccio found a taking-off point for his longest and most notable work. Not only did the plague give him the mechanical excuse for assembling the young men and young women who told those stories which make up the *Decameron*. It created the necessary moral atmosphere.

"I purpose," he announced in his proem, "for the succor and solace of ladies in love—unto others the needle and the spindle and the reel suffice—to recount a hundred stories or fables or parables or histories or whatever you like to call them."

"Most noble damsels," he said in his conclusion, "for whose consolation I have addressed myself to so long a labor."

It might also be added that both then and later he gave out the impression that the book was assembled at the direct command of a princess who has been supposed, variously, to have been either Queen Giovanna or Fiammetta.

He adduced, moreover, as his reason for choosing this audience:

"And who will deny that it is better to give this comfort"—i.e., of these stories—"to lovesick ladies than to men? For these, shamefast and fearful, are obliged to hold hid within their bosoms the fires of love, and constrained by the wishes, the pleasures, the commandments of fathers, mothers, brothers,

VMANA COSA ELHAVER COMPASSIONE
AGLI AFFLITTI. e come che a ciafchuna pfona ftia
bene a choloro maffimamête e richiefto liquali gia hâ
no di conforto hauuto mifteri: & hânolo trouato in al
cuno fra liquali fe alcuno mai nebbexogli fu caro o gra
ne riceuete piacere .Io forio uno di quelli p cio che dal
la mia prima giouenezza infino a quefto tempo foltra
modo effendo ftato accefo da altiffimo & nobile amo
re forfe piu affai chella mia baffa conditione non pare
be narrandolo io fi richiedeffe : quantunque doppo
coloro che difcreti erano: & alla cui noticia puêne:io ne fuffi lodato & da mol
to piu reputato. Non dimeno mi fu egli di grâdiffima fatica a foffrire:certo
non per crudelta della donna amata:ma per fouecchio amore nella mente con
cepto da pocho regolato appetito .ilquale percio a niuno regolato côueneuo
le termine milafcia contento ftate piu di noia che di bifogno nô era fpeffe uol
te fentire mi faceua. Nella qual Inoia tanto refrigerio mi porfero li piaceuoli
ragionamenn dalcuno amico & le delefteuole fue côfolatiõe che io porto fer

THE FIRST PAGE OF THE DECAMERON

FROM THE EDITION OF 1492

and husbands, to spend most of their time shut up in the narrow compass of their chambers, and sitting idle, as it were, to revolve in their minds various thoughts which it is not possible should still be merry."

Even making allowance for a certain amount of fooling—and it must be noted that as Boccaccio wrote the *Decameron* he at least posed as being far too much the man of the world to be entirely serious—those words could hardly have been written or this point of view taken even as little as half a dozen years before they actually were. The plague, however, by giving men and women alike a sudden and demoralizing sense of insecurity, had generated a new attitude. By its ravages, good and bad were destroyed impartially. Sheep were not sorted from goats. Deity, therefore, did not seem to be so close, or so watchful, or so benevolent as it had heretofore. Of course, there were some who reverted into almost revivalistic religion, but on the whole those who survived, like most who live through a deluge, were more interested in acquiring such scraps of human pleasure as are here below available, than in speculating too heavily in celestial real estate. It was a reckless generation, rather than a corrupt generation. It was an unmoral one, rather than an immoral one. But the manifestations were about the same.

The frame of the book is as follows:

On a certain Tuesday while the death is at its height, seven young ladies foregather in the Church of Santa Maria Novella in Florence. Whatever their real names may have been—and Boccaccio allows us to think that each one was an actual person —he calls them Pampinea, Fiammetta, Filomena, Emilia, Lauretta, Neifile, and Elisa. Pampinea, the eldest, is but eight and twenty. The youngest, presumably Elisa, is no more than eighteen.

As they gather there, they discuss the plague, and Pampinea suggests that they leave the city. What is the use of staying there when there is nothing around but death and sadness? Why not save themselves as their friends and acquaintances have already done? The others agree with her, until Filomena interposes an objection:

"Ladies," she says, "although that which Pampinea tells us is well said, it is not right to hasten too much, as it appears you would like to do. Remember that we are all women, and none of us is childish enough not to realize how unreasonable women are among themselves, and how little they know how to order themselves without a man to help them. We are fickle, willful, suspicious, faint-hearted and timorous. For that reason I know that if we do not take some other guidance than our own, our company will far too soon be dissolved, and with less honor to ourselves than would be fitting."

Elisa supports her. She is right. Men are the head of women, and without their assistance, rarely does any womanly enterprise come to a good end. But how can they get these men?

At that moment, three young gentlemen enter the church. They are not so young, however, that the youngest of them is less than twenty-five years old. Of these one is called Panfilo, the second Filostrato, and the third Dioneo. Furthermore, it happens that each one of them is in love with one of three young ladies, that they are all related to the other four.

Pampinea sees them:

"Look! Fortune is favorable to our beginnings, and has thrown in our way young men of worth and discretion, who will gladly be both our guides and our servitors, if we do not disdain to accept them in that capacity."

At this Neifile blushes, she happening to be one of those who are beloved by one of the young men:

"For God's sake, Pampinea, be careful what you say! I am afraid that, without any fault on our part or on theirs, scandal will result if we take them with us."

"That is of no importance," says Filomena. "For my part, as long as I live honestly and my own conscience does not prick me, let any one who wishes say the contrary: God and the truth will take up arms for me. Therefore, if they are disposed to come, we may truly say, as Pampinea did, that fortune is favorable to us."

Her reasoning carries the day, and the plans, therefore, are broached to the young men. Let us all retire to a near-by villa, taking with us our servants and all that is needful to our comfort, and there wait until the ravages of the disease have spent themselves. They agree gladly. All, therefore, set out the next morning to a place "not more than two short miles from the city" which was almost certainly that large edifice not far from Settignano, known to-day as the Poggio Gherardi. Later they transfer to a second villa. This may have been the Villa Rasponi, but was more probably the Villa Palmieri. There on soft lawns and under brooding trees, they feast on fine wines and delicate foods. There they play lutes, take strolls, and go swimming in a little lake in a small depression that is still known as the Valley of Ladies. There, too, they begin telling their stories.

The idea originates with Pampinea. Dioneo tells her that he has left his cares behind him within the city gates, and that if they are not going to make merry here, he would prefer to go back to them. To avoid this, she suggests that each one be chosen as ruler for a day, and that on that day the one chosen be responsible not only for the management of their affairs but also for the group's amusement. She is Queen of the first day, and for entertainment bids each one in turn tell a story. At the end one of their number is asked to sing a song. Her plan is so successful that it is carried on by those who follow her. There are two intervals of two days each—each Friday, and each Saturday—for religious offices, and because on Saturday it was "the usance of the ladies to wash their heads and to do away all dust and all uncleanliness which had befallen them for the labors of the past week." All in all, then, the action of the *Decameron* lasts exactly two weeks. There are ten narrators. Exactly one hundred stories are told.

And these one hundred stories form not only one of the merriest and most entertaining collections ever penned by hand of mortal: they give also a complete and lively picture of the whole Fourteenth Century western world. Geographically the range is from England to Alexandria, from Portugal to Asia Minor, while even in Italy nearly the whole stretch of the peninsula is touched upon. Palermo, rising handsomely under its half circle of rugged mountains, is the scene of one story, and Venice that of another. Landolfo Ruffolo starts his adventures along "the seacoast from Reggio to Gaeta which is commonly held to be very nearly the most delightful part of Italy." He comes specifically from Ravello, a small place situated on a hillside "pretty near Salerno, overlooking the sea, which the country folk call Amalfi-side, full of little towns and gardens and springs, and of men who are as rich and active in trade as any in the world." Andreuccio, the protagonist of the next story, comes from Perugia. A few stories on, Bernabo is from Genoa. Montferrat, Verona, Bologna, Treviso, Pisa, Pavia, Pistoia, Milan, Rome, Messina, Brescia, Ravenna, Prato, Siena, Arezzo, are among the Italian cities represented. A tale is laid on the road near Ferrara. Two touch the island of

Lipari. One Trapani in Sicily. One Barletta in farthest Apulia. One the Romagna. One a convent in the Lunigiana. One a convent in Lombardy. Indeed, only two places are specially favored. As is fitting, these are Florence and Naples. Four stories deal with the place where Boccaccio spent his early manhood, while perhaps as many more deal with what might be called the Neapolitan country. Florence receives even better treatment. Including such towns in the neighborhood as Fiesole, Varlungo, his own Certaldo, and an unnamed hamlet "in the plain of the Mugnone," the city by the Arno is the scene of nearly thirty.

The same comprehensive diversity applies to the cast of characters. King Charles of Naples figures in one story, and Chichibio, cook to a Florentine burgher, and a most plausible and witty rogue at that, appears in another. Here we have the generous-hearted Ser Federigo who sacrifices his last possession, a fine falcon, to the woman he loves but who has never even looked upon him. Here Messer Gentile de' Carisendi who, having rescued the woman he loves from the grave, turns her over to her husband. Here Madame Beritola, loyal to her husband through the long years of his imprisonment. Here Cisti, the baker, respectful yet independent, who was so quick to offer his excellent bottling of wine to Messer Geri Spina and the delegates of Pope Boniface, so tactful yet firm in his determination that this offer should not be abused by Messer Geri's servants. In juxtaposition, we have Jancofiore of Palermo, one of those lady "barberesses"—"very fair of their persons, yet sworn enemies to honesty" who are given not only "to shave men, but altogether to flay them"—and the arch-rogue Ser Ciapelletto of Prato. Every class is represented. There is King Pedro of Aragon and Prince Tancred of Salerno. There is Rinaldo d'Asti, a merchant; Saladin, the knightly sultan; Messer Ghino di Tacco, a bandit; the Marquis of Saluzzo; the poet Cecco Angiolari; Giotto, the painter; Pietro de' Tresanti, a poor trader; Stecchi, Martellino and Marchese, three jugglers; a wool-comber called Gianni Lotteringhi; the Bishop of Florence, the Abbot of Cluny; the parish priest of Varlungo. There is the wife of the Marquis of Montferrat, the wife of a humble innkeeper, the nuns of a convent near Florence. There is the daughter of the King of England; the betrothed of the King of Algarvie; the mistress of the Lord of Ferrara. Men and women out of every corner of the late Middle Ages, they come crowding up to us, various and individual. It is as if, possessed of some magic carpet having power over time as well as space, we had been transported back over the space of six centuries. Or, as if equipped with the enchanted rod borrowed from Merlin, we had been able to conjure some of the brightly-colored paintings that hang on the walls of galleries in Florence, Perugia and Siena into glittering and vivacious life.

The same variety applies to the stories. Here one concerns itself with a wise retort made by a citizen of Florence; there one with a crude practical joke played on a simple painter, or an even simpler doctor, or a raw judge from the marches of Ancona. Here we have the gory tale of a woman who kills herself after finding out that she has eaten the heart of her lover. Here an account of a merchant who calmly turns pirate when his legitimate ventures do not turn out well. Here one of another merchant who is tricked by the most transparent of devices. There one of a third who is blown by the ill-wind of being robbed and beaten to the bath and bed, and into the arms of a fair lady who was intended for another. The very tone is constantly different. Here—though it must be admitted that tales of this sort are rare—we have an account of necro-

mancy and enchanted gardens, and there one redolent of the
very smell and feel of popular life in one of the suburbs of
Naples. Here a whole day—the last—devoted entirely to
stories dealing with acts of impossible nobleness. The famous
history of patient Griselda is one of these. There two days—
the seventh and eighth—concerned only with "the deceits
which for love or for their own preservation women have
played on their husbands" and "with the tricks which all day
long women play men or men women or men one another."
Monna Beatrice who appears in the first of these days makes a
good contrast to Griselda. Unfaithful to her husband, she ar-
ranges that he should be cudgeled roundly in his own garden
by the very man who has cuckolded him. And that he should
accept that very cudgeling as a proof of her fidelity. Black
could not possibly be more neatly opposed to white.

Yet it must not be deduced from this that Giovanni had no
favorite themes. Though he cast his eyes on the whole world
around him, certain aspects of it interested him more than
others, or at least seemed to him to afford better subjects. Two
in particular. The first of these was love, and it was, likewise,
the principal one. Indeed, very nearly nine stories out of every
ten deal with this engrossing passion, and with all sorts of its
consequences. There are comedies of love and tragedies of
love. Love makes men and women clever, dishonest, resolute,
brave, generous, unscrupulous, and heroic. The untaught
Cimon becomes civilized on account of love, yet it is because
of love that Monna Beatrice's husband, as related above, is
laid about on the shoulders and rear end with a good stout
staff. Gerbino dies for love, and Gianni da Procida, condemned to burn on account of love, asks only that his face be
turned toward his beloved. On the other hand, it is because
of love that the scholar Rinieri is obliged to pace up and down

all night in the snow, while the fair Elena and her fancy man laugh at him behind closed windows. Thus tears and laughter interplay.

But whichever of these is called forth, the emotion itself is always treated in the same manner. That is, that however it manifests itself, it is fine and laudable. That is, that it is so natural and compelling that it justifies whatever may ensue.

Prince Tancred informs his daughter that he has discovered that she has taken a groom for her paramour.

Ghismonda replies thus:

"It should have been manifest to thee, Tancred, since thou art of flesh and blood, that thou had begotten a daughter of flesh and blood, and not of stone and iron. And thou shouldst have remembered, and shouldst still remember for all thou art old, what and of what nature are the laws of youth, and with what potency they work."

Having been married, she goes on, and having known, therefore, what pleasure it is to give satisfaction to her desires, only made them the stronger. In consequence, it seemed necessary to get a lover. She considered that she had fulfilled her obligations to her father when she did her utmost to see that no shame should ensue to either him or her as a result.

Monna Filippa of Prato is brought to trial for having a lover. The penalty is death. On trial she asks the provost to demand of her husband if she had not always contented him. The husband replies in the affirmative.

"Then my lord provost, if he hath taken of me that which was needful and pleasing to him, what, I ask you, was or am I to do with that which remaineth over or above his requirements? Should I cast it to the dogs? Was I not far better to gratify a gentleman withal who hath loved me better than himself?"

Tedaldo Elisei, disguised as a pilgrim, returns to Florence. There he enters into conversation with Ermellina who had once been his mistress. Not knowing who he is, she tells him how she once loved a certain Tedaldo but was swerved from her love by a priest who convinced her she was sinning.

This is his answer:

"Granted even that we allow that which the friar who rebuked you said to you: to wit, that it is a grievous sin to break the marriage vow, is it not a far greater one to rob a man and yet a greater one to slay him or to drive him into exile? Every one must allow this. For a woman to have converse with a man is a sin of nature, but to rob him or slay him or drive him into exile proceeds from malignity of mind."

Indeed, only two derelictions having anything to do with love seem to have been recognized by Boccaccio. The first was to love insincerely, but how we are to distinguish the counterfeit emotion from the real one is a matter of which he neglects to inform us. A hint seems to be given in two stories where canny ladies attempt to receive remuneration for their infidelities. We are expected to laugh as at cheaters cheated when they are tricked out of receiving the same. The other failing was for a woman to refuse love to the man enamored of her. This, to be sure, is, in Boccaccio's opinion, so rare an occurrence that it but few times finds its way into the pattern of the stories. But it is so dire an offense that Boccaccio reserves for illustrating its punishment one of his unfrequent excursions into the supernatural. Nastagio degli Onesti is enabled to win the love of a cold and haughty lady of the Traversari family by showing her the fate of another of her kind. The pine woods near Ravenna are haunted. Through them every Friday hastes a fair lady pursued by a knight with hounds. After a long chase, she is overtaken and torn to pieces. While living she, too, was cold and haughty. This is her eternal doom.

The second theme much favored by Boccaccio was that offered to him by the all too human failings of the churchmen.

"Fair ladies," says Panfilo, "it occurs to me to tell you a little story against those who continually offend against us, without being open to retaliation on our part. To wit, the clergy, who have proclaimed a crusade against our wives, and who, whenever they get one of the latter into their power, conceive themselves to have gained forgiveness of fault and penalty, no less than if they had brought the Sultan bound from Alexandria to Avignon. And for this, the wretched laymen cannot return them the like, although they do wreak their ire upon the priests' mothers and sisters, their sweethearts and their daughters, assailing them with no less ardor than the others do their wives."

"The lewd and filthy life of the clergy," says Filostrato, "in many things a constant mark for malice, as it were, gives occasion without much difficulty to those who have a mind to speak of, to gird at, and to rebuke it."

With these preludes, Boccaccio introduces us to such a series of merry rogues, sly hypocrites, and even arch frauds as to make us see readily why the Catholic Church, when it came later to polish up its tarnished façades, felt obliged to regard him with hostility. We have already taken note of Fra Cipolla "the jolliest rascal in the world" with his quick wit and his trumped-up holy relics. We have already paused to look at the parish priest of Varlungo so "lusty of his person" in the service of just that, which by his holy vows, he should have abjured. But those are only the most vivid members of an extremely numerous company. There is brother Alberto of Imola who makes his way to the bedchamber of a silly Venetian lady by impersonating the Archangel Gabriel who he says was in love with her. There is the abbess of a convent in Lombardy "very famous for its sanctity and religion" who, rushing from her chamber to upbraid a young nun who had been caught with her lover, has the bad fortune to seize, in the dark, the breeches of the priest who, unknown to the rest, is sharing it with her, and wrap them around her head in place of her coif. Nor is it only such warm-hearted indiscretions which are discussed. The sixth story of the first day, which relates the story of a holy inquisitor "who was a devotee of St. John Goldenbeard," and of the cutting rebuke administered to him by "an honest layman," is aimed at what Boccaccio regarded as another typically clerical failing, namely, avarice and "brothswilling hypocrisy." It should be pointed out, incidentally, that when in the Sixteenth Century, an expurgated edition of the *Decameron* was brought out under church approval, it was such stories rather than the book's general outspokenness that was disapproved of. For nuns and abbots were substituted lords and ladies. But even the broadest of the stories were otherwise unchanged.

Yet it was not, curiously enough, in a tale dealing directly with the church, that his satiric attack on the churchmen advanced most effectively, and on the widest front. Boccaccio was not, however much quoted by the Lutherans, a forerunner of Martin Luther, and only once was the Church as a whole the target of his sentences. Then the protagonist of his story was Abraham, a worthy Jew.

Jeannot de Chivigné, a merchant of Paris, is very anxious to convert to Christianity this person, who is a friend of his. Abraham refuses to abandon the faith of his fathers until he has seen Rome and judged the other's religion at its principal home. Fearing the result, Jeannot tries to dissuade him, but when Abraham tells him that under no other circumstances will he be converted, he lets him go.

The Jew immediately hurries to Rome where he is entertained by his brethren. There he begins cautiously to make inquiry as to the habits of the Pope and the Cardinals and the other members of the Papal court.

"And with what he himself noted, being a mighty quick-witted man, and with what he gathered from others, he found all, from highest to lowest, most shamefully given to lust, and that not only in the way of nature, but after the Sodomitical fashion, without any restraint of remorse or shamefastness, so that to obtain any favor there, the influence of courtesans and of catamites was of no small power. Moreover, he saw them to be universally gluttons, winebibbers, drunkards and slaves to their bellies after the fashion of beasts, and more than anything else to lust. Looking further, he saw them to be so covetous and greedy for money that they bought and sold indifferently human and even Christian blood as well as things sacred, whatever they might be, whether pertaining to sacraments or to benefices, making a great traffic and having more brokers therefor than folk at Paris for their cloth and other merchandise. Manifest simony they had christened 'procuration' and gluttony 'sustenation,' as if God did not understand —let be the meaning of words—even the intention of depraved minds, and would suffer Himself, after the fashion of men, to be duped by the names of things."

All this—together with much else which, according to Boccaccio, must be left unsaid—is supremely displeasing to the Jew who is a sober and a modest man, so he straightway returns to Paris where he is met by Jeannot who expects nothing less than the Jew's conversion. Jeannot asks him what he thought of the Holy Father and his court.

"This!" answers the Jew with some vehemence. "God give them one and all ill!"

Then he recounts what he saw. There was no piety or devoutness or good example in the whole city; instead, nothing but lust, covetousness, and gluttony, and worse too, if worse there could be. It was a smithy of things rather diabolical than divine. The very Pope himself, and in consequence all others, act more as if they were trying to banish the Christian religion from the earth, than to be its foundation and support.

"And since I saw also," is the Jew's surprising conclusion, "that this after which they strive does not come to pass, but that your religion continually increases and waxes still brighter and more glorious, it seems to me that I discern that the Holy Spirit is indeed its support and foundation as of that which is true and holy above all others. For that reason, although I was formerly obstinate and insensible to your exhortations and would not be persuaded to embrace your faith, I now tell you frankly that nothing in the world could keep me from being a Christian. Let us, then, to church, and there have me baptized according to the right and ordinance of your holy faith."

Such, then, were the subjects of which Boccaccio chose to make use of in the great work in which his genius flowered. The stories that he wove around these subjects he took where he could find them. Some are from the classic authors that he studied. Some are from the French *fabliaux*. Some are from such crude collections of medieval stories as "The Seven Sages" or the *Gesta Romanorum*. Some are from the earlier collections of *novelle* such as the *Cento Novelle Antiche* or *L'Avventuroso Ciciliano*. Some are from the crude anecdotes told by the street gossips. Some are things that actually occurred in Florence. Some few he may actually have made up.

To them he applied his various qualities much as a sculptor

applies his chisels to a rough block of marble, for with Boccaccio, as with almost any artist worthy of the name, story and subject were as much part of his medium as pen, ink and parchment were. They were not ultimate ends, but the means to an ultimate end. His mastery of prose, for instance: for, despite all its involutions and its classic Latin resonances, his was the first writing of the modern world which aimed at, and to some extent achieved, both exactness and vividness on one hand, and organic and inherent beauty on the other. His sense of realism: the skill in which he conveyed the external world; the skill with which he used exterior correctness to lend force and conviction to his compositions. His sense of character: in this he anticipated and at times even equaled such masters as Shakespeare and the French novelists; with a few exceptions the people of his stories are not animated abstractions, but men and women of the world around him.

Finally he applied that civilized blend of skepticism, humor, a sense of proportion and a slightly disillusioned tolerance which we denominate irony. In a way, that was the strongest quality of all.

And not only the strongest but to a large extent the most surprising, for it is the one quality that was well-nigh utterly lacking in all who had preceded him. Before Boccaccio, there had been little literary finesse. Writing had been either white or black. Men were either deadly serious, as was the case with Dante who represented this point of view at its best, and with monks like Helinand and Caesar of Hesterbach who represented it at its worst. Or else they were out and out clowns like the buffoons of the piazza, the crude reciters of the *fabliaux,* the rough-and-tumble strokes of whose humor seemed to have been administered with a bludgeon or a quarterstaff.

Boccaccio gibed very well with neither of these. As an artist he was as serious as Dante, but he was animated by no great and humorless moral purpose. As a comedian he winged the same shafts as the street rhyme-makers, but he laughed nowhere crudely and riotously. His amusement was expressed in a smile.

Nowhere is this better illustrated than in his remarks directed at those who censured what they termed the licentiousness of his writings. They are found in the introduction to the fourth day of the *Decameron,* and in the epilogue to the whole book. They are extremely appropriate even to-day.

He wrote too much of love and thought too much of pleasing the ladies?

Why not? Why should he think it shame to seek to please those whom Guido Cavalcanti and Dante Alighieri, when already stricken in years, and Messer Cino da Pistoia, when a very old man, held in honor and whose approval was very dear to them?

He used unseemly words and takes overmuch license?

"This I deny, for the reason that there is nothing so unseemly as to be forbidden unto any one, if he but express it in seemly terms, as it seems to me I have here very aptly done."

These stories will do great harm?

But almost everything that there is has in it the potentiality of both good and evil. "Who does not know that wine, though according to Cinciglione and Scolajo and many others an excellent thing for people in health, is hurtful unto one who has the fever? Shall we say, then, because it harms the fever that it is evil? Who does not know that fire is most useful, no, necessary to mortals? Shall we say that because it burns houses and villages and cities that it is evil? Arms, similarly, assure the welfare of those who desire to live in peace, and yet often they slay men, not from any malice of their own, but from the perversity of those that use them. *Corrupt mind never understood word healthily, and even as seemly words do not profit a depraved mind, so those which are not seemly do not avail to corrupt the well-disposed, any more than mire can sully the rays of the sun, or earthly foulness the beauties of the sky.*"

Then irrepressible entertainment flickers across his lips:

"There are also some ladies who will say that there are some stories here which had better been away. Granted. But I could not, nor should write any except those actually related. Therefore those who told them should have told them goodly, and I would have written them goodly. But if people will even pretend that I am both the writer and the inventor of these tales—which I am not—I say that I should not take shame to myself that they were not all goodly. For there is no craftsman living, barring God, who does everything alike well and completely. In a multitude of things diversity will of necessity be found. No field was ever tilled so well but that nettles or thistles or somewhat of briers or other weeds might be found therein mingled with the better herbs. Besides, having to speak to simple lasses, such as you for the most part are, it would have been folly to go seeking and wearying myself to find very choice and exquisite matters, and to use great pains to speak very measuredly."

It is this last quality—his sense of irony—that gives, too, the key to the only one of the riddles of the identity of the persons in the frame story that so far any one has been able to solve.

It has been suggested that each of the three young men of that gay assemblage who tell all these stories represents Boccaccio at a different point in his career. Reading the above lines, this seems very credible. But in that case Panfilo—young Boccaccio in the flush of amorous success—and Filostrato—the melancholy and lovelorn Boccaccio—have become Dioneo, that "merriest springald in the world" who is so "full of games and quips" and so empty of all reverence. That gay gentleman, who insists on telling his tale last and on being exempted from conforming to the subject assigned so that he can end each day on the note of some riotous and full-blooded comedy, that irrepressible and self-confident funmaker, who, when called on to give in his turn the sentimental song with which each day is concluded, offers instead the first lines of half a dozen tap-room jingles which are so outspoken that even the ladies of this tolerant group will not permit him to go on with them, is the one character in the troupe of story-tellers that stands out with anything like reality. If he does not represent Boccaccio as he actually was, he represents him as he wished to be, or as he imagined he was.

But more probably he represents the actual Boccaccio.

In the one description of Boccaccio's appearance which is still extant, he is set forth as follows:

"The poet was rather stout of figure, but tall. His face was round, but his nose had a slight depression over the nostrils. His chin was cleft, and when he smiled he was extremely handsome. He was jocund and merry of aspect, and in his speech pleasant and human. And he delighted very much in conversation."

These words of Filippo Villani seem to apply to the sort of man he must have been at the time he was finishing the *Decameron*.

Physically, then, he had matured greatly since the days when he had been a good-looking slender youth making love to Fiammetta.

The interior maturing which went on during the same period must have been of very much the same order.

And it could, hardly, have been any less.

CHAPTER XVIII

THE description of the plague, which, as we have already seen, serves as an introduction to the *Decameron,* indicates plainly that whenever individual tales may have been written, the book as a whole could not have been commenced or for that matter even conceived before 1348. And although the fact that at least the first three days were issued before the whole was finished, seems to be shown by Boccaccio's feeling that it was necessary to answer some of his critics in the introduction to the fourth day, the complete work was not published—or to be more accurate—allowed to circulate until 1353. Giovanni, then,—just as had Dante Alighieri before him— commenced his most important book *"nel mezzo del cammin di nostra vita"*: midway along the high road of our life. Specifically, since the Biblical and accepted span of these our days was threescore years and ten, when he was thirty-five. He finished it when he was forty. Five years, thus—and precisely those five years when he should have been, and actually was, at the height of his powers—were devoted to its composition. But even for so vast a book, five years was considerable time, assuming, that is, that its writer had no other occupations.

What other occupations did Giovanni have during this period? A great many. Documents regarding this particular half decade are hardly any more plentiful than they are for any other period, yet even those that survive show a man so engaged in various activities that, far from wondering how he consumed all this time on a single book, we are astonished that he finished it at all.

To begin with he was involved in an extremely exacting family responsibility. His stepmother died during the plague, and his father—whom we know to have been alive in July, 1348, dead by January, 1350—lived at most only slightly more than a year longer. In consequence, Boccaccio suddenly found himself the guardian of his half brother Jacopo. The boy was not quite six years old—he was born in May, 1344—and it is not difficult, therefore, to imagine what Giovanni's feelings must have been. A bachelor, a "womanless" man with this veritable baby to clothe and feed and to look after! A poet and a student and a dreamer with a young imp on his hands to disturb his philosophical quiet! Yet for the moment at least he did not shrink from what he must have conceived to be his duty or from any of its implications, and on January 26, 1350, he drew up a paper in which he legally assumed the obligation. Possibly the reason was that he did not know what a nuisance it would be. Possibly he remembered his own neglected and unhappy youth.

It was this matter that brought him back to Florence, for in spite of its realism, the description of the plague's ravages in that city was not the work of an eyewitness. We have Boccaccio's specific word that he was elsewhere, and that elsewhere was probably Naples. It was his return to Florence that necessitated his other activities. By establishing himself in this republican city, he lost all his chances of royal or of princely patronage. Furthermore he soon discovered that the small inheritance from his father was not nearly enough to live on. His first step was to attempt to disburden himself of Jacopo. After a year's effort he threw up the sponge and petitioned to be relieved of the guardianship. Let some one else better qualified to hold the position be named, was his demand. On May, 1351, this request was granted and two Florentine notaries were designated to succeed him. His second step was to seek out such government offices and employments as were available. Not, either, apparently, without a certain amount of success.

We have record of five of his appointments. In the fall of 1350 he was sent on a mission to the Romagna. Its nature is not known but it was while engaged in this that he met Dante's daughter Sister Beatrice who was a nun in the convent of Santo Stefano dell 'Uliva near Ravenna. In January of the next year he was one of the chamberlains of the Florentine Treasury. This was a fiscal office and it called for a man of known integrity. Its salary was sixteen gold florins monthly. In February he was one of the commissioners who helped negotiate the treaty by which Florence bought the city of Prato from the royal house of Naples. In December he was sent as ambassador to Louis, Duke of Brandenburg. His object was to secure Louis' assistance in the war Florence was waging against John Visconti, Archbishop of Milan, and though he was not successful, it is not probable that any Florentine could have been. This trip took him at least as far as the Tyrol, and is possibly the one vaguely referred to by Marcantonio Niccolletti who, writing in the Sixteenth Century, relates a tradition that Boccaccio made a trip to Cividale di Friuli to see Lapo and Loteringo da Certaldo, his relatives, and from there visited Udine and Pola where he admired the Roman ruins. Finally, in 1353, we have another vague mission to Ravenna. Nor is there any reason to suppose—just because we lack documentary evidence—that these were his only activities during these years.

As can be seen, none of these offices were of any stupendous importance. Or at best, but one was. None, however, was trifling. The fact, therefore, that he held them shows that he was a man respected by his community. That, however, he was more than respected,—that he was honored, that he was regarded as a man of soundness, of presentability, of persuasive eloquence, and of great ability, was indicated by his next appointment. On April 30, 1354, he was designated as Florentine ambassador to the Pope himself, who then held his court at Avignon. His embassy was to last forty-five days, but on June 30th of the same year note is made in the Florentine archives that it was extended an additional fifteen. With him was associated one Bernardo Cambi, but if there is any question as to who headed the mission it will be dispelled by a glance at the documents which record it. The ambassadorial stipends are there set down. "Dominus Johannes de Boccachii" is to receive four Florentine pounds and ten soldi *per diem,* with an allowance of three horses. "Bernardus Cambii" is allowed only a single mount. His salary is twenty soldi—or exactly one Florentine pound.

And the mission they went on was, it happens, of extraordinary importance. Once again a German prince stood on the threshold of Italy. Charles IV, grandson of the great Henry, had succeeded Louis of Bavaria and he was about to march down the peninsula. Florence, as usual, was alarmed. And this time she did not know just what the Pope's attitude would be. It was thought indeed that Clement VI had swerved from the customary Papal policy and was favoring his traditional rival.

First of all, then, Boccaccio was to assure the Pope "that which was evident," namely that Florence was, as always, devoted to the Papal cause.

Second "he was to relate to His Holiness that the illustrious King of the Romans and of Bohemia had announced by his licitors and legates to the City of Florence and to the cities of his realm that he would arrive shortly in Italian parts, the which announcement caused great astonishment to those who heard it, for the reason that it was not clear to the City of Florence whether or not he so descended with the knowledge of the High Pontiff. Therefore the said city, desiring strongly, as has thus far been her custom, to deviate in no way from the Sacred Mother Church, wishes to be made certain of the Apostolic Will so that she can cautiously proceed in her actions and can carry on negotiations subject to the Apostolic approval."

Next he was to find out what—if it was true that Charles descended without papal permission—it was the Church's wish that Florence was to do. He was to say that he had no other instructions than to carry out the will of the High Pontiff.

Finally, "whatever precise and final answer shall be given to the above-mentioned requests by his Apostolic Holiness, the said ambassador should return with as swift steps as possible."

In addition to the above matters, he was expected to attempt to secure the appointment of Claro de' Peruzzi to the bishopric of Perugia and to regain favor for certain noblemen who had become estranged from the Papacy. The mission, therefore, makes a clean-cut commentary on the reputation of Boccaccio. This is extremely important. Aside from his own references to criticisms, we have little evidence as to just how the *Decameron* was received. Petrarch, we know, was not shocked at it, and that even so distinguished a knight as Mainardo Cavalcanti not only read it eagerly but was prepared to give it to his wife to peruse we know from Boccaccio's protest—written to be sure when he was nearly sixty—against permitting so noble a woman to read his "hardly decent" trifles. Neither of them, of course, took it very seriously, both regarding it as merely entertainment.

And that must have been the way it was regarded by the generality. At any rate, that it could not have shocked many, seems proved by this appointment. Boccaccio's abilities and likeabilities might have gained him his other offices, but certainly if he was regarded only as a lewd, irreverent fellow, even cynical Florence would have hardly picked him to head a mission to the Holy Father. Not, certainly, at a moment when they were bidding so anxiously for the latter's friendship and aid.

CHAPTER XIX

IT was just after he had returned from his long and hazardous voyage to the south of France that Boccaccio was given
another, and for the time being, his last public appointment. In a document which carried the same date—June 30,
1354—as that in which the extension of his embassy to Avignon
was noted, he and Bernardo Cambi were again associated on a
diplomatic errand. By the same Florentine republic and paid
the same wages, they were designated to make a six-day
journey "in behalf of the said city in the direction of the Val
d'Elsa and especially to the neighborhood of Certaldo."

This time, however, it was not an Apostolic Prince, the
powerful and sanctified successor to St. Peter, that they were
sent to wait upon. A new disturbing element, more pressing,
though in the long run considerably less dangerous than Papal
intrigue, now threatened the tranquillity of the wool merchants. The age of imperial domination having pretty well
ended, the age of brigands, which was to mature into the age
of great captains, was beginning. Attracted by the high pay
offered in the wars between city and city, attracted even more
by the opportunity for rich and easy plunder held out by the
disorganized state of the peninsula, a new type of barbarian
was swarming through the Alpine passes. Nearly as destructive as Hun, Visigoth, or Vandal, these men gave themselves
the romantic-sounding appellation of soldiers of fortune, and
so fierce and bloody were they that the names of some of their
leaders are, actually, still words of terror. There was Duke

Werner, self-styled "enemy of God, of pity and of mercy."
There was Conrad of Lando with his "Great Company."
Finally there was the Englishman Sir John Hawkwood—
Giovanni Aguto, to the Italians—in whom, as Sacchetti puts it,
"there was neither love nor faith"; who rebuked two priests
who said to him "God grant you peace" because "I live by war,
and peace would ruin me"; who ravaged the peninsula so indis-
criminately that the very places he had done most hurt to were
forced to employ him and honor him as the only way to end
his harm.

The first of these men to turn his attention to the city of
the red lily was one Montreal, a renegade French Knight
Hospitaler who because of his Italian activities has gone down
in history as Fra Moriale. He headed an actual army of fifteen
hundred horsemen and about two thousand foot soldiers. With
these he overran the territory of Arezzo and Siena. Finally,
however, the Sienese defeated him at Quercegrossa, and thus
barred from their land, there was only one direction in which
he could turn. That was toward Florence. He determined,
therefore, to enter the Florentine territory. The Florentines
learned of this, and, immediately, following old custom, fell
to wrangling. Should they fight him or should they pay him?
In the meanwhile they sent, one after the other, three citizens
to treat with him. No results were forthcoming so a fourth mission was sent out headed by Giovanni. It was to head off, by
plausible talking, these men who only understood two languages—that of steel, and that of gold and silver—that Boccaccio and Cambi were sent.

Yet in spite of that, apparently they succeeded. Or at any
rate—for Boccaccio's exact part in the negotiations is not
known—the Florentines did. They had made up their minds
at last that they were willing to pay a large sum of money,

and at the same time they were prepared to fight, if necessary. Action—especially after his recent defeat—was the last thing that Fra Moriale wanted and money—then as always—was the first thing, so he agreed to go elsewhere. The bribe was fixed at twenty-eight thousand florins, of which three thousand were to be paid secretly to the officers, honor among those particular thieves enjoying, it would seem, temporary leave of absence. The money was given over at Montevarchi, underneath the Chianti mountains, and they moved away.

It was this episode that gave Boccaccio probably his one close-up view of the only aspect of Italian life that was still unfamiliar to him. He had known princes and had lived upon terms of intimacy with both great and little merchants. He had talked with country people and had watched the city's various artisans engaged in their labors. Now he saw close-to, and with his own eyes, those men of blood and iron, whom merchants and princes alike were willing to employ unscrupulously in their never-ending struggles for dominion. He saw those who had burned the countryman's houses, carried off his crops and violated his wife and daughters. He saw those, to meet whose insatiable demands for pay and ransom, the artisan was ground with taxes.

Nor did he like what he saw.

And presently he inveighed against the same, choosing, however, rather unfortunately, one of his Latin poems for the expression of these sentiments which did not, in consequence, reach the wide audience that they should have.

The place is in the seventh eclogue where Florida—Florence—disputes with Daphnis—the Emperor Charles IV. In response to the emperor's taunts, Florida replies that at least she is a free woman.

"Free?" is the substance of Daphnis' answer. "Free when

you have introduced all these mercenary troops into Italy? This rabble chased by famine from Germanic forests? These wretches that you should have put to flight with a scourge?"

Florida does not defend these men. Her answer is, instead, to accuse Daphnis of being responsible for having introduced them.

"Why should you boast of what you ought to be ashamed of? It is from your country that these men have descended."

It is not surprising. It did not take particularly clear eyes to see the danger of admitting, of abetting these irresponsible bands. Boccaccio was not anticipating Machiavelli, was not theorizing politically, was not doing anything remarkable whatsoever when he descried their presence on the peninsula. He was merely exercising common sense. But this simple quality was lacking just where, tragically enough, it is almost always lacking, in the men who had control of things. Governing a city or a nation is so much a matter of immediate decisions that there is rarely ever found a ruler who will look at large consequences. As is almost always the case, Boccaccio, the man of theory, was essentially right, and the rulers of the country, the men of action, were essentially wrong. As is almost always the case, the man of theory was disregarded. It could hardly have been otherwise, but this did not make it any less distressing. For, of the fully five centuries of acute misery which were to ensue to Italy, it was certainly a principal cause.

CHAPTER XX

I T was not, however, in holding public office that this part of Boccaccio's life alone was occupied. It was not alone in setting down on paper the *Decameron*. One other happening took place during this span of five years, and both as regards Boccaccio himself, and as regards the whole history of Italian culture, it was an extremely important one. This was his meeting with the poet, Francesco Petrarca. It occurred toward the end of 1350 when the latter halted at Florence on his way to take part in the Papal jubilee that marked the conclusion of the half century. Boccaccio, at the time, was thirty-seven years old.

Petrarch himself gives us an account of this:

"Some years ago," he wrote the younger man, "it happened that I was making a swift voyage across Central Italy. It was midwinter, yet you hurried forth to meet me not only with your affection, which is the footstep of the soul, but in person, impelled by a marvelous desire to see one you had never yet beheld. And you sent ahead of you a fine piece of verse, thus showing first the aspect of your genius and then your own aspect to the person you were minded to love. It was evening and the daylight was already fading when—just as I was returning from my long exile and at last stood within the walls of my city—you came to welcome me with more courtesy and with far greater respect than I merited. Thus you renewed the poetic interview which the King of Arcadia—'who in the fire of his youth longed to speak with the hero and press his hand'—had with Anchises. For, although I did not, like him, stand 'above all others,' your zeal was no less ardent. True, you did not conduct me 'within the walls of Pheneus' but into the holy place of your own friendship. Nor did I give you 'a superb quiver and some arrows of Lycia' but my sincere and enduring affection. While acknowledging my inferiority in many respects, in this one I will concede it to neither Nisus, nor to Pythias, nor to Laelius. Farewell."

This almost chance acquaintance, here described with so many borrowings from the *Aeneid*, ripened shortly into what was to be virtually the most distinguished literary friendship in the whole course of history. By comparison, Shakespeare and the whole Mermaid Tavern crowd were but gallant drinking companions, Byron and Shelley only rather uncongenial fellow exiles, bound together by the superficial resemblance of their rebellions and their fates. Here, on the other hand, we have two great and serious artists, each one of whom is still virtually unequaled in his own particular line, held together by such a bond of common purpose and mutual regard, that, despite those vicissitudes which kept them apart except on less than half a dozen brief occasions, it could be said of them "that it seemed as if in two bodies there were held but a single spirit." The human soul being by its very nature isolated and lonely and this being especially true in the case of men of genius, such a happy occurrence does not take place very many times.

Boccaccio had long been an admirer of Petrarch, with whose works—if we can accept as exact a statement made in a letter written at the time of the poet's death to Francesco da Brossano, Petrarch's son-in-law—he had been familiar since the earlier days of his stay at Naples. Next to Dante, he regarded Laura's lover as second in greatness among writers of Italian, and he placed both of these men on a par with the ancients.

It was indeed this man who was responsible for the fact that we possess so little of Giovanni's earlier poetry, for so inferior did his own roughly put together madrigals and sonnets seem to Boccaccio in comparison with the polished products of the other man's pen, that in despair he set fire to—as worthless— a great part of all that he had composed.

Now Petrarch was given the opportunity to reciprocate these feelings, and apparently—at least to some extent—he did so. Far too egotistical, far too sure of himself, even to approach Boccaccio's self-effacement, he let, nevertheless, his heart go out to the younger Florentine with something that approximated warmth of feeling. After their first meeting, he wrote Boccaccio from Rome, and his bright letter, with its compact descriptions of his traveling companions of whom one "by his mature age and his religious calling," another "by his knowledge and the flow of his words," the rest "by their experience and their amiability made the journey pass pleasantly"; with its brief philosophical *impressions de voyage;* with its account of the deplorable accident which befell him—near Bolsena his leg was painfully bruised and crushed by the kick of a horse— has just such an intimate and conversational nature as could only have been possible between men who were in sympathy with each other. "I pen these lines, still lying in bed, as my handwriting must show you," he said, and he dated the letter from "Rome, in the silence of the middle of the night." On the way back he again halted at Florence, and was again entertained by Boccaccio. When the next year Boccaccio persuaded his city to offer Petrarch the chair of letters in her newly founded university; when in April he himself made the long journey to Padua, as Florentine ambassador, to invite Petrarch to accept the same, he touched the latter at his weakest point, namely, his vanity. It happened that

Petrarch did not accept this post, although had he done so he would have received back all the property of which a sentence of banishment had deprived his father. Apparently he preferred the calm of exile to native turbulence. Nevertheless he was flattered by it. He divined, too, who was responsible and was grateful to him. Boccaccio—so Petrarch must have reasoned—might have tried to win this position for himself, but instead he worked to have it given to me. His friendship for Giovanni was sealed by this generous act.

And this friendship and this mutual admiration lasted just as long as either of the two men were living. Petrarch never came to Florence again. Indeed, when he failed to accept the proffered professorship, Florence angrily rescinded all the decrees they had made in his favor. Boccaccio, however, visited Petrarch several times.

At the city where he came to present the offer:

"I think that you will remember, my very good master, how three years have not gone by since I came to you in Padua as the ambassador of our Senate, and having discharged my commission I stayed with you for several days longer which were passed by us in almost the same way. You devoted your time to your sacred studies. I, eager for your compositions, made copies of them for myself. When, however, the day sank toward evening, we both made an end of our labors and went into your garden, adorned since the coming of spring with leaves and flowers. There, alternately sitting and talking, we passed such of the day as remained in placid and praiseworthy leisure."

At Milan. We have a note in the hand of Petrarch dated March 16, 1359, in which he says that he has just planted three laurel trees and that they would probably prosper since the day was propitious for the plant sacred to poets. On it, Boccaccio, himself a poet, had arrived to visit him.

By the slow somber canals, under the flamboyant sunsets of Venice. He visited Petrarch at Venice twice.

Here we have four occasions when the two great men were together, when they were able to talk calmly and at peace of the great things that interested them. The sad state of Italy. The white beauty of the classics that men, who had long stumbled among the dank, gloomy catacombs of the Middle Ages, were suddenly coming upon. The perils of the human soul.

Besides that, they corresponded frequently. Boccaccio, in his intense hero-worship of Petrarch, preserved nearly everything the latter wrote to him. We have, therefore, no less than twenty-eight epistles sent to him during the course of their friendship. Petrarch was less careful and only three of Boccaccio's letters to him are still in existence. One of these, however, is labeled *"unum ex mille"*—one out of a thousand—and nearly every Petrarch letter mentions one from Boccaccio which called it forth. The exaggeration, therefore, is not very great.

These letters dealt with every imaginable subject. Petrarch wrote Boccaccio concerning the annoyances of his private life, concerning an ardent young scholar of Ravenna who was aiding him in his studies, concerning his grief over the death of his son and of his friends.

He wrote Boccaccio to attack putting faith in astrologers. Speaking of one who had announced that on a certain day the stars would be favorable to a given undertaking, he said:

"It is very astonishing that from the beginning of the world to now the stars have never before been in these exact places. And this despite the fact that in their frequent revolutions they must have covered the whole sky."

He wrote Boccaccio to poke fun at taking doctors too seriously.

"Once upon a time—I don't remember just when—you wrote me that you had been seriously ill, but that you had been cured, thanks to God and to the help of a doctor. I answered you that I was extremely surprised to see such a vulgar error in so cultivated a mind. I said that it was God and your strong constitution that had saved you. Now you tell me that in your illness you had no recourse to a doctor, and I am no longer surprised that you got well so quickly. The best way for a sick man to get well is to leave doctors alone."

Boccaccio wrote Petrarch to tell him of his many journeys, to send him notes for a life of San Pier Damiano which he had collected, to borrow manuscripts, and to discuss problems of literature and scholarship. He wrote complaining about his health, and he wrote complaining about Petrarch's politics. He wrote over and over again asking for Petrarch's poems, for Petrarch's letters, for Petrarch's essays and studies, for anything that Petrarch ever wrote.

They also exchanged many courtesies. Boccaccio sent Petrarch Dante's "Comedy," St. Augustine's "Commentary on the Psalms of David," a Cicero and a Varro.

"What has added to the charm of the book," Petrarch wrote acknowledging the last of these, "is that it was copied out by your own hand. That places you in my opinion in the same rank as those two heroes of the Latin language."

Over and over again, Petrarch invited Boccaccio to visit him. My house which is really your house, he said. My books which are really your books. The plague once more rages in Florence? Come to Venice, then, where your last visit was not nearly long enough. You will have the fairest season of the year, no cares but the pleasant service of the Muses, a healthy house which you already know, good companionship. Benintendi, the chancellor of the city, is here. Donato, the grammarian. At night there will be long conversations under the stars, as we glide in a gondola under the darkling palaces. Or if you fear the Venetian weather we will take a trip to Trieste or to Capo d'Istria. We will hunt for the source of the river Timavus named by Vergil.

They took unfailing interest in each other.

To see Petrarch, Boccaccio, middle-aged and stout, was willing to make a long hazardous journey across Central Italy at the foulest season of the year. He was willing to disregard the advice of friends, to risk bandits, to risk storms, and to undergo the perils and inconveniences of the worst roads in all of Italy.

If Boccaccio did not write Petrarch for a certain length of time, the latter was worried.

"As for you, to tell the truth, our friend Donato and I are very much afraid that you too have departed from this life. It does not seem possible that if you were alive you would have failed to write us, knowing, we believe, in what sorrow and anxiety you left us."

Even in Petrarch's death, the two were united.

When his will was opened it was found that Petrarch had left fifty florins to Boccaccio to buy a fur cloak to wear when he sat up late at night at his studies.

But it would have been possible to buy many cloaks even though trimmed with fur for that sum of money.

Petrach knew very well his friend's poverty. In this delicate way, he tried to help it out.

The man to whom Boccaccio was thus bound by so many ties and interests occupied a position not only unique in Italian history, but nearly so in the whole history of letters. Not only was he a great poet, and that—for all his reliance on verbal dexterity and subtlety of mood rather than on grandeur of idea—he most certainly was: he was recognized as a great poet, and was so recognized when he could still almost be called a young man. Not only was he a great scholar: men hailed him as a great scholar. He was not, therefore, like Dante—who though his inferior in sheer, superficial technique, was immeasurably more profound—obliged to wander from court to court, only moderately well known and perhaps even regarded as something of a nuisance, while he carried, half-finished in his baggage, the passport to supernal regions. He was not like Cino da Pistoia compelled to weave his rhythms in the intervals of the dull practice and duller teaching of law. In his youth, Pope, kings, and the greatest duke in all Italy, contended for the honor of his services. In his old age, two embattled armies suspended hostilities so that he could float down the river between them to his destination. The best minds of the period were on terms of intimacy with him. He could go where he wanted to. He could stay where, and do what, he pleased.

He was born at Arezzo on the twentieth day of July in the year 1304. His father, Petracco d'Incisa, a Florentine notary, was expelled from Florence by that same decree of the year 1302 which condemned Dante to perpetual exile, and he was engaged on the very night of his son's birth in a senseless enterprise which took away definitely any chance of his being allowed to return. With other members of his faction he attempted to reënter the city by force, but was repulsed in a night battle. Petrarch's formative years, therefore, were spent in exile. First in the little hamlet of Incisa where, although even as the crow flies it was twenty kilometers distant from Florence, he was able to learn the strong, colorful Tuscan idiom which he was to wield so successfully. Then at Pisa.

Finally at Avignon. His father wished him to become an advocate, and in consequence he studied for a while at both Montpellier and at Bologna. Like many poets, however, he detested what he regarded as the tricky illiberalities of the legal profession. Indeed, so deep was his determination never to enter it, that there is a well-founded story that Petracco found it necessary to fling his son's books of rhetoric and poetry into the fire, saving, however, Vergil and Cicero half-burned from the flames at the latter's passionate entreaties.

But Petracco died when his son was only twenty-two and from then on he was free to do as he wished. He was in Bologna at the time, but he returned forthwith to Avignon. There, or at Vaucluse near-by, he lived until he was approaching fifty. He made, to be sure, one long trip which took him to Paris, Ghent, Liège, and Cologne, as well as four to Rome, two to Naples, and others to the various cities of Italy. But for the most part he remained in France. He entered priestly orders so as to make patronage easier. He carried on his literary and scholastic activities. He corresponded with his many friends: Ludwig of Ham, the Roman Lello, Giovanni Barilli, Giacomo Colonna. He supported enthusiastically the visionary revolution of Cola da Rienzi, that impractical and bewildered "last of the Romans" who imagined futilely that he could reconstruct the strong iron of the *"populus Romanus"* out of the medieval city's miscellaneous rabble. It was only when his life began to decline, when a great part of his work had been accomplished that he found that he could no longer tolerate this "Babylon of the West, worse than the Eastern one because nearer." When, in 1353, he entered his peninsula to reside there, he came more as a stranger than as one returning to his own home.

Yet he never left again. Milan, Venice, and Padua, claimed

him, as we have already seen, at various periods, and it was at Arquà, a little village in the Euganean Hills, that he passed his last days. His end was at once beautiful and appropriate. On the morning of July 19, 1374, when he lacked but a day of being seventy, his servants entered his library and found the old poet—who had worked late into the night before—bent over among his books, his head supported by his arms. He appeared to be asleep and in one sense he actually was asleep. He was at last on terms of equality with his beloved classic authors. He was one of the great dead.

It was this long stay at Avignon that gave its particular cast to the genius of Petrarch. Not because he there met Laura. The lady of his sonnets was a real person, and may well even have been the good-looking wife of Hugh de Sade as was set forth in the Eighteenth Century by the latter's learned descendant. Laura, however, was not necessary to Petrarch's shaping. Or to put it in a better way, his attachment for her was so distant and so much merely his poetic fancy, that if he had not seen her at her devotions on that fragrant April morning of his twenty-third year, he would, probably, have found another Laura. She was neither Fiammetta, a goddess of the body, an unclothed and golden-haired Venus arising, like the one painted by Botticelli, from the small waves of a blue ocean, nor a Beatrice made fiery by the fierce glow of her spiritual halo. She was fair and she was beloved, but she was dim and evanescent.

What made his stay at Avignon important was that it gave him the viewpoint of an exile, that it made him theoretical and abstract. No wonder he scorned the Italian tongue and regarded it as fit only for works that were trifling. His pope was a Frenchman and his prelates spoke the international language of Latin. No wonder that the thin ceremony of a coronation with a crown of laurel on the steps of the Campidoglio was more desirable to him than the applause of his fellow country-men. Italy was, but for one voice he could not appreciate, still inarticulate. His countrymen were the dead Romans. The same thing can be said of his foolish devotion to the cause of Cola di Rienzi. In the peninsula, a new modern world was about to come into being. Dante, in a way, prepared for it, and Boccaccio, though perhaps unconsciously, was expressing it. But how could Petrarch, at Avignon, know anything about it? How could his Pope and his Cardinals? How could his benefice-seeking churchmen with their plans and counter-plans? It was the muck that was seething and germinating, and these men lived in high altitudes. When Petrarch tired of this, when he found the atmosphere too thin and too false, it was not to crude earth that he descended. He withdrew into his own heart. He intensified his study of men dead a thousand years before him. He wrote a book upon the charms of the solitary life.

It is for that reason exceedingly fortunate that the meeting between Petrarch and Boccaccio did not take place any sooner. Boccaccio's modesty and his ingrained penchant for effacing himself placed him immediately under the spell of Petrarch. Fully as great, probably even greater than the other man, he had absolutely no idea of this, and it seemed to him that where his writings differed from Petrarch's, they were poor and worthless. He therefore set out pretty self-consiously to fol-low the trails Petrarch had blazed. Did Petrarch despise Italian? Well, then, he too would despise Italian. Did Petrarch set scholarship above creativeness? He, too, would do likewise. Petrarch being—as he said in one of his eclogues —the only one who could lead him to Sappho—divine poetry— he would follow Petrarch to the last detail. True, when he was a boy, song in the vulgar tongue had pleased him, but now that he was of another age, other loves were more fitting. One is glad, therefore, that Boccaccio had already written the *Decameron*. For while opinions may differ as to whether that book, or Petrarch's collection of sonnets, is the more worth saving, there is no question but that it far surpasses any other thing that Petrarch ever wrote. It is one of the valued items in a rare and golden heritage. It is what Milton said that a good book must always be: "the precious lifeblood of a master spirit." In consequence, it has been "embalmed and treasured to a life beyond life."

And yet for all that it must not be believed that Boccaccio, in his relationship to Petrarch, was merely servile. Because he believed Petrarch to be eminently greater as a man of letters, he followed him as a man of letters.

In other matters, however, he kept his independence. He refused, for instance, to allow Petrarch to persist in his childish scorn of Dante. He guessed correctly that Petrarch was jealous, and although he could never quite overcome this jealousy, he at least forced him to a grudging acknowledgment of Dante's merits.

He was always critical of Petrarch's relation to Italian politics, and when the poet took service with John Visconti, who was the arch-enemy of Florence, this criticism became outspoken.

"In the words of another," he said, " 'I am forbidden to talk yet I cannot remain silent.' "

Then he opened up with his artillery.

What had taken their old Silvanus—Petrarch—from them? Had wicked Egone—John Visconti—and incestuous Cressida—money—been able to do that which neither white-haired Argus—King Robert—nor even Pan himself—the Pope—who rules over all the others been able to do? If the Sorgues, the Parma and the Brenta had grown muddied, could no other river than the Ticino quench his thirst? But leaving aside matters pertaining to war, what was this admirer and cultivator of solitude doing girdled by the multitude? What was he who was accustomed to praise so highly the life of freedom and of honest poverty, doing under a foreign yoke, doing adorned with evil gain?

"And now, my illustrious master, although there remain many further things which I could say against him, I do not wish to expose any more. But what will you say, you who are more indignant and more eloquent than I am? What will my venerable Monicus (Petrarch's brother Gherardo) say? What will his Socrates (Ludwig of Ham), his Ideo (Giovanni Barilli), his Pythias (Barbato of Sulmona) say? What will all those many others who for so long have regarded him as almost divine and as unique among men, who have admired him and have praised him to the skies? I think that they will all condemn him, and will feel bitterly disappointed. And so, knowing how much faith he has in you, I beg you that you will talk to him, and with your example lead him back from his wicked crime, and that out of this heinous man you will compel such decorousness and such counsel that you will restore him to his ancient fame, and to us, and to you, and to our woods bring back our pleasant and beloved friend."

This letter needs little comment. Though apparently talking to Petrarch about a third person, it is Petrarch that it actually is criticizing. That he actually sent it to the man he so worshiped tells us a lot about Boccaccio.

But it tells us even more about Petrarch, who read the letter, and answered it, but neither changed his course nor resented it. This says a great deal for him. Very petty in some things, oversensitive in regard to his work, and extremely jealous about its position, he must, none the less, have an essential bigness. Few men of letters, few men of any sort, for that matter, would allow their best friends to write them with such bitter candidness and still have their friendship unaffected by it. Students of the Fourteenth Century have a tendency either to play up Boccaccio at the expense of Petrarch, or Petrarch at the expense of Boccaccio. This is as foolish as the Tennyson-Browning and Dickens-Thackeray controversies which used to occupy modern readers. Both of them were exceedingly great men.

CHAPTER XXI

THE return from Naples marked, as has already been shown, the end of Boccaccio's youth. In the same way, the completion of the *Decameron* set a period to his maturity. From then on, he began to decline. He was not old in the modern sense of the word, and even in terms of his own life he still had a third left to live. But those twenty-one years —at least in comparison with the twenty-one which immediately preceded them—had a certain emptiness. Not only was his work to fall off—and after the *Decameron* he produced, really, no single thing that could, in any sense, be termed a masterpiece: his actual character began to break up. Nowhere is this better indicated than in his change of moral attitude. There had always been a streak of the Dark Ages—however well concealed—in this modern prose writer, and that streak now came into the open. The man who had boasted in the *Amorosa Visione* that the thing to do was to enjoy the world while one could, that there would be time to repent somewhat later, began—all at once—to wonder whether or not that time were not almost on him. The level-headed scorner of superstition began to be timorous about those very shadows he had heretofore made mock of. The joyous, if unconscious, pagan began to feel, think, talk, and write like a monk.

A single event has been held to be responsible. That, however, was not really the case. Instead, various factors contributed. Petrarch's influence, as has already been pointed out, was one of these. The natural processes of disintegration were an-

other. Nevertheless, the traditional single event was extremely
important. It is worth, therefore, discussing in detail.

Some time during the year 1354—probably just after his
return from Avignon on his mission to the Pope—Boccaccio
and a friend were discussing various subjects. Among others,
that of fair ladies came up. Those of old time were mentioned
and lauded, but few of the present day were found worthy of
praise, until his friend happened to mention a certain widow.
So superlative were her various qualities, he said, that she was
like an Alexander among women. She was generous, had
great common sense, and a fine way of speaking. Besides that,
and more important, she was both good to look upon, and not
lacking in charity.

Boccaccio's old instinct as an amorist was aroused.

"Any one could call himself lucky if fortune so favored him
that such a woman gave him her love," he said.

He made a half resolve that he would be the person so
favored, and very soon that half resolve became a whole
resolve.

He had gone where he had imagined she would be, and
knowing only that she was clad in black, had picked out one
of the many so dressed, who seemed particularly attractive
to him.

Then, as he was wondering whether or not she were the
person they had discussed, he had overheard two women
talking.

"Look, my dear, and aren't widow's weeds very becoming
to that lady?"

"Which lady? There are many dressed that way."

"The third one on the bench is the one that I am talking
about."

From the name they used, he realized that it was the widow that his friend had told him about.

Immediately he had fallen in love with her.

He wrote her a letter setting this forth, and begging her to return his affection. Presently she answered him in a short note which said neither yes nor no, but which seemed, none the less, to give him encouragement. He wrote again. She would have him, he now knew. His joy mounted.

Then one day as he was walking along the street he saw her with a group of other ladies, all of whom he knew. They were looking at him, and they were smiling.

Words suddenly came to him across the interval.

They were her words.

"Do you see that poor bumpkin? He's in love with me! Oughtn't I to consider myself lucky though?"

In a daze of humiliation and chagrin, he realized what had happened: that he was being made sport of, that he had been led on and encouraged for no other reason than to make him look ridiculous.

Then, piece by piece, the rest of the story became plain to him.

She already had a lover—just such a cocky and audacious Florentine young man as Boccaccio used to make his stories of—and to avoid that lover's suspicions she had shown him Boccaccio's letters. In the intervals of their love making, they must have arisen to look at and laugh at his outpourings. She had flouted the idea that she could even look at such a person —that fat halfwit, that pumpkin, Master Soupladle—while the lover had boasted valiantly—in the safety of her bedroom—of the beatings he would have liked to give him.

"God give him the itch," he had cried. "Why doesn't he go back and pick onions and leave gentlewomen alone?"

It was, even, the lover who had written the letter, and now probably the whole malicious city of Florence was tittering.

Boccaccio's own estimation of his love-making abilities, of his smooth expertness as a man of the world, must have afforded one point where his vanity was vulnerable, and he felt, therefore, completely deflated.

"Ah, me," he bewailed, "but it is an obscene and unbecoming thing for a man—let be noble, which I don't claim to be, but even one accustomed to associating with worthy persons, and at least well-enough, if not overweeningly acquainted with the ways of the world—to be pointed out by the finger of one woman to other women just as if he were the village idiot!"

For a while, indeed, by his own admission, so completely deflated was he, that he thought of killing himself, but he decided—quite possibly with good enough reason—that to do this would be only to give satisfaction to the person who had made such a fool of him.

Instead, therefore, he determined on revenge.

And this revenge he got very completely with the one weapon that he was most skilled in using.

He wrote a book. Calling it *Il Corbaccio*—almost, "The Old Crow"—and in it narrating his encounter with the scornful lady's husband in a woeful infernal region which he says was known variously as "The Labyrinth of Love," "The Enchanted Valley," "The Pigsty of Venus," or "The Vale of Sighs and Tears," he made it an excuse, among other things, for taking you satirically behind the scenes, and revealing unkindly just those things that a widow, who was just beginning to be a little sensitive owing to the fact that she was not quite so freshly youthful as she would like her lovers to believe, would least like the outside world to know.

The pretext is a moral sermon. The husband first tells

Boccaccio that man, having been created but a little lower than the angels and being a truly noble creature, should have nothing to do with woman who is really a sort of animal. He then inveighs against love. Next against women in general. Finally against his former wife. He concludes by pledging Boccaccio, apparently on the grounds of morals and religion, to devote himself to perpetual vendetta. After that, with the dawn, he disappears in a ruddy glow, returning to serve out his time in that purgatory, to which—so he indicates—the woman who had been his wife, helped—when he was still living—to send him.

It is in this book that we see for the first time the new Boccaccio. Consider, for example, his general remarks upon women. His satire, when he chooses to use it, is still very effective, but his tolerance has entirely vanished. Quite often he is ill-tempered and testy. Quite often even stingingly rude.

Woman is an imperfect creature, governed by a thousand evil and abominable passions.

No other creature is less cleanly than woman.

All a woman is interested in, is prestige. Born to be a servant, she wishes to dominate everything and everybody. She wishes, too, to wear the symbols of ruling. Crowns, girdles, robes of gold and of vair, and all sorts of ornaments.

All a woman is interested in, is new and lewd fashions. Discontent with sensible clothes, she wishes to be clad like some courtezan.

All a woman is interested in, is her lovers. Her passions are fiery and insatiable. She does not care who satisfies them: servant, laborer, miller, or even black Ethiopian. It is one and the same.

Woman is timid when it comes to doing good. When her husband wishes her to go on a ship, she becomes seasick. She is afraid of a mouse, and the slightest small noise makes her tremble. Yet when she has something illicit to do, she is as brave as the bravest. For her lover, she will climb to the roof of the very highest tower.

All the thoughts of women, all their zeal, is put into nothing else than robbing, lording it over, and deceiving men.

A woman will marry a slobbering old man whose eyes are gummy and whose hands and head tremble, if only he is rich and she thinks there is some chance of being soon a widow.

"Poor students"—this is the most cutting stricture—"suffer cold and hunger and wakefulness, and after many years they realize that they have learned but little. Women, when they have been to church one morning and that hardly long enough to hear a mass, know how the firmament turns; how many stars there are in heaven and how great they are; what are the courses of the sun and of the planets; how lightning, thunder, the rainbow, hail and everything else in the air is made; how the tide goes out and comes in again, and how the earth produces its fruits. They know what is being done in India and Spain; how the houses of the Ethiopians are constructed; where the Nile rises; and whether crystal is made from snow borne by the north wind or from something else. They know with whom their she-neighbor sleeps; by whom another one was made pregnant and in what month the child will be born; how many lovers a third one has; and who gave her the ring she has and who the girdle. They know how many eggs their neighbor's hen lays in a year and how many spindles are worn out weaving a dozen yards of linen. In short they return completely informed of everything the Romans and the Greeks and the Trojans ever did, and if no one else better is around, they gabble on ceaselessly about this with the servant, the baker's wife, the market woman and the laundress, and they are very much put out if any one rebukes them for so doing."

The remarks which he puts in the mouth of the husband concerning the lady who was so ill-advised as to reject him, are of much the same order. Somewhat more specific, however. She was only interested in her ancestry and in proving that she was of better blood than the man who married her, he says. Her foodstuffs had to be of the best, and the great variety of dainties—fat capons, jugged hare *alla parmigiana,* milk-fed veal, partridges, pheasants, fat thrushes, doves, soup *alla lombarda,* strips of macaroni, fritters flavored with elderberry, white puddings, and such tidbits as cherries, figs, and melons—which she had to have—nearly brought him to ruin. Wine was also a weakness, and it had to be of the most expensive brands, such as white Sardinian and Greco. Her beauty was entirely artificial. The house was like a chemical laboratory with its various vials and retorts, and she was so covered with unguents that when her husband tried to kiss her he stuck to her lips. Even before he died, she needed half a dozen lovers. She went to church, true, but her real paternosters were romances of Lancelot and Guinevere, Tristram and Isolde. So irascible was she that when a fly lit on her face and she could not kill it, she used to snatch up a broom and pursue it from room to room until you almost wondered if she would not blow up.

But it was not in these disclosures that Boccaccio dealt his unkindest counterstrokes.

Her husband makes public her age.

Though you think she is young, he says, and though she pretends that she is twenty-eight, she is really nearer forty than thirty. Her hair is already graying and it is only by careful arrangement that she can conceal this fact. You should see her with her maid when she is doing this.

"This net is not yellow enough," she goes on, "and this hangs too much over there. Push that part up a little, and pull that one down so that it covers my forehead. Take out that pin which you put below my ear and set it over there a little, and tighten out that wrinkle that it gives me under my chin. Take away the glass and lift up that piece of cloth that crosses my cheek under the left eye."

Then suddenly she flies into a rage.

"Oh, go away!" she cries. "You're good for nothing but to wash dishpans. Go away, and call me Madame So-and-so."

Yet when she is through she licks her fingers like a cat, looks at herself first one way and then the other and seems very much pleased with herself.

It would be hard to believe that this does not represent some actual scene.

Her husband also describes her in the early morning, squatting and spitting in front of the fire, haggard and unkempt, and clad in a dirty dressing gown.

He tears every illusion away from her. How could Boccaccio possibly have fallen for such tawdriness!

Two things should have kept him from so doing, he says. First of all Boccaccio's age. If his white hair does not deceive the husband, Boccaccio has been out of swaddling clothes for at least forty years, and has known worldly things for at least five-and-twenty. Second, his study of philosophy which should, certainly, have taught him what women really amounted to.

"You ought to have seen that love is a passion that blinds the soul, unmakes the intellect, dulls the memory, dissipates every earthly faculty, wastes the body, is the enemy of both youth and age, is death, and the mother of vices and the dweller of empty places. You ought to have seen that it is a thing without reason, order, or any stability whatsoever. You ought to have seen that it is a vice of the mind and a destroyer of all freedom."

One thinks of the sheaves of mediæval rhymes in French, Latin, Italian, Spanish, Portuguese, English, Dutch, German, and Scandinavian, to say nothing, probably, of every other language that then existed, which man, abetted by the priestly conception of woman as the arch-temptress, had flung against the fair enemy:

> Woman, I tell you, is a dwelling place of demons,
> She is a stinking rose, she is a poison sweet...
>
> Better by far with a serpent to crawl,
> Than to crawl with a woman, and I lie not at all....

And perhaps a hundred thousand others.

Boccaccio, supposedly, had advanced far beyond this dark and unkind point of view, and certainly the *Decameron,* though saying many things that a present-day feminist would hardly like, was written by a man who was far beyond it. But underneath we are all very much the product of the forces that have made us, and it took only the sting of one personal humiliation to cause Giovanni to revert to type. Let us not be too hard on him, however. Remember that his keenness was now dulling. Remember that he was now beginning to feel years.

CHAPTER XXII

IT must have been shortly after the completion of *Il Corbaccio* that Boccaccio set his hand to a new and very dissimilar task. This was the writing of the first of the two works which he devoted to his great predecessor, Dante Alighieri. The date in which he wrote his "Life of Dante"—known also as "Pamphlet in Praise of Dante" or as "Concerning the Origin, Life, Habits, and Studies of the Illustrious Poet, Dante Alighieri of Florence, and Concerning the Works Composed by Him"—can be surmised only from internal evidence. To make this difficult, there is an array of various texts; and even when this has been straightened out, there remain two versions, one long and the other short, yet both apparently equally authentic, for the confusion of critics. It seems probable, however, that one of these but represents an earlier draft of the other. It seems almost certain that the "Life" was written sometime between 1355 and 1359, or at about the time when he was trying to convince Petrarch of Dante's great eminence. Possibly then—though there is no supporting evidence—it was part of his propaganda. It should be noted, also, that of the two dates, the earlier one seems likely to be the correct one. If a single year has to be fixed upon, the most probable is 1355.

The book is extremely interesting. Among other reasons, because it was the first really complete biographical study of the poet ever written. Besides that, it came from the hand of a man singularly well-qualified to compose it. Boccaccio had

been an admirer of Dante from his earliest years, and he was
—or at least very nearly—the first Dante "student" in the whole
of history. He was nine years old when Dante died, and he
must, therefore, have talked to many Florentines who had
known the great poet personally. He had copied out nearly
all of Dante's writings—both for his own benefit and for the
benefit of others—and had pored over them hour after hour
trying to work out their most hidden meanings. He had
known and talked with Dante's daughter, Sister Beatrice, and
on more than one occasion had been to Ravenna which held
the poet's ashes, and which must have been filled with his
memory. Consequently what he says had and still should
have, considerable authority. Modern criticism has frequently
tried to show the unreliability of some of his statements, and it
is perhaps true that he was not infallible, being, for one thing, a
little overwilling to accept gossip for fact. There is, nevertheless, such a thing as too great skepticism. Boccaccio was, after
all, fairly near to Dante, nearer than most who would like to
disprove him, and one should, therefore, be wary in disbeliev-
ing him. There is no reason, for instance, that he should not
have known what he was talking about when he identified
Beatrice with a real person, namely Bice, the daughter of Folco
Portinari, or when he spoke of a voyage to Paris. In fact, anything Boccaccio says, that cannot definitely be disproven,
should at least tentatively be accepted as so.

The "Life of Dante" begins with an attack.

"Solon," Boccaccio says, "whose heart was reputed to be a
divine temple of human wisdom, and whose sacred laws still
remain to men of to-day as plain testimony of ancient justice,
was, according to what they related, in the habit of saying that
every republic, just as every man did, stood on two feet. Of
which, he gravely added, the right one was to leave no crime

unpunished, the left one to leave no good deed without reward."

Florence, however, did not, apparently, heed that remark, as witness her treatment of this poet. For instead of rewarding him, she punished him. She drove him into exile and took all his goods away. She tried to defame his character, and forced him to die, and be buried, in a foreign city.

"Oh wicked thought!" Boccaccio cries. "Oh unworthy deed, oh mean example, oh prophecy of future ruin! If it were possible to hide from the eyes of God who sees all, every other Florentine iniquity, would not this alone be enough to bring down on her His anger?"

He makes what he considers the answer:

"Certainly yes."

The book then goes on with the story of the person it is considering. It gives Dante's own version of his ancestry, tracing his descent, on one hand, from the Roman Frangipanni, the Florentine Elisei, the famous Cacciaguida, and on the other from a damsel of the Ferrarese family of Aldighieri. It tells of his early studies. It relates that, unlike the others of his day, he did not devote himself to making money, but to "the praiseworthy pursuit of fame." It tells how he read the poets, not only studying Vergil, Horace, Ovid, Statius and many another famous in antiquity, but also striving to imitate them. It relates how, just as he went to Paris later, so in his youth he went to Bologna. It tells how he became a philosopher as well as a poet. It tells of his love for Bice and it tells of the death of his beloved. "By which death, Dante was plunged into such sorrow and affliction, and shed so many tears, that his friends and relatives expected him to die also." It makes mention of his public career, and after that tells of his exile. It tells how his friends, even his wife, were disloyal to him. It sketches his

years of wandering. How he went to Verona, where he was
sheltered by Messer Alberto della Scala. How he returned to
the Casentino, from whence he could look down on his city.
How he went to the Lunigiana, to the mountains near Urbino,
to Bologna, to Padua, to Verona again. How he visited France,
and how he waited on the Emperor Henry, and tried to persuade him to attack Florence. How in the end he went to
Ravenna where he was received with courtesy and honor by
Messer Guido Novello da Polenta; where he breathed his last,
almost of exhaustion, at the not too decrepit age of fifty-six;
where he was buried reverently; where his body rests even
to-day.

Besides that it sets down a physical picture of the man.

"Our poet, then, was of medium height, and after he reached
the age of maturity he walked always with a slight stoop; his
way of carrying himself was sedate and calm, and he was
always clad in the plainest clothes, as was befitting to a man
of his gravity. His face was long, his nose aquiline, his eyes
neither large nor small, his jaw long, and his under lip was
thrust out further than his upper lip. He was dark in complexion, his hair was black and curly, and his face always sad
and very thoughtful. For that reason it happened that one
day, as he passed near a gate in Verona whereby many women
were sitting—the fame of his works being already well-known,
and particularly that part of his Comedy which he called 'The
Inferno'—one of them said softly, yet not so softly but that he
and those with him heard it:

"'Do you see that man? He goes to hell and comes back
again whenever he wants to, and he brings back news of those
who are down there.'

"To which the other replied simply:

"'Indeed, you must speak the truth. Do you see how his

beard is all curly and his face blackened by the heat and the smoke which is below?'

"Hearing which words spoken behind him and realizing that they came from the woman's actual belief, he was very much amused at them, and entirely satisfied that they should think thus, he continued, smiling slightly, on his way."

Besides that, it builds up the legend of his character.

In his public and private affairs, Boccaccio relates, Dante was orderly and self-controlled, and he was more courteous and polite than any other.

In his meats and in his drink, he was extremely temperate. He liked delicacies as well as the next man, but for the most part he lived on plain food.

In his youth, he delighted in music and song. Those proficient in either, were sure to be numbered among his acquaintances.

He liked, similarly, to be alone and far removed from the crowd, so that his thoughts would not be interrupted, and if a thought which pleased him greatly did come to him when he was with a crowd, and anything regarding something else were asked him, rather than that his imaginations should be broken in on, he would answer nothing at all.

He was devoted to study. Once at Siena, finding in a certain drug store a book that he had long been seeking, and having no better place to which he could go, he sat down on a bench in front of the store, and began to read. There was a festival going on at the time, and among other things it included jousts and passages at arms. He never lifted his eyes but in spite of the noise kept on reading. It was sunset when he finished the book. Friends asked him how he had been able to concentrate in the midst of such a splendid celebration. He said that he had never noticed it at all.

His intellect was fine. Once at Paris, fourteen questions were proposed to him at the same time by fourteen learned theologians. He answered all of them, and then met all of the objections to his answers.

True, he was fond of honors and of pomp.

"Yet what of it? What life is so humble that it is not moved by the sweetness of glory?"

True, he wanted to be crowned with laurel at the font of the Baptistry in Florence. Yes. But he would not make any compromise of his principles to obtain this coronation.

The book even records the mysterious finding, by Dante's sons, of the lost last cantos of the *Paradiso* after their whereabouts had been indicated in a vision.

Thus the whole outline of Dante as we now imagine him was suggested in its limited span.

Yet for all that, it is not any more for what it tells us of the author of the "Divine Comedy" than for what it tells us of its own author that this book is valuable. It shows us his loyalty, his modesty and his sense of proportion. It shows his keenness of perception, his industriousness, his level-headedness, and his sense of realism. It shows, too, his independence.

Boccaccio is quite willing to criticize his great idol. He does plainly when he comes to discuss Dante's Ghibellinism. It is a pity, he says, that such a great man should have been susceptible to such violent party spirit. He does also, when he comes to discuss the moot question of Dante's carnality. He is not afraid to assert, without mincing, that the poet was devoted to this "natural and almost necessary," yet at the same time quite "inexcusable" failing, not only in his youth but in his maturity.

"Yet who," he says candidly, "among mortals could be a just judge to condemn him for it? Not I."

More than anything else, however, it shows his new violent misogynism.

Expressing his disapproval of Dante's relatives, who, he asserts, forced the poet to marry so that he would forget his sorrow for the death of Beatrice, he says:

"He, accustomed to wake long in his sacred studies, was wont oftentimes to converse with emperors, kings, and other great princes as an equal, and to talk with philosophers, and to entertain pleasing poets, and hearing of the woes of others, thus to mitigate his own. Now, with those who pleased his new lady and at the time that was suitable to her, he was obliged to listen to the chatter of women, and if he did not wish further annoyance, not only agree with what they said, but even praise it. He, accustomed, when the vulgar crowd annoyed him, to withdraw to some solitary part, and there in speculation to consider what spirit moved the sky, whence came the life of those on earth, and what are the causes of things, or to let his fancies wander, or to compose some of those things which, after he is dead, have made him known to future generations, now not only was taken from such sweet thoughts whenever his new lady wished it, but must take with him, when he did go, one badly suited to the tenor of such things. He who was in the habit of laughing, weeping, singing, or sighing according to the sweet or sad mood which had possession of him, had now to render account not only of the more important things, but of the slightest sigh, showing her what moved him, whence it came, and whither it went, she thinking that his joy must have come from the love of another, his sorrow from hatred of her. Oh, what an ineffable weariness to live with such a creature, to talk with her, and finally to grow old and die!"

He then goes on into another tirade against women.

Think of the expense of marrying one of them. The clothes.

The ornaments. The rooms filled with needless dainties. The men servants and the maid servants. The nurses. The chambermaids. The feasts. The presents to the relatives of your wife.

Think of their reputation. If a woman is good-looking who doubts that she will soon have many lovers?

Think of the trouble they make. The wrangling. The quarrels with the servants.

And so forth and so on, through a long list to repeat which would but be tedious.

"Yet you must not believe," he concludes ironically, "that for the above reasons I have come to the opinion that men should never marry. Quite the contrary. I praise marriage. But not for every one. Let philosophers, then, leave marriage to rich imbeciles, to noble lords, and to day laborers, and let them delight themselves instead with philosophy, who is a better wife than all of them."

It is not hard to deduce that the lines must have been written at about the same time that he set down *Il Corbaccio*.

The mood also bears resemblance to that in which he found himself when he penned similar remarks at the end of his observations on Samson in a Latin book, the *De Casibus virorum illustrium*, which he would shortly bring to a conclusion.

"A pleasant but a deadly evil is woman," he there said.

Yet he betrayed himself in his description of this evil.

"Her pink and white complexion," he went on; "her large, grave, black, and gleaming eyes; her sweet and musical voice; her glittering golden hair; her little mouth; her lips red as coral; her neatly chiselled nose; her delicate and ivory neck, which rises slenderly and straight from her curved, full shoulders; the firm elevation of her bosom, which slowly heaves, and is entirely spotless; her round, slightly rising breasts, which are divided one from the other by a little space; her plump and even arms; her small and gentle hands; her distended fingers; her delicate and snow-white body; her flesh like ivory; her tiny and soft feet; her strong flanks; her swelling thighs; her firm and rounded legs; and the rest of her body of medium height—neither too tall nor yet too little, that is."

O Lord—in other words—deliver me from a temptation that is still singularly attractive to me!

It has been noted that Boccaccio was changing.

But a man does not change completely overnight.

CHAPTER XXIII

THERE was to be one further step in the intellectual disintegration of Boccaccio, and so dramatically incredible was it, yet at the same time so ironically appropriate, that it is to be questioned whether even an Anatole France or a James Branch Cabell inventing a life for the novel writer, could have improved on it. This was what is known as the "conversion" of Boccaccio. *Il diavolo invecchiato, si fece frate,* runs an Italian proverb: when the devil grows old, he turns monk. At one time it was thought that this, actually, was what had happened, and while it must now be admitted that the authority on which it was once believed that Giovanni really did enter holy orders, quite possibly existed only in the imagination of an Eighteenth Century commentator whose bias was distinctly Catholic, in substance, if not in letter, the wise saying was justified.

The satirist of Fra Cipolla was the victim of the persuasions of a friar whose devices must have been fully as crude and as transparent. Early in the year 1362, his studies were interrupted by a strange visitor. A Carthusian monk of Siena, by name Joachim Ciani, appeared at Boccaccio's house and demanded that he be listened to. Admitted, he announced melodramatically that he was the bearer of a deathbed message from another Carthusian, also of Siena, a certain Blessed Pietro Petroni. Boccaccio was to die shortly, the message was, and for that reason he should abandon his unholy studies. He should give up his profane devotion to the Muses, and prepare to confront his Maker. Joachim said that after seeing Boccaccio at Florence he was going to Naples, from whence he would sail for France and England where he had other persons to visit. On his return he would seek out Petrarch for whom he had the same tidings and same warning. Apparently he gave signs and mentioned things supposedly secret in such a way as to lend conviction to what he said.

Boccaccio was astounded. He might have reflected—as he once certainly would have—that the self-assurance and effrontery of most monks was quite enough—when the issue of saving a soul was at stake—to lead them into any fraud whatsoever that happened to serve their purpose. Instead—perhaps because it but confirmed his own growing apprehensions—he believed Joachim's warning implicitly and was plunged, therefore, into a daze of horror. The world that he loved so dearly and so inordinately was fading, it was about to break up into shreds of riven mist like the unsubstantial vision that it really was, and ahead loomed only the crackling fires of hell or the bleak wastes of purgatory. Was it too late to do anything? The monk said no. His first impulse seems, therefore, to have been to do whatever Joachim had commanded. He would destroy his books. He would give up every study except the study of things religious.

Then, apparently, he had an afterthought. Petrarch, his great friend, was mentioned in the monk's warnings? Petrarch would know the answer. Why not, then, pour out his doubts and fears to Petrarch? The epistle that he sent for this purpose is not now in existence, yet we have good reason to feel sure that it was a confused and panicky one. Nevertheless, it saved him, for it brought back an answer that, for all the fact that some of the points it made seem almost as mediæval as Boccaccio's superstitions, was so full of level-headedness and common sense and of fine generous affection, that its reasoning could hardly be resisted.

"Your letter, my dear brother," it began, "has worried me extraordinarily. As I read it, I was filled with great astonishment, and great sorrow. After I had finished it, one and the other had disappeared."

Then it went on to consider the matters broached by Boccaccio.

As to the validity of the message, Petrarch would judge that better when the messenger visited him.

"I will question his age, his brow, his eyes, his character, his appearance, his gestures, his way of walking, his way of carrying himself, his very voice, his words, and more than anything else the things he says and what his object seems to be. I do not minimize the authority of prophecy. All that Christ says is true. It is not possible for verity to lie. Yet I ask myself if the author of this prophecy is Christ, or whether some one else, as so often happens, has not borrowed the name of Christ to lend conviction to his imposture."

As to the fact that Boccaccio had little time to live:

"Were you, a man of your years, ignorant of that fact even before he came to see you?"

Our life is but an instant, and since the prophet told him that he had a few more years to live, he should be thankful, for he might not have that much.

As to his grief at leaving this world, he should not be sorry. Remember what Cicero said in his Tusculan orations: "The best thing of all is not to be born at all, failing that to die early." Remember the words of Ecclesiastes: "Wherefore I praised the dead which are already dead more than the living which are yet alive; yea, better is he than both they, which hath not yet been, who hath not yet seen the evil work that is done under the sun." Remember Job's cry: "Let the day perish wherein I was born."

"Since life is full of dangers, uncertainties and evils, it follows that the end of this ill thing is good and desirable."

It is not really the end of life that one should weep for but its beginning.

As to his renouncing his studies, that advice might be fitting if he were merely a beginner, for certainly it would be foolish for an old man to begin so profane a study as that of letters. Boccaccio, however, was an experienced writer. Why should his one consolation be taken away from him? Did not many of the philosophers devote themselves to study in their old age? When Cato was an old man, he began to learn Greek. Varro still read and studied when he was a hundred. He left life before he left his love of study. Homer practiced poetry when he was old and blind. When Socrates was old, he took up the study of music. Besides that, were not many of the saints men of education? The thing to do was not so much to abandon his studies as to chasten them, and to chasten his own life as well. Ignorance, however devoted, is not to be compared with the piety of a man of education.

Finally, as to buying Boccaccio's books:

"I will not deny that I am flattered that you prefer me to have them above all others. I will not deny that I am eager for books, as you say, and if I did deny it, all that I have written would give the lie to me. And although I do not like to buy what really belongs to me"—Petrarch held that all that belonged to him belonged to his friends and vice versa—"I do not wish that the books of so great a man should be scattered here and there, and should be handled, as would happen, by profane hands. For that reason I am willing that just as we have had but one heart between us though our bodies have been separated, so, after we have gone, these materials of our study should rest forever unseparated in a holy and sanctified dwelling place which would be a perpetual memorial to both of us." He could not name a price, however, as Boccaccio asked him to, as he did not know either the titles or the number or the value. If, however, Boccaccio sent him a list he would do so. "Then if by any chance you decide to spend with me what little time remains to both of us—something which I have always desired, and which it seems to me you have sometimes promised—you will find your books placed among those which I have been able to gather, and you will see that instead of losing something you once had, you have gained something new."

CHAPTER XXIV

THERE seems but little doubt that this moving letter, with its warmth of feeling, and its soundness of advice, acted as a much needed steadier. At any rate, it prevented Boccaccio from doing anything wild or hysterical. But it did not—and apparently it was not intended to—stand in the way of something like a complete change of feeling. Under the influence of Petrarch's friendship, Giovanni had come, as has already been noted, to regard all his writings in Italian with suspicion. His new religiousness made him look on them with horror: they might have brought him to damnation. He would keep on writing, but from now on all that he set down would be serious in tone, and elevated in purpose. There would be no glittering poems, ornate romances, or light-hearted tales gathered together for the diversion of fair ladies. From now on he would write for men, and the men he wrote for would be men of gravity and erudition. He never swerved from this intention. Various important items came from his study in his thirteen remaining years, but they all lay in the realm of scholarship and learning. Not a single piece of creative or imaginative writing was the product of his industrious pen.

The first of these new works—which he sponsored rather than wrote—was the earliest modern translation of Homer into a western language. This rendering of the Greek poet into Latin prose, in a sense, however, hardly belongs to the phase of Boccaccio's life which was instituted by the monk's visit, for it

was virtually completed when he was called on by the imperti-
nent Ciani. It was begun, in fact, in 1360, and was the result
of a collaboration. On the circumstances leading up to this,
Boccaccio makes some comment in the last book of the *De
Genealogia deorum gentilium:*

"Was it not I"—he there boasts, not without justification—
"who persuaded Leontius Pilate, whom I found in Venetia
en route to the western Babylon, to make the long journey to
my fatherland? Was it not I who took him into my own
home, and kept him there as my guest for a long time, and
who arranged, too, that he should be enrolled among the professors of the University of Florence, and should be paid a
salary out of the public funds? It was I too, moreover, who at
my own expense brought back to Etruria the books of Homer,
and of the other Greeks, which had departed thence many
centuries ago, never to return again. It was I who, in private,
first heard Leontius Pilate read the *Iliad* in the Latin language,
and who first arranged that Homer's writings should be read
in public. And if I did not understand them well, yet I com-
prehended what I could. Nor do I doubt that if that peregrine
man had but stayed with us longer, I would have compre-
hended all."

Apparently he met Leontius in Milan when the scholar
visited Petrarch there in 1359, and Leontius was able to convince both him and his illustrious host that he had been at one
time a student of Barlaam, the distinguished Calabrese bishop
of Gerace, who had once been a teacher of Petrarch. He said
that he was on his way to Avignon, where he was seeking
employment. Both Boccaccio and Petrarch were extremely
anxious that Homer and Plato should be translated into Latin,
and here—since Petrarch knew no Greek whatsoever, and
Boccaccio but little—was some one who would do it for them.

Furthermore, Boccaccio thought he saw an opportunity of meeting some of the expenses of this undertaking by having created, and securing for Leontius a Florentine Greek professorship. He succeeded, brought Leontius to Florence, and for nearly three years entertained him in his own home. During the intervals of the latter's public lectures, he tutored Boccaccio privately. We know the method that was pursued. Leontius would read aloud a passage of Homer, and Boccaccio would ask him questions concerning it. He would then take down voluminous notes on the answers.

During the intervals of Leontius' public lectures, they toiled also at the production for which their association is now largely remembered. Together—this must be the case, for Leontius was as crude in his knowledge of Latin as he was supposedly learned in the language he was translating—they tortured the sonorous hexameters of the father of poetry into an awkward but equivalent Latin. First the *Iliad,* and then the *Odyssey.* In a way, it was as important an accomplishment as anything with which Boccaccio ever was associated, for it was the first tangible achievement of the revival of learning. It was the first step toward making these books widely known.

Yet for all its glory, the task could not have been a pleasant one. Leontius was something of a ruffian. According to Boccaccio, he was a man of hideous appearance. He had the face of a scoundrel, a long and unkempt beard, and disordered black hair. His manners were as rude as his appearance, and his temperament gloomy and changeable. Petrarch bore out this description. He called him "a great beast." "Our Leontius," he said, "is really from Calabria. He likes to think that he is from Thessaly, as if it were more noble to be a Greek than an Italian. I suspect, however, that when he is in Greece he calls himself an Italian just as he calls himself a Greek here.

In each case he wishes to take advantage of the glamor of being a foreigner." Not an attractive picture, at all.

It was with this insufferable person—who had another vice, too, that of personal filthiness—that Boccaccio was obliged to put up for three winters and two summers. It must have been extremely irritating. One thing consoled him, however. He was learning what he wanted to learn. He was being led into a new and gleaming country. This consolation, he must have repeated to himself over and over. "As I found out myself, he was very learned in Greek letters, and his knowledge of Greek history was inexhaustible." In other words, because of this, nearly everything should be forgiven him. Here we see a beginning of the patience and enthusiasm which would soon grasp the whole peninsula. Here we have the precursor of a long line that would run from Niccolo Niccoli to Poggio Bracciolini and Pico della Mirandola. It is pathetic, therefore, that it must be related that even the learning which Leontius had to offer was of an extremely doubtful quality. To Boccaccio in his eagerness, and to Petrarch, who clasped lovingly the great masterpieces which he could not read, it seemed, indeed, of crystal clarity. So, to parched desert wanderers, does the most tepid, brackish stream seem cool and refreshing. But in reality it was otherwise. The fountain of Greek language and learning to which Leontius led them was, in fact, as muddied and impure as the spring torrents of his native Bruttium. Yet these two men had to drink from it eagerly, for it was the only fountain which they had.

It was Petrarch who saw this the more clearly.

"I now wish to warn you of another thing," he wrote Boccaccio, "so that I will not be obliged to repent later of having kept silent. If, as you say, the translation is to be made into prose, consider how St. Jerome expressed himself on this subject in the preface of the *De tempora* of Eusebius, which he rendered into Latin. 'If any one,' he says, 'does not believe that translation alters the grace of the original, let him render Homer word for word into Latin; I will even say more, let him translate it into prose. He will see words in ridiculous order and the greatest of the poets but stammer.' I tell you this so that you will take care, while yet there is time, that so great a labor be not in vain."

He then went on:

"However, for my part, I wish that the thing may be done, whether well or ill. I am so ravenous for great literature that, just as he who has a great appetite for food, does not require the skill of an expert cook, so I await with keen impatience whatever food for my soul there may be made. And in truth, the morsel, which the same Leontius, translating the beginning of Homer into Latin prose, gave me as a sample of the whole work, even though it confirmed the opinion of Jerome, has not ceased to please me. It contains indeed a secret charm, like certain ingredients which one has not quite succeeded in turning into jelly, which lack form, but which keep their fragrance and their flavor. May he continue then with the aid of heaven, and may he return us Homer who has been lost to us."

He last sounded a note of caution:

"In asking me for the volume of Plato which I have with me, and which escaped the fire of my Transalpine house, you give me a proof of your ardor, and I will hold it at your disposal. But take care that he is not unseemly enough to reunite in a single volume these two great princes of Greece, and that the weight of these two geniuses does not break down his mortal shoulders. Let him undertake, God aiding him, one of the two, and first he that wrote several centuries before the other."

It was as if he appreciated fully the bearded Calabrian's limitations, and was anxious to have some translation from his pen, before Leontius tired of the settled life that was so unsuited to his temperament. It was as if he anticipated a sudden unannounced departure.

And if this is so, he guessed, certainly, with correctness.

Toward the spring of 1362, Leontius left Florence abruptly. He stopped at Venice for a while, where Petrarch, as Boccaccio had done before him, put up with his bad breeding for the sake of his supposed erudition. But even Venice could not hold him long. Flinging curses at an Italy whose gravest fault in regard to him was, really, that it had received him too courteously, he set sail for Constantinople. Petrarch did not attempt to retain him; he sent him off, giving him as a traveling companion, a volume of the comedian Terence. "I noticed that he seemed pleased by it, and I have since often wondered what this ill-natured Greek could possibly have had in common with the gay-hearted African." No sooner, however, had Leontius reached the Greek capital than he began to regret Italy. He wrote Petrarch begging him to invite him back again. Petrarch disregarded the letter.

"I will never send for him either by letter or by messenger," he wrote Boccaccio. "Let him stay in the place where he has chosen, and let him live sadly, where he went insolently. He who despised the charms of Florence—which would have been shameful under any circumstances, and was all the more so considering his poverty—let him now suffer the misery of Byzantium with equally loud groans. He who condemned the fair fields of Italy, let him grow old, without my stopping him, in the forests of Thessaly; let him be food for the worms of Greece. He could have helped us in our studies if he had only been a human being and had not been made a beast by his overweening rudeness and his love of change. Let him follow then, and keep for his own, his manners, his beard and his reputation. Let him reap what he has sown. Let him cook what he has reaped. Let him eat what he has prepared."

It was not to be expected, however, that a man of this disposition would allow some one else thus to dispose of his destinies. When, therefore, Leontius realized that Petrarch would not invite him, he decided to come on his own initiative. In the summer of 1365, he took ship for Italy. But he was destined never to reach there. He had already passed the Bosphorus, the Propontus, the Hellespont, the Ægean and Ionian seas, and indeed all the seas of Greece, he was already plowing the Adriatic, when disaster overtook him. A storm suddenly arose. The sailors ran to their posts and Leontius was lashed to a mast. He seemed secure there, and indeed he should have been. All at once, however, the sky cracked, and a swift flash of lightning stabbed and glittered. It struck the very spar to which the philosopher was bound, reducing it and him to cinders. All around were flattened to the deck both by the stroke and by their terror.

"Such," Petrarch wrote, "was the end of our Leontius. His poor baggage and his thumb-worn books were brought to safety thanks to the honesty of the sailors and their little value. I will have them looked through to see whether the Sophocles and the Euripides and some others which he promised to find for me are among them. His shapeless and half burned body was thrown into the sea. He who in another letter which I sent you, I destined to the worms of Greece, is food, alas, for the fishes of Italy."

It was not, however, the end of the troubles that he caused.

His erratic disposition had occasioned serious delay to Petrarch in his passionate desire to have the two Greek epics in a form in which he could read them, for when he left Florence the work was in such chaos that it took Boccaccio the better part of five years to put it in order. This was extremely distressing to Petrarch who wrote Giovanni frequently, and sometimes even with an irritable impatience, imploring him to send the manuscript. Perhaps he thought that he would die before it reached him. But impatience could have no effect, and by its nature the work went on slowly. First one part was sent and then another. It was not, however, until the early days of 1367, that the last lines of the *Odyssey*—copied out, as were all the others, by the actual hand of Boccaccio—came into his possession. Then Boccaccio had rendered his friend the greatest service that was in his power. Then Petrarch's greatest dream had come true.

CHAPTER XXV

BUT it was not only in such a stupendous work of translation and editorship that Boccaccio's remaining years were to be occupied. He made also four compilations in the Latin language of such classical, historical and geographical knowledge as was then available. Curiously enough, for the moment these far surpassed in popularity all that we now regard as his more important writings. So much so, indeed, that one of his early biographers, in discussing his works, could list them with an air of importance, and then briefly add: "He wrote also many books in the vernacular, filled with lightness and vanity, but also with the sauce of sentiment and the sweet suavity of melodious language, such as the 'Book of a Hundred Novels,' the 'Corbatius' and the 'Philostratus.'" The names of these Latin volumes have already appeared in this story. One was the *De casibus virorum illustrium,* later paraphrased into English poetry by John Lydgate under the apt title of "The Fall of Princes." This book, in a series of historic episodes beginning with "our first colleague Adam" and concluding at the bloody court of Naples, sets forth the dizzy mutability of fortune. How the mighty are fallen! is its theme. A second was the *De claris mulieribus*—"The Book of Great Ladies." From the first mother to the ruling queen of Naples, it describes all those of the feminine sex who had escaped being forgotten. A third was the *De Genealogia deorum gentilium*—"The Genealogy of the Pagan Gods." This is a handbook or a compendium—virtually the earliest known—

of classic mythology. The fourth one was his dictionary of names of places, the *De montibus, silvis, fontibus, lacubus, fluminibus, stagnis seu paludibus, de nominibus maris*—"The Book of Mountains, Forests, Springs, Lakes, Rivers, Swamps or Marshes, and of the Names of Oceans." Its title virtually describes what it contains.

There was, too, really a fifth book, although because it was never published as such, it is not usually included in the list of Boccaccio's compositions. In that collection of scholarly notes, written in Boccaccio's own hand, which is preserved in the Laurentian library at Florence, and is known as the Boccaccio *zibaldone* or miscellany, he has set down the rough draft of the greater part of a history of the Tartars. It is supposedly an adaptation of a treatise on the same subject by a royal Armenian monk, Aytoun, but the changes and improvements are enough to warrant us accepting it as a Boccaccio original. It shows him, therefore, as having still another interest. But the whole miscellany is illuminating in this capacity. Not only does it contain numerous transcripts from classic and mediæval authors, all carefully annotated. Not only are there copies of letters and poems by Petrarch and by Zanobi da Strada. There is a full and vivid account of the discovery of the Canary Islands in the summer of 1341 by two ships sent from Lisbon by the King of Portugal, and manned by Florentine, Genovese, Catalan and Spanish sailors. The information came from letters sent to Florence by Florentine merchants "who were in Seville, a city of lower Spain," yet it was as colorful and as full of detail as if Boccaccio had himself been a member of the expedition. Apparently there was nothing whatsoever which had to do with the world he lived in, in which he was not interested, and about which he did not want to know.

The exact years in which these Latin books were written

are still matters of controversy. Since there was no printing, there was no publication with the date set conveniently on the title page. Guesses have been made, however, and there is much reason for accepting them as fairly accurate. Because, for instance, the *De claris mulieribus* was dedicated to Andrea Acciaiuoli, sister of Niccolo, and because Giovanni is known to have quarreled with that great man in 1363, the year earlier has been assigned as the latest in which it could have been published. Since it refers to that lady as the Countess of Altavilla, and since her second marriage, by which she acquired this title, did not take place until 1357, another limit is established. A date can be found for the *De Casibus virorum illustrium* in the same way. References to the battle of Poitiers, and to the arrival in England, as a prisoner, of King John of France, show that it must have been written later than 1357. A colloquy between Petrarch and Boccaccio, in which the former rebukes his friend for his sloth in prosecuting this work, brings us probably to Giovanni's 1363 visit to Milan. Its dedication to Mainardo Cavalcanti, and its mention of the latter's son for whom Boccaccio stood sponsor—Mainardo was not married until 1372—indicate that it was not published until 1373. The *De Genealogia deorum gentilium* was perhaps the earliest begun. It was composed at the request of King Hugh of Cyprus who died in 1359, but the conversation between Boccaccio and Donnino of Parma, one of the former's nobles who had been given the mission of persuading Giovanni to undertake the task, which is recorded in the introduction, seems to have taken place when Boccaccio was really young. We know, furthermore, that King Hugh had made the acquaintance of Boccaccio's father in Paris as far back as 1332. The book was not, however, released until at least 1372, and then without Boccaccio's consent, and in a state which he regarded as unfinished. At the latter's request, he lent Ugo di San Severino, one of his patrons, a copy. Ugo showed it to Pietro da Monteforte, who admired it so greatly that he circulated it on his own initiative. The book of lakes and mountains was composed, on Boccaccio's own assertion, during the intervals of a graver occupation. Presumably during the intervals of his writing the *De Genealogia*. The miscellany could not have been set down before 1341, and is believed not to have been laid aside later than 1363 or 1364. Thus it can be seen that at whatever date individual items were written, the production of the group as a whole occupied nearly all the last years of Boccaccio's life. That is about all that can be said about them, for that really,—if you eliminate matters of merely technical import—is about all that is known.

Yet it is quite enough, for except as curiosities, these books have to-day only a few points of interest. They were to enjoy approximately two centuries of being widely read and intensely admired. They were to be translated into nearly every language of Europe. Then they were to sink into as complete oblivion. It is the common fate of scholarship. That these books were carefully worked out, the numerous versions and the many thorough revisions seem to indicate; and if they had not been veritable treasuries of knowledge, they would not have been turned to so frequently during the Renaissance. But they are now out of date, since all their learning has been replaced by newer learning. If we read the *De Casibus virorum illustrium* at all, it is only to hunt out such an illuminating passage of self-portraiture as the remarks at the conclusion of the chapter on Samson which have already been cited, or because, though inaccurate, Boccaccio's observations on Walter of Brienne, and on Philippa of Catania, have at least the virtue of coming from a contemporary, and possibly from an eye-witness.

One episode in the *De claris mulieribus*—the story of the priest
of Anubis who persuades the chaste Roman lady Paulina to
share his bed with him under the impression that he is the god
himself who wishes to beget a son from her—has the sprightli-
ness of a tale from the *Decameron*. Indeed, it is almost iden-
tical with the story of Fra Alberto and the Venetian lady. The
rest of the book—whether it deals with Eve; Cleopatra; that
charming and scandalous fiction of the Middle Ages, the lady
Pope, the Papessa Giovanna; or Queen Giovanna of Naples—
has only the interest that it confirms our impression of Boccaccio's attitude toward women, both as expressed in *Il Corbaccio,*
and in his romances. The geographical dictionary reflects his
admiration of Petrarch in its description of the fountain of
Sorgues, near which the poet lived; and it tells us, as we have
already seen, in the passages on the Arno and the Elsa, something of Boccaccio's own boyhood. If it were not for the last
two books of the *De Genealogia deorum gentilium,* that enormous and laboriously put together mass of information regarding fable and mythology, would gather dust, never disturbed,
in the shelves of old libraries. It would be as forgotten as the
encyclopedic volumes of his old teacher, Paul of Perugia, by
which it was inspired, and from which so great a part, if not
indeed most, of its information was drawn.

It is, therefore, rather surprising that these two last books
are among the most animated of all the things that Boccaccio
ever wrote. The first—Book XIV—is a defense of poetry. It
attempts to explain why a career as a man of letters is justified.
The second—Book XV—is his own apology. It gives his defense for having become a writer. It makes an explanation of
why, and of how, he became what he was.

It is this book that is the more important, for it is a principal,
and on many points the only, source of information as to the

THE PAPAESSA GIOVANNA

FROM A 1473 EDITION OF THE DE CLARIS MULIERIBUS

early life of Boccaccio. We have already drawn from it profusely. It establishes, among other things, Boccaccio's early devotion to letters, the opposition of his father, and his years of business and of law study. The other book, is, however, more interesting. Poetry, Boccaccio therein says, has been attacked by the jurists, the doctors, and the theologians. These say that poetry is a nullity, not worthy of the attention of a rational being; that it is a collection of lies; that it is either meaningless or morally baneful, or it is so obscure that we cannot understand it; that at best the poets are the apes of the philosophers. Hence all good men will follow Boethius and Jerome in condemning poetry, they will follow Plato in banishing poets from the city. Point by point Boccaccio meets these objections, and his answers flame with almost holy conviction.

It is not a nullity:

"Poetry is a certain fervor of exquisite invention, and of exquisite writing and speaking what one has invented. It is an unusual interweaving of words and thoughts, concealing truth under the beauteous veil of fable."

Again:

"Although they"—Plautus and Terence—"intended nothing beyond what the letter implies, yet by their genius they describe the manners and words of various men, and if these things have not actually taken place, yet since they are universal, they could have taken place."

It is not a collection of lies:

"I say this, because a lie, in my opinion, is a certain falsehood much resembling the truth, through which the truth is repressed and the false expressed, and that for the purpose of injuring or benefitting some one. The poets do not lie, they invent, and if their inventions be lies, so too are those of St. John the Apocalypse."

It is not even meaningless:

When Dante "depicted the double-membered Gryphon dragging the car on the summit of Mount Severus, accompanied by the seven candle-sticks and the seven nymphs and the rest of the triumphal pomp," did they think he did this "merely to show he knew how to compose rhymes and fables"? Who would be "so insane as to suppose that that most illustrious and most Christian man, Francis Petrarch, spent so many vigils, so many sacred meditations, so many hours, days and years simply in depicting Gallus demanding his pipe of Tyrrhenus, or Pamphilus and Mitius contending with each other?"

No one who had read Petrarch's other works, Boccaccio asserts.

Then he continues:

"I might in addition adduce my own bucolic poem, whose meaning I well know, but I think it is better to omit that because I am not yet of such worth that I ought to mingle with illustrious men."

Nor is that all:

"We must believe"—further—"that it is not only illustrious men who have put into their poems profound meanings, but there is never an old woman doting on the home hearth in the watches of the winter nights, who, when she tells of Orcus or the Fates or of witches—about which they oftenest make up their stories—does not, as she invents and repeats them, conceal beneath her narrative some meaning, according to the measure of her narrow powers—a meaning sometimes by no means to be derided—through which she wishes either to terrify the little boys, or divert the girls, or to make old people laugh, or at least to show forth the power of fortune."

Poets are obscure?

So too are the philosophers and the writers of the Scriptures.

It is well to conceal precious truths, lest by too easy accessibility, they become cheap.

Finally—it has been said that poets are the apes of the philosophers.

"If they had said that they were the apes of nature, it might have been endured, since according to his powers, the poet tries to describe in lofty song whatever is done by nature herself. If these critics choose to look, they will see the movements of the sky and of the stars, the noise and sweep of the winds, and the noisy crackling of flames, the roar of the waves, the height of mountains, the shadow of the woods, the course of rivers, so clearly described that the things themselves would seem to be contained in the few lines of the songs. In this sense, I will admit that poets are apes, and I think it a most honorable endeavor to strive by art after that which nature does by power."

Naturally the need for some of these defenses has vanished. It is not, for instance, now necessary for a poet to defend the truth of his fictions. But they are none the less compelling, and not even Sir Philip Sidney or Percy Bysshe Shelley was to surpass them in eloquence. They gleam amid the tedium of much crabbed dullness with a warm-hearted and glittering effulgence. It is as if they wished to prove to us that, for all that Boccaccio was aging, his heart still beat valiantly; that he was still filled with a leaping and exalting fire; that—at least at moments—he was still gorgeously young.

CHAPTER XXVI

THE years during which Boccaccio was engaged in the composition of these erudite works were passed, so it seems, in much the same way as those during the course of which he had written the *Decameron*. It is known, to be sure, that he departed from Florence, returning to his ancestral Certaldo.

"As I have already told you," he wrote Pino dei Rossi in his letter consoling the latter for his exile which was a consequence of his part in disturbances which took place in 1360, "I have retired to Certaldo, and there I have commenced—with much less difficulty than I expected—to enjoy living again. I have begun to wear rough country clothes and to enjoy country food. And not seeing the ambitions and annoyances and troublesomeness of my fellow citizens has brought such solace to my spirit, that I tell you that if I could only be sure that I would never hear of such things again, it would bring me great peace."

In other respects, however, his mode of life was unchanged, and even those words may be taken as something of a literary gesture. For the moment, "the hills and meadows, the trees with their green leaves and their vari-colored flowers" might indeed seem preferable to "the feverish and incessant turmoils of the townsfolk." For the moment, "the song of the nightingales and of the other birds" might bring him more joy than "the deceits and the disloyalties" of the Florentines. For the moment, able—after a hectic and active existence—"to retire

with his little books" whenever he wished to, it might seem
to him that "mortal as I am, I here taste eternal felicity."

But this mood could not last. There is good reason to suppose that in spite of his pronunciamento, Boccaccio returned
to Florence again and again, and there is documentary evidence that on at least one occasion he found civic employment
there. In April, 1368, he was member of an advisory committee
which had charge of alterations to the oratory of the Or' San
Michele. Nor could the fresh Tuscan air take away from him
his restless love of travel. Between 1362 and 1368, he made at
least five and possibly six long voyages.

The first of these—in the fall of 1362 and in the spring of
1363—took him to Naples, and then back the whole length of
the Italian peninsula to Venice. The second—two years later—
was a new mission to the Pope at Avignon. The third—in
1367—was another trip to Venice. The fourth—toward the end
of that year, and in the beginning of 1368—was to Rome and to
Viterbo. The fifth—in the ensuing fall—was to Venice and
to Padua. Besides these, there is a hypothetical residence at
Ravenna during the early months of 1367. There is considerable doubt, to be sure, that this actually took place, for the
letter to Petrarch by which it is supposedly established, is now
pretty well conceded to date from an earlier visit. But even
without it, Boccaccio stands out as an extraordinary and energetic journeyer. Especially when you consider not only the
sheer uncomfortableness but the actual danger of moving about
Italy at this time. Especially when you remember that like
another famous John—Shakespeare's John Falstaff—Giovanni
grew old and was fat.

In a certain sense, this journey to the south of France, all
these wanderings up and down the Italian peninsula, were but
repetitions of Boccaccio's earlier travels. They cannot be passed

by without comment, however. What they tell us, gives a most animated contact with the period in which Giovanni was living. It also adds a few more significant touches to the portrait of a man of letters which is being painted, making him stand out more vividly and more clear.

The embassy to Avignon was connected with the last phases of what has been termed the Pope's "Babylonian captivity." Guillaume de Grimoard, elected High Pontiff in succession to Clement VI, had taken the significant title of Urban V. The Spaniard, Cardinal Gil Albornoz, first of the series of great Papal generals who were to raise St. Peter's spiritual hegemony into an important temporal power, had reduced most of the turbulent Ghibellines. He had even tamed Boccaccio's former patron, Francesco degli Ordelaffi, and the latter's gallant wife, Monna Cia, who was as good a captain as her husband was. The word was abroad that what saint and poet and patriot had so ardently longed for was about to transpire: that the head of the Christian religion was about to return to Rome. Florence, naturally, was particularly pleased. Then she heard something that took part of her joy away. Urban was coming under the auspices of, and would be accompanied by, the emperor, Charles IV. It was to ascertain whether or not this were true that Boccaccio was appointed ambassador. He was also to attempt to prevent it. His instructions included a long list of Florentine services to the Pope which he was to enumerate in arguing her case. He was directed to certain cardinals, supposedly favorable to Florence, to whom he was to appeal. He was authorized to put five galleys at the Pope's disposal, if he decided to enter Italy by sea, and five hundred soldiers, if he decided to enter Italy by land.

It goes without saying that his mission was not successful. The Pope, who had at last come to an understanding with

the emperor, could hardly have risked alienating so valuable
a friendship for anything that might be promised him by a
people as notoriously volatile as the Florentines. Besides, he
must have known that he could count on a certain amount of
Florentine help whatever he did. Florence was so deeply
involved in the Papal cause and had been for so long a time
that she could hardly have extricated herself. As far as
Boccaccio was concerned, however, the voyage must have been
a pleasant one. Although he could not take the time—as he
would have liked to—for a detour to visit Petrarch at Pavia,
he halted for a while at Genoa where he was entertained by
Riquiero Grimaldi and his son.

At Avignon, he had an even greater joy. He met Petrarch's
old friend, Philip de Cabassoles, formerly Bishop of Cavaillon.

"But to end my complaints,"—this is Petrarch's account of
the occasion, and he refers to his disappointment that Boccaccio had not sufficiently extended his trip to pay a call
on him—"with a congratulation, I am very happy that in
Babylon itself, you saw those friends whom death has left me,
and especially him, who, as you say, is really my father: my
dear Philip, Patriarch of Jerusalem. To describe him in a few
words, he is a man fully as great as his great rank, and he
would not be below that of Pope either, if one day that honor,
of which he is worthy, were bestowed on his merits. You write
me that although he had never before known you, he held
you in his arms for a long time, and that in the presence of
the lord high Pope himself, and of the astonished cardinals,
he clasped you, as another myself, in the embraces of true
friendship."

After this greeting, Philip inquired tenderly for news of the
great poet, and the two aging men, united by this common interest, held long conversations together. Philip begged Boccac-

cio to use his influence to secure him an example of Petrarch's "The Solitary Life." Although the book was dedicated to him, he had never owned a copy. Boccaccio evidently promised to do his best for him. There is something extremely human about this little interlude, and it shakes away very effectively the dry dust of nearly half a dozen centuries. It makes the three persons about which it centers suddenly seem warm, and made of flesh and blood. We almost forget that they are not still living men.

The trip to Venice in 1367 was a direct consequence of this trip to Avignon. Boccaccio made it to rectify his omission in not going to Pavia two years previously. In the midst of spring rains, and against the advice of his friends, he left Certaldo on March 24 for the north of Italy. He succeeded in crossing the Apennines, but when he reached Bologna, it was to learn that Petrarch no longer occupied his house by the Grand Canal. He determined to continue, however, wishing to see Petrarch's daughter, Francesca, and his son-in-law, Francesco da Brossano. When, approaching the city, he learned, by encountering the latter, that even Francesco would not be there, he had gone too far to return, so he kept on.

There were several very illuminating matters connected with this visit. It was at this time, for instance, that an incident occurred which showed how extremely sensitive Boccaccio was to his moral reputation. He himself tells about it. Writing to Petrarch to tell him how he was sheltered by Francesco Allegri, a young Florentine, he added:

"I relate you this in so many words so that I may excuse myself for not having taken advantage, this time, of what, in your letter, you so generously offered me. Yet if none of these friends had been there to receive a stranger, I would have gone to an inn rather than to stay with your Francesca while her husband was away. For although you know the integrity of my attitude toward what is yours both in this and in many other matters, all the rest may not know it. And so to make clear that I am honorable—although certainly my white hair, my mature age, my fatness and my feeble body ought to take away all suspicion—I thought to stay away, so that the false thinking of the evil-minded could not find a footprint where indeed there was none. You well know how in matters like this ill report has more power than the truth has."

It was on this visit, too, that he saw Petrarch's small granddaughter who reminded him—as has already been noted—so movingly of his own little Violante.

There was one other significant episode connected with this visit. It throws much light on the often-debated subject of Boccaccio's poverty. Apparently this enemy of such long standing did not abandon her attacks even in the latter years of his life. His Renaissance biographers, dwelling upon the enormous amount of copying of manuscripts which he did, point out that since he was too poor to buy books he had to manufacture his own. It would seem, however, that his want was even greater than that. In spite of his great distinction, and in spite of the many offices he held, it would seem that he often lacked the very means of life.

When Francesco returned, he arranged a series of entertainments for Boccaccio. Dinners were given, distinguished guests invited, everything done to make Boccaccio have an enjoyable time.

"But besides all these things—if you do not know it"— Giovanni wrote Petrarch, and it makes one furious that this should have to be true of so great a spirit,—"realizing how poor I was, he drew me aside just as, at a late hour, I was leaving the city, and grasping my frail arm in his giant's hand, without saying a word he handed me a liberal present. Then escaping and calling good-by at the same moment, he made off, leaving me to condemn both myself and what I had permitted. All I can say is: May God return it to him many times!"

The mission to Rome and to Viterbo was really a continuation of his embassy to Avignon. Pope Urban was now in Italy, where he would remain until the death of Cardinal Albornoz removed his ablest protector. Then, tiring of Italian bickerings, and in spite of the prophecy made by St. Bridget—it was actually fulfilled—that he would die shortly if he went back to France, he would return to his place of exile.

Once again Boccaccio was sent to determine what were to be his policies. This is the Pope's comment:

"We have graciously received our son Giovanni Boccaccio, your ambassador, both in consideration of those sending him and because of his own worth. We listened diligently to what he expounded patiently on behalf of your affairs. And what, in the interest of God, and for our own and the public good, we deem should be carried out and reformed, especially in Italy, we have told him in our answer. This he will be able to inform you verbally." If—as far as politics were concerned —it was diplomatically non-committal, it at least paid a nice Papal tribute.

It was on this trip also that Boccaccio was charged with the inspection of the Florentine militia. This was the last bureaucratic duty that he fulfilled.

The 1368 trip to Padua and Venice was the last visit that he paid to Petrarch. He visited the poet in the former city during October, while in November he stayed, in Venice, with Donato degli Albanzati—Donato the Grammarian, to whom he had dedicated his sixteen eclogues. This also was his last excursion to the north.

But it was not, really, any of the above discussed journeys that was—as far as Boccaccio was concerned—the most interesting. That qualification belonged to the one that he made just before these four: his 1362 journey to Naples. For one thing, it was at this time that he made his last strenuous attempt to secure for himself some kind of worldly security. For another, it marked, in an extremely dramatic manner, the culmination of his relations with Niccolo Acciaiuoli, who had been his boyhood friend.

Something has already been said of this man. He was born in Florence in 1310, and as was the case with Boccaccio, his father—Acciaiuolo Acciaiuoli—was a merchant of great wealth and influence, but of low plebeian origin. Like Boccaccio, too, he went to Naples in his youth. In 1331—when he was twenty-one years old—he transferred himself to the city where his grandfather Bartolomeo Acciaiuoli, when he sold feathers and cloth to Queen Beatrice, wife of Charles I, had been one of the first Florentines to do business. But there his resemblance to Giovanni came to an end. Instead of wasting his time—as it seemed to a Florentine—in the unremunerative pursuit of learning, he set all his attention to advancing himself. He secured the good graces—by the bed-room route, it is asserted —of King Robert's sister, Catherine of Courtnay, the so-called empress of Constantinople, and became guardian of her children. Through her he received favor after favor. Before he was thirty—as we have seen—he had led an important and successful expedition to Greece, where he had recovered lands belonging to Catherine's family, and by the time he was thirty-one he was rich enough to endow Florence with one of her most magnificent religious buildings. He meant this for his final resting place, and he and his son Lorenzo now rest there. You can see them to-day. Lorenzo, a typical

knight, his face candid, alert, courageous, yet just a little stupid.
His hair cut in the Florentine fashion. Niccolo, the type of a
modern railroad builder. His forehead unusually broad, yet
a general effect of angularity due to his pointed beard. They
are carved out of noble marble.

Yet even that did not represent the height of his glory. His
masterstroke was when he literally dragooned his unwilling
ward, Prince Luigi, into marrying Queen Giovanna, after the
murder of Andrew of Hungary. For a moment that seemed
to be his downfall. But when Louis of Hungary withdrew
and Luigi was able to return, he was not forgotten. Made
royal lieutenant and seneschal of the kingdom, the Florentine
who had entered Naples with but one servant only two decades
earlier, became the first man of the realm. Then he was able
to indulge in that taste for magnificence, which was to appear later in the Medici, and which seems to have been common to all successful Florentines. He visited his native city,
where his lavish entertainments, coming at a time—this was in
1355—when Florence had not yet completely recovered from
the failure of her banking houses, caused a certain amount
of scandal. He took revenge on Florentine lack of friendliness
at the time of his flight by forcing Florence—under threat of
reprisals against her merchants who were established in Naples
—to remit all taxes on his property held in her territory. He
condescendingly gave her unasked advice on how to manage
her affairs. But the light of his new greatness shone most
refulgently in Naples. He began to beautify the southern
capital and southern kingdom with a series of resplendent
edifices. He set out to become a patron of letters. For his
own glory and for the glory of the city, he set out to make
Naples—as it had been under King Robert—a center of the
literary world.

It was this last purpose that seemed to give Giovanni an opportunity of realizing his life-long desire of establishing himself there under a powerful patron. He had long thought of Niccolo as a possible benefactor. It can be recalled how, in the days of his youth, he deplored the latter's departure for the Morea. There exists also a letter which he wrote to Zanobi da Strada in 1353 in which his ironic comments on the latter's service of Acciaiuoli, and his strictures against Niccolo's lack of emotion when he learned that his son Lorenzo had died, seem but to cover over a certain hinting. So, too, does his assertion that he was as happy with his "few little books" as kings were with their diadems. *The lady doth protest too much, methinks.* Was he not really suggesting to Zanobi that he was not quite so content as he sounded? Was he not hoping for a look of favor? Besides this, one of the eclogues gives a clear indication that, in 1355, he was on the point of going to Naples, if indeed he did not actually start to go there. He was turned back, however, by a fear of his reception. Now, however, the long-waited-for moment was at hand. Not only did Acciaiuoli—who had lost the services of Zanobi through the latter's transference to Avignon, and through his death there—actually want him. Acciaiuoli's secretary was a friend of his. He was Francesco Nelli, one of those who in 1350 had received and entertained Petrarch with him. Nelli, too, joined in the urging. Boccaccio, therefore, naturally felt that his troubles were over. He not only left Florence: he brought with him his half brother Jacopo, then twenty years old. So he thought, they bid the Tuscan city good-by forever. So he thought, both of their fortunes were now made.

Yet the sequel turned out to be quite different from what he had imagined. For one thing, Niccolo was extremely occupied with other matters, and he hardly noted Boccaccio's

arrival. For another, he had not brought Giovanni to Naples
simply to carry on his study of literature: he wanted Boccaccio
to write a eulogistic biography of him. When he discovered
that Boccaccio did not wish to do this, he lost a good deal of his
interest in him. He sent the writer and his brother to a filthy
and unsanitary hovel that was covered with spider-webs and
dry dust, and that had been used for so many foul and evil-
smelling purposes that Boccaccio referred to it as "the sewer."
The bed—which he was obliged to share with Jacopo—was
made of interwoven wattles, and its last occupant having been
a muleteer, it was but half covered with a stinking coverlet.
A single lantern gave the place a cold and a half-dead light,
and Boccaccio was not even alone there: it was occupied by a
whole crowd of Niccolo's meaner domestics. He was obliged
to eat there, too. The food was foul and revolting. Finally
he could stand it no longer. He had arrived in Naples in
November, and after two months of such treatment he accepted
the invitation of Mainardo Cavalcanti, a young Florentine
knight who was rising to new honors in the kingdom and
would later succeed Niccolo as seneschal. He sent his brother
to an inn.

Then Niccolo apparently reconsidered. He invited Boccaccio
to his villa at Tripergoli near Baia. But there Giovanni's
situation was no better than before. Once again he was given
a tiny room, while his bed was so disgusting that a young
Neapolitan who came to call on him, seeing it, rode back to
Pozzuoli in indignation, and sent him a new one from his own
house. As a climax to all, hardly was Boccaccio established
than Niccolo decided to return to the city. Bag and baggage,
he set out, leaving Giovanni behind with his books and his few
belongings. There was no inn, and Giovanni with his single
servant literally did not know where to turn, until finally

Nelli sent for him. He brought him back, however, to the same Neapolitan cesspool which he had already fled from. This was more than Giovanni could stand. Mainardo Cavalcanti was not in Naples, having gone to Sant' Eramo on the queen's service, and there was no one else he could turn to. Six miserable months had been wasted, and he determined, therefore, to leave the kingdom. He bid good-by to Nelli, who did not, apparently, think that he would really go, and without further ado, departed. First he went to Sulmona where he paid a visit to his old friend Barbato. Then he went to Venice, whither he had long been invited by Petrarch. When he got there, insult was added to injury. He received a letter from Nelli. In it, he was chided for leaving. Nelli called him "impetuous." He implied that he was soft and effeminate. He said that he was "a man of glass."

It was this rebuke that was responsible for the fact that we know so many facts connected with this unfortunate sojourn. Stung to something very like rage, Boccaccio dipped his pen into the same corrosive fluid which he had used in writing of *Il Corbaccio*. He indited an answer.

"I had it in mind to have kept silent," he began; "you with your sarcastic letter have moved me into speech. And certainly I am very sorry, for it is not always fitting for an honest man to spread abroad that which he has indeed suffered, lest it should be thought that he had made a goad of his tongue, and while he is telling the truth, he be reputed a slanderer. However, since innocence has a duty to defend herself, and since I, who have been offended against, am the one accused, I must needs resort to words."

Then he gave a bitter account of the inconsiderate way in which he had been treated.

Next he launched into an ironic portrayal of Acciaiuoli.

That "great man," he said, that "Mæcenas," wanted him to write his biography, yet what had he ever done to justify immortality?

He laid claim to being a great general?

"In how many battles, then, did he find himself? How many disorganized routs did he restore to discipline? How many fugitives did he halt? How many hostile armies did he overthrow? What loot, what plunder, what spoils, what standards of war, what enemy camps did he capture? What provinces did he subdue? Let him say. Let any one else say. I have heard nothing of them."

He felt that he should be recognized, not only as a patron, but as a practitioner of letters?

A laugh was in order.

The same treatment was applied to his claim for renown because of the numerous buildings he had erected, and to his claim of great magnanimity of character. It was true, Boccaccio admitted, that at times no one was a more generous pardoner than Acciaiuoli, but that was only when he could not get revenge.

The magnate had, besides, one other serious and annoying fault, which, Boccaccio said, although it was known to all, he would expose only to Nelli.

"'Oftentimes he goes into an inner chamber, and there, so that it will seem that he has much to do which is of grave importance to the kingdom, guards are placed, and no one is permitted to enter. Many come, among them often the great men of the kingdom. They fill the courtyard in front of his door, and in a humble voice ask for time to speak to him. The answers that the guards give are something to laugh at. To some they say that he is having conference with some one. To others that he is saying the divine office. To others that, wearied with public affairs, he is snatching a little repose. And suchlike drivel. Whereas, after all, he does nothing whatsoever except that which was said of the emperor Domitian who wished the same things said of him that this man does: that is, he wounds flies with his dagger. Or what I rather believe to be true—for although I am neither one of his menials, nor ever wish to be, yet I know the customs of his chamber —he has a commode brought into his private room, and there, as in a chair of majesty, he sits, and surrounded by his women —I will not say whores, for although they are neither sisters, nor relatives, nor nieces, they are not so low as that—he holds, to the discordant rumbling of his belly, and while easing his inwards of their malodorous burden, his great councils, and disposes the affairs of his kingdom, designates the prefectures, gives justice by word of mouth, dictates, writes, and corrects letters to the kings of the world, the Pope, and to his other friends, not only his women, but his Greeks and his jesters overlooking the same; while the poor fools in the courtyard believe that he, having been received into the consistory of the gods, together with them holds solemn parliament regarding the universal affairs of the state."

There is, naturally, some exaggeration to this, as to any other portrait by a satirist. The eminence to which Acciaiuoli rose so swiftly, and by his own ingenuity, controverts flatly any assertion that he lacked ability, and even Boccaccio's scorn of his erstwhile friend's literary abilities was not entirely justified. The very passages in which he ridicules these concede that Acciaiuoli's interests lay in the right direction. They also pay tribute, if somewhat grudgingly, to a composition by Niccolo on the deeds of the Knights of the Holy Sepulchre which was written in the French language, which "although filled with incorrect and laughable matters" was "perhaps

memorable, and"—in subject at least—"worthy of the verse of
Homer." That was something for a man so occupied in other
matters as was Acciaiuoli. But the main outlines were certainly correct, and so if the Grand Seneschal wished to have
posterity blind to his limitations, he acted with scant wisdom
in thus irritating Giovanni. Furthermore it represented but
a beginning of what Boccaccio felt he had in him to say on the
subject.

"I write you, therefore," he concluded, "making use of my
liberty and of my being away from the power of others, so
that you may realize that it is a childish thing to stir up a
beehive, and not to expect to be stung in the face by the swarm.
Certainly if you but slightly shake a burning bough innumerable sparks fly up. Let him beware, and let you beware, too,
that you do not rouse me into invectives. You will see that I
have more skill in that occupation than you imagine. You
have washed me with cold water: I have not shaved you, as
I should have, with a saw-toothed razor. But what has not
been done, will be, if you do not keep silent. So may God
protect you!"

What are the exact conclusions which should be drawn from
this burst of furiousness? The letter was never sent. Nelli
died of the plague and Petrarch apparently persuaded Boccaccio that it would now be more dignified to say nothing.
After all he had wasted considerable time and abased himself
very thoroughly before finally deciding to leave. Possibly he
realized that for quite a few months and in the hope of
advantage, he had been nearly as fawning as Acciaiuoli's
"Greeks," regarding whom he was so sarcastic. Possibly the
reason that his rage subsided once he had given expression to
it, was that he was no more angry at Acciaiuoli than he had
been, in the last analysis, at himself.

CHAPTER XXVII

THE group of voyages which have been above discussed brought Boccaccio through 1368. The next year—his fifty-seventh—and the greater part of 1370 were spent, as far as can be determined, at Certaldo. In the autumn of that year, however, Giovanni set out again on the long road to the south. Despite his disillusions, despite the fact that Fiammetta no longer lived—she had died, apparently, during the Great Plague—despite the rebuffs that he had received there at the hands of Acciaiuoli and Nelli during his last visit, the glittering city where he had spent the most glamorous period of his existence still exerted her strong spell over him. It was as if the place were some bright El Dorado of the spirit, more golden and resplendent than any actual city, and so indeed was it in his imagining. Petrarch—whom Boccaccio so greatly admired—had the utmost difficulty to persuade Giovanni to make a few short visits, yet it had only to be hinted that he would be welcome in Naples for him to pack up his books and his belongings and start out thither. Disappointed each time he arrived there, it never seemed to have occurred to him, each time he planned a new voyage, that this time he would be disappointed again.

His last excursion seems to have been made somewhat impetuously. "My fatherland, which I left very indignantly last autumn," is a phrase from a letter written the next year. Just why he was indignant is not, however, recorded. Was he criticized for something that he did or wrote, and did he, over-

sensitive as he was apt to be, take umbrage thereat? Was he
promised some office and then not given the same? Or did
he merely have one of his periodic outbursts of spleen against
the materialistic Florentines who were interested only in the
scorned "mechanic arts," and was he fleeing Florence, therefore, much as some modern American writer becomes an angry
expatriate in Paris or on the Riviera? The last of these seems
a very plausible guess.

Nor can much more be said of his journey southward, or of
his stay at the southern capital. It is believed that it was
while he was en route that he paid his celebrated visit to the
monastery of Montecassino. Benvenuto da Imola tells of this
in his commentary on Dante. He relates how his "master"
Boccaccio paused there, and how, desiring to see the library,
he humbly asked—"being of a very courteous disposition"—one
of the monks to show it to him. And how when this was
done, he found it without door and with a leaking roof, filled
with dust and with most of the manuscripts cut to pieces. And
how when full of sorrow that such rare and ancient works of
so great men of genius should thus be lost, he came forth weeping. And how he asked a monk why it happened that these
precious manuscripts should be treated so. And how the
monk replied that it happened because some of his colleagues,
to gain four or five *soldi,* used to erase the sheepskins and
make psalters for children and breviaries for ladies out of
them. It was an insolence and a tragedy which had been acted
and reënacted all over western Europe during the last thousand
years. Boccaccio was, however, one of the first persons able
to appreciate its significance. If he wept, he knew the reason
for his tears.

It was also during this trip that he contemplated a visit to
the monastery of San Stefano in Calabria. When he first ar-

rived in Naples, he met Niccolo da Montefalcone, a boyhood friend, who said that he was now abbot of this place. Niccolo discoursed so eloquently on the "pleasant solitude" which surrounded the monastery, as well as of "the supply of books, the splashing fountains, the healthfulness of the situation, the abundance of all good things, and the mildness of the climate" that Boccaccio assumed that he had been invited there. He immediately took counsel with his friends as to whether or not, and as to how, he should make the voyage. In the meantime Niccolo incontinently departed. Boccaccio flew into one of his rages. He wrote the monk an angry letter in the very superscription of which he questioned whether or not Niccolo were really the abbot, or were but a simple monk, thereby implying that perhaps Niccolo had overstepped his authority in inviting him. He then affected gratefulness to Niccolo because he had been the first one "to take the fog out of his eyes." He apologized for his own simplicity. He had supposed, he began superciliously, that because of "the coming on of white hair, age and illness, and because he presided over a sacred order, the youthful lightness of any man would have vanished, his unseemly feelings would have been suppressed, and his manners have changed for the better." This did not seem to be the case. He then took a fling at Niccolo's age. He reminded him, among other things, that trees that were fair in the springtime with their leaves and flowers were bare in autumn. After this he recovered temporarily his good humor and assured Niccolo that he would not treat him as he himself had been treated. He even suggested a return to Naples. His last sentences, however, shot another shaft of sarcasm. Would Niccolo at least send the manuscript of Tacitus which he had *borrowed* "so as not to render in vain all my labor" and so "the book will not receive any further damage"? His temper had not, apparently, mellowed very appreciably with the years. He was, indeed, not a pleasant person to annoy.

Yet it was not only in such ill-flavored querulousness, that his days at Naples were spent. His letters to Jacopo Pizzinghe, praising the latter for his poetical accomplishments, and to Matteo d'Ambrosio, a youthful admirer, show him in contact with the literary activities of the kingdom. He was entertained by his old friend Mainardo Cavalcanti, now become—after Niccolo Acciaiuoli's death— the first man in the kingdom. He was offered patronage by Ugo di San Severino, both in the latter's own name and in the name of Queen Giovanna. He was also offered patronage—with complete liberty of action—by James of Majora, Queen Giovanna's chivalrous, if foolhardy third husband, who had just returned from captivity after one of his characteristically gallant, but ill-fated adventures, this time against the bloody monarch Henry of Trastamare who ruled in the north of Spain.

But he saw fit to accept none of these offers, for by now he was beginning to be homesick. Once again Naples had failed to come up to his expectations. Once again he was ready to depart for his own country. His books called him. His friends called him. He longed for Certaldese tranquillity. He reached Certaldo in the early summer of 1371. He was never to leave Tuscany again.

This, however, was not because he was not tempted, for on June 21 he was visited by a servant of Niccolo Orsini, Count Palatine and Count of Nola. The servant brought a message from his master, who invited Boccaccio to pass his remaining days on his estate between Rome and Tuscany. Giovanni was duly grateful, but by now he had lost his interest in travel. Though but fifty-eight the hard life of the Fourteenth Century made him old, almost broken. Besides that, he was growing weary. He wrote Count Orsini a letter thanking him for the generosity of his offer, but saying that he could not accept it. He was too old to change his habits, he said, and having been accustomed to live in independence all his life, he could not now support a yoke. He had a small estate which he had inherited from his father and that was enough to support his few needs. Only a few years, he felt, remained to him, and for that length of time he could support, without too much hardship, his poverty. He wanted to pass these, however, in his own country, and to be buried by the ashes of his forefathers. If, however, he ever altered this decision, he assured Niccolo, he would indeed come to him rather than to any one else, although others had invited him previously. But that did not seem to be likely, as he had made up his mind.

CHAPTER XXVIII

YET despite the gloomy tone of this dejected-sounding letter, Boccaccio's life was not yet over with. Before the bleak tomb gaped to receive him he had at least one more public function to fulfill. It was one of the most important which was ever assigned to him. On August 25, 1373, the Florentine republic appointed him the first public lecturer on Dante that the world had ever known. He was to serve in this capacity for a year and was to expound the whole "Divine Comedy." His salary was to be one hundred golden florins. The diary of one Guido Monaldo, a Florentine citizen, gives the date for the beginning of this exposition. "On Sunday the twenty-third day of October in the city of Florence, Master Giovanni Boccaccio commenced to read Dante," it records. The place where he gave these lectures was on the steps of the church of Santo Stefano. It used to be believed that this was the Church of Santo Stefano al Ponte Vecchio, now the Church of Santo Stefano and Santo Cecilia just off the Via Por Santa Maria, the narrow Florentine street which flows into that bridge with its famous jewel shops. Benvenuto da Imola, who listened to the lectures, makes it plain, however, that they were given at the Church of Santo Stefano alla Badia. This building which is no longer standing was—next to the Baptistery—the second oldest church in Florence.

The very fact that Boccaccio was invited to deliver these lectures makes an interesting commentary on the evolution of Florentine feelings. It was but seventy-one years ago—not more than a single lifetime—that Dante had been expelled from the city. "And if any one of the above-mentioned persons," ran the stern decree of March 10, 1302, by which he was exiled, "shall at any time come into the power of the said city, he shall be so burned with fire that he shall die." Dante's bitter pride and his association with the emperor Henry VII, on whom he called to wipe out "the stinking fox" whose lips fouled the River Arno, "the viper" who "devoured its own entrails," "the sick sheep which by the contagion of its own ill defiles the whole herd,"—did not increase his popularity. For a while it was almost dangerous to admire him. But with the increasing fame of his book, and with, too, the break-up— under the stress of new issues—of the old parties and the formation of new political alignments, a new attitude came into being. In opposition to Dante's detractors, there sprang up a whole race of defenders. Imitators and writers of rhymed eulogies came into being. Annotators and interpreters appeared. These were followed by rewritings—there being always available a sufficiency of little men who imagine they can improve on the work of genius—new explanations, rubrics, *capitoli,* and compendiums. Private tutors seeking employment gave as one of their qualifications that they could "also expound Dante." Soon a definite Dante cult was flourishing.

"On behalf of a great many Florentine citizens," stated the petition of the summer of 1373, "who desire, as much for themselves as for other citizens who wish to attain virtue, as well for their children and posterity, to be instructed in the book of Dante,—from which even the unlettered can learn how to avoid evil and how to acquire good quite as much as eloquence of language,—it is hereby reverently petitioned of you, the lords Priors of the Arts, and the Gonfalonier of Justice of the City and People of Florence, that, in so far as you deem it fitting to have this provided for and carried out, you may choose a worthy and learned man, and one well instructed in this sort of poetry, to read, on all days not holidays, and consecutively as in such matters is customary, for that length of time which you deem fit but not for longer than a year, that book which is commonly known as *el Dante,* so that all who wish may hear it. And that you may give him what salary you wish for the said year, but not more than one hundred gold florins, and according to the rules, forms, articles, and conditions which seem fitting to you. And that the chamberlains of the city treasury shall give out and pay the said salary in the money of the said city to the person thus chosen in two payments: that is to say, one-half should be paid to him toward the end of the month of December, and the other half toward the end of the month of April, without any retention for taxes."

The vote taken on this petition is extremely illuminating. On August 12, the Council of the Captain and of the People, cast one hundred and eighty-six affirmative ballots—black beans—and nineteen negative ballots—white beans. The following day the Council of the Podestà returned an even more impressive majority in favor of the lectures. The "ayes" were one hundred and fourteen in number; the "nays" only seven. Thus, out of somewhat more than three hundred votes, only twenty-six—less than one in ten—were against honoring the great poet. It has been suggested that these votes came from members of those families whose ancestors had been relegated to Hell or otherwise branded by Dante in his *Comedia.* This does not seem to be at all improbable.

It was entirely natural, then, that when these lectures had been determined on, Boccaccio should have been the man selected to give them. His life of Dante which had now been in circulation for at least fourteen, and possibly eighteen years, called attention to the fact that he was the greatest living Dante authority. His prose rubrics on the Divine Comedy, and his *capitoli* in *terza rima,* which gave the arguments of the *Inferno,* the *Purgatorio,* and the *Paradiso,* further added to that reputation. Moreover, his various Latin works and their wide and enthusiastic reception made him the best known man of letters in a city, which was—with many of the great men of the Renaissance already born, with the Turks, who were to take Constantinople in but eighty years, already in Bulgaria—on the very verge of the Revival of Learning. A group of the younger humanists, such as Coluccio Salutati and Benvenuto da Imola, already centered about him as their master. When, therefore, less than two weeks after the vote, the city fathers appointed "Dominus Johannes de Certaldo, *honorabilis civis florentinus,*" they did only what was the obvious. It was approximately two months later, as we already know, that he began his lessons. We can assume that the interval was consumed in their careful preparation.

And we know pretty well what these lectures consisted of, for the manuscript of his commentary on the first sixteen cantos of the *Inferno,* and on part of the seventeenth still exists. *"Voi signori,"* these notes begin, "You, gentlemen—" which tells us that they were those on which the lessons were based rather than a rough draft of something he was preparing for readers. They then proceed to an invocation by a quotation from Vergil, after Boccaccio has modestly pointed out his own limitations. They next proceed to a discussion of the meaning of the title *Comedia.* After that he takes up the significance of Dante's own name. It is not, Boccaccio points out—though he is not now generally agreed with—an abbreviation of Durante, but is symbolic of one who gives freely: i.e.,

a form of the verb *dare,* Dante, the giver. After that he makes
retraction and apologizes in advance for any spiritual errors.
If such exist, they are unwitting and unintentional. Then he
goes on with his detailed and lengthy explanation of the text.
Each canto is commented on twice. First its literal meaning
is examined, and then its allegorical meaning. Phrase by
phrase—sometimes even word by word—he has turned on
"The Divine Comedy" his critical attention. The astonishing
thing is that it emerges from this hard test still great poetry.
It is like gold, in that no ordinary acid can dull its gleam.

An examination of Boccaccio's treatment of one canto will
illustrate sufficiently his method. Let us take the fifth one of
the *Inferno.* It is in this one, that Dante tells the story of Paolo
and Francesca, possibly the most well known and the most
moving in his whole book.

Boccaccio begins by quoting the opening line.

"Cosi discesco del cerchio primaio. Having descended thus
from the first circle."

"In the present canto," he goes on, "just as in the ones before
it, the author continues with the matters he has already begun.
He showed in the preceding canto how he and Vergil, having
left the other four poets, came by another road from the
place where there was still light into a place where there was
none. In the beginning of this canto, continuing what he had
already undertaken, he shows how they went down into the
second circle of hell. And the author in this canto accom-
plishes six things. First of all, as we have already shown, he
goes on with what he has already begun, making it plain what
place he has come to. Second, he relates how he found there
a devil who was the examiner of these sinners. Third, he
relates what sins they punish in this circle and how the sins
are punished. Fourth, he names some of the sinners who are

punished with this woe. Fifth he speaks with certain of the sinners who are here being punished. Sixth and last, he describes what happened to him as the result of this speaking."

Nor was he even content to let the intelligence of his listeners determine the exact and fairly obvious points at which these various arbitrary divisions began.

"The second part begins with: *'Stavvi Minos.* Here Minos stands,'" he explains. "The third with: *'Ora incommincian.* And now begin.' The fourth with: *'La prima di color.* The first of these.' The fifth with: *'Poscia ch'io ebbi.* After I had.' The sixth and last with: *'Mentre che l'uno spirto.* While thus one spirit.'"

It is the so-called professorial method—which does libel, however, to a great many eloquent and convincing professors— in its most rudimentary form.

The same elementary nature is characteristic of all the other comments.

"Stavvi Minos" has moved Boccaccio to a long mythological treatise on the origin and history of the famous Cretan monarch, whose enormous palaces gave rise to the fantastic story which added the word "labyrinth" to most western languages, and who was fabricated by the Florentine poet into a judge over the infernal regions. The other persons named among the damned have affected him similarly, and the stories, therefore, of Semiramis, Dido, Cleopatra, Helen, "the great Achilles," Paris, and Tristan are related, all of them except the last one, at some length. Nor was he content to tell simply the version of the story which he himself believed. Various accounts of these mythological persons are given, and with the same careful seriousness that you might have expected him to use, had they been actual persons. Once he actually disagrees with Dante's judgment. He proves to his

own satisfaction—and by resort to an amazing chronology—
that Æneas could not possibly have been the lover of Dido.

"Dido then was a chaste woman and she killed herself so
as not to break faith with the memory of Sichæus. But the
author follows, as in so many other matters, the opinion of
Vergil."

All of which subtilizing about two figures who are at best
legendary, and more probably wholly fictitious, would be little
more than amusing, but for the comment that it makes on
Boccaccio's character. Here we have another evidence of his
intellectual independence. As—though greatly influenced by
him—he had not allowed Petrarch to change his intellectual
judgments, so he would not follow even Dante if it led him
against his own convictions.

The same independence and the same care is shown in his
comment on the story of Paolo and Francesca. If anything,
the treatment is more detailed. Here, for example, is a passage:

" 'When I replied.' To the question of Vergil, that is. "I thus
began.' To say. 'Alas, by what sweet sighs?' Sweet sighs
seem to be those which come from the certain hope that you
will obtain the thing you love. 'How many desires?' He almost says 'what great?' 'Led these two persons.' Paolo and
Francesca. 'To the dolorous state.' That is to death."

But it is not only these minuscula that are given by Boccaccio.
Lest Dante's admirers should not know it, Giovanni relates the
whole story of the two lovers. He tells how there was a long
feud between Messer Guido Vecchio da Polenta, who was
lord of Ravenna, and the Malatesta family of Rimini. He tells
how it was ended by a treaty, one of the provisions of which
was that Guido would give his daughter in marriage to Gianciotto, son of Malatesta. He goes on with how, Gianciotto
being deformed, it was arranged—so that Francesca should not

take a dislike to him, and refuse to marry him—that she should be shown his brother "Polo," and be informed that this was the person she was to wed. And with how she fell in love with this "Polo," and with how after she was married to Gianciotto, she began to have illicit commerce with Polo. "But how she actually joined herself to him, I have never heard told, except what the author here writes." Dante, it will be remembered, described the two lovers as reading the tale of Lancelot and Guinevere. "It is possible that so it happened, but I think that this more likely was a fiction invented around that which may have taken place, than anything which really occurred." And how she and Paolo persisted in this familiarity. And how Gianciotto finally learned about it. And how he pretended to go to Rimini, and returning swiftly, found Paolo and Francesca locked into a chamber together. And how Paolo, both for his own safety, and to clear Francesca's name, attempted to escape through a trap door, but was prevented when a strap of his armor caught on a nail. And how Gianciotto, trying to slay him with his rapier, inadvertently first slew Francesca. And how he then slew Paolo. And how finally the two lovers were buried in the same grave.

This story being so like one of those that Boccaccio would have gladly romanticized in the days when he wrote the *Decameron,* his attitude toward it as he delivered the lectures is a matter of great interest.

"*Amor ch'a nullo amato amar perdona,*" wrote Dante. "Love that denial takes from none beloved."

"That," is Boccaccio's comment, "with due reverence to the author, does not of necessity follow with this kind of love, but it does truly follow with chaste love, as the same author clearly shows in the twenty-second canto of the following book, where he says:

> Let its pure flame
> From virtue flow, and love can never fail
> To warm another's bosom, so the light
> Shine manifestly forth."

Dante made Francesca, even in Hell, take some consolation
from the fact that even there Paolo was not separated from
her.

"That," noted Boccaccio, "according to the Catholic faith,
one should not believe. For the divine justice does not wish
that any damned spirit should have, in any form whatsoever,
anything which conforms to his desire, or that he should know
any pleasure or consolation at all: and it would, therefore, be
directly contrary to the same, if this lady—which Dante tries
to show in his words—took any pleasure from being in the
company of her lover."

This was the man who had won and wooed Fiammetta, and
it was he—as has been said and reiterated—who in the *Amorosa
Visione* had refused to mount the steep stairs of virtue until he
had tasted all of earthly joy.

Yet even at this late date, Boccaccio had not—any more than
he had ten years previously—forgotten entirely what had once
allured him.

In the account of Helen, he described how the painter Zeuxis,
wishing to make a portrait of that paragon of all women and
of all time, had chosen the five fairest damsels of Croton, and
with them beside him, and aided by the verse of Homer, had
made a picture which was accepted as that of her whose face
had launched a thousand ships, of her who by the award of
Aphrodite had been set forth as the fairest woman in the
world.

"By which device," said Boccaccio, "it is possible that the
illustrious master was able to achieve her lineaments, her

color, the form of her body. But we cannot believe that the brush and the palette knife could make a picture of the liveliness of her eyes, the winsomeness of her whole face, her affability, her heavenly laugh, the varying expressions of her features, her modest words, and the quality of her actions. Such a thing could only be accomplished by nature."

Furthermore, in his explanation of the symbolical meaning of the canto, while denouncing lust and commenting fiercely on the depraved Florentine customs, he showed the same bias. Explaining why these sinners were not thrust even farther into hell he said that theirs—as he knew only too well—was a natural sin, and not one that proceeded from an evil mind. The sharpest penalties awaited those whose intention as well as whose acts were perverse. *"Caïna attende chi a vita ci spense,"* Dante made Francesca say. "Cain awaits that man who split our life." Boccaccio was not at all prepared to disagree with this conclusion on the part of Alighieri. Unlawful love was, indeed, so he now thought, a grievous sin. But not so grievous as the sin of him who, even to avenge unlawful sin, slew his own wife and his own brother.

It was in this manner, and with this same detailed fullness, that—as far as he went—Boccaccio dealt with every aspect of "The Divine Comedy." Apparently the lectures were meticulously prepared. Apparently, too, the whole scheme of what he was going to say was worked out before he spoke the first words. For references like this are frequent: "As you will see when I come to the fifteenth canto of this book;" "This will be more fully treated in the twentieth canto;" etc., etc. Nor can the fact that Boccaccio, in illustrating his points, often quoted verbatim long passages from his earlier writings be taken as indicative either of mental decrepitude or of hasty preparation. The whole tone of his commentary shows that it was addressed to an audience which was not likely to have read either the *De Genealogia* or the *De Casibus*. In the short time which he had at his disposal to organize his series of lectures, there was plenty for him to do without wasting his time doing over again work that he had already done.

And yet for all his care, his lectures were not received with an entire absence of criticism. The notes on which he based them became such a standard, that for nearly two centuries there was hardly a commentator who did not draw on them widely, and quite often without acknowledgment, yet as they were delivered they excited hostility. The reason was, apparently, that it was regarded as a sacrilege and a profanation, to lay bare the thoughts of so great a man as Dante to the vulgar mob.

Boccaccio seems to have agreed with these charges, for in a series of sonnets, aimed apparently at answering his detractors, he pointed to his ill health and said that it must be a punishment for his impertinence. He said, too, that he was not responsible for what he had done. His friends had urged him to the undertaking, while both his foolish hope of glorifying Dante and his own always pressing poverty had prevented him from returning a negative answer. However, while he could not undo what he had already done, he was not likely to continue in his error; an ungrateful people, interested only in gain, would not long listen to his discourses. Therefore let his enemies accept his pardon: he would not sin again.

Nor is this attitude at all surprising, for Boccaccio's views had almost always been just exactly those of them who criticized him. He had long had a most vehement scorn of what he called the rabble, and in the prologue to the third book of *De Genealogia deorum gentilium,* he described a dream related by the philosopher Numenius, the moral of which was that to ex-

pose the sacred secrets of religion or of knowledge to the
generality, was, in effect, to let them out as prostitutes. This
too was the view taken in his defense of poetry, in Book
XIV of that same work of learning. He was, therefore, going against his own long-held theory when he spoke at all,
and there was, in consequence—as the saying goes,—more
truth than poetry to his answering sonnets. That fact,
incidentally, might also offer another explanation for the elementary nature of his comments. Probably even the most
rudimentary Florentine did not need to have an explanation of what an oar or an anchor was. To define these was,
however, the method Boccaccio chose—though perhaps unconsciously—to express his contempt. Certainly his mild
treatment of those who criticized him, was not due to the fact
that he had lost his powers of invective. At about this time
he wrote two sonnets to a "wicked priest" with whom he had
quarreled. His suggestion to the latter that he wipe out his
own shame before he carp against the faults of some one else,
followed by the unkind suggestion that it was generally
known that the other had murdered his own illegitimate child
and then cast his body into a privy, show that he had not lost
any of his capabilities for either anger or cutting scorn.

CHAPTER XXIX

THESE lectures on Dante marked the last public appearance of Boccaccio. Despite their eloquence, his mind, as has already been noted, had long passed its zenith. It had, in fact, declined rapidly ever since he wrote the *Decameron*. Now his body was about to fail too, for the insistencies of old age could be gainsaid no longer. The tragic and inevitable break-up—all the more tragic since it concerned one who could not be easily replaced, namely a man of genius —had at last confronted him. He was drawing near the end.

It was some time before this that he received the first warning, though it is hardly possible that either the illnesses referred to in some of Petrarch's letters of a decade earlier, or the one he hinted about in a Latin poem sent to Zanobi da Strada as far back as 1355 were the same as the one which ultimately destroyed him. However, in September, 1372, more than a year before the lectures, he penned this letter from Certaldo to Mainardo Cavalcanti in Naples.

"You will wonder, illustrious knight," he said, "why I have so long delayed in writing you, and without doubt I would be very much to blame if I did not have a very excellent, but sad reason for my tardiness. You must have heard, if I am not mistaken, that I have been very sick. Alas, I say *have been,* just as if I were not still. For I still am, and what is worse, have not the slightest hope for a quick recovery."

He then went into a description of his symptoms, and from them it has been judged that what he suffered from was diabetes. It may be slightly problematical, however, as to whether or not a physician can diagnose a patient who is separated from his office and his instruments by something like six hundred years.

"First of all," he said, "I had, and still have a continual itching, a dry scrofula, to take away the flakes and scales of which, day and night hardly suffice my busy nails. In addition to that, I have a weighty heaviness of the stomach, continual pain in my kidneys, a swelling of my spleen, burning bile, a suffocating cough, hoarseness, a splitting headache, and indeed so many other ills, that if I enumerated them you would say readily that my whole body languished, and that all my humours were at war among themselves. As a result of this, it is difficult for me even to look up at the sky. My body is heavy. My step uncertain. My hand trembles. I am pale as a ghost. I have lost all appetite and everything is distasteful to me. I hate writing, and those very books which used to delight me are now abhorrent. The strength of my spirit is failing. My memory is almost gone, and my intellect is fading. All my thoughts turn to the sepulcher and death."

This first attack was followed by a short respite, and then suddenly Boccaccio was stricken again.

"For on the day I am speaking about, at about sunset, as I lay on my bed, weak and worn out and hardly able to move, a burning fever suddenly attacked me with such great force that at its first onslaught I thought that I was done for and laid myself down on my poor wretched bed, never expecting to get out of it on my own feet. And as the night grew later, the fever grew more fierce until finally, tormented by the deadly burning and by a fierce headache, I began to groan softly, although it is not my custom to act in this way, and to toss hither and thither, hoping by my motions and by the swishing of my garments, to elude its heat. And since in my struggles against the immense forces of so great a fire, I felt myself weakened and exhausted, I decided I was near my end, and despairing of the present life, I began to think of the future, and knowing that I, sinful man, as soon as I left my body, would have to appear before the Judge who knows all things, and considering in my own mind how severe a scrutiny of my sins His just anger would make, so great a fear took hold of me that I trembled all over and, although ashamed of myself, I began weeping from the bottom of my heart."

There was in the same room an old servant of his, and she certainly, though in a way that was not intentional, saved his life. For seeing him in this state, and believing him to be vanquished by his illness, she commenced to weep in a disordered manner, at the same time begging him to keep up his spirits. "I then in the midst of my fever could not help laughing at her foolishness." This laughter seemed to restore his courage. His pain increased until finally he thought that it would burn up his body, and he lay there calmly awaiting the end. But the end did not come, and at last the sky brightened into morning. Then the servant ran out, and called in a group of the neighbors. There is a nice implication of Boccaccio's relations to them in the way they all hurried to his aid.

"They all wondered that I was still alive, and having nothing to do but to take care of me, busied themselves about giving me advice. They begged me to call the doctor, which I scorned doing, since I was accustomed to entrust to nature the cure of whatsoever ill. But finally so that it would not seem that I refused one more from miserliness than because of my poor opinion of doctors, I summoned one. And I don't want you to think that he was a new Apollo, who they say was the first one to discover herbs, or an Æsculapius from Epidaurus, or a Hippocrates of Chios. He was a man who spent his time curing rustics, yet at that he was pleasant and sensible. He, having seen my fiery scabs, the indication of an inflamed liver, said that it would be necessary for him to drive out the superfluous and harmful matter, and that the usual cure was needed. By this I could be fully healed, but if I put it off for even a single day, I would die in four days. And he gave the reasons. I was frightened, I admit, and I ordered that the commands of the doctor be carried out immediately. The instruments for operating on me, the iron, and the fire, were prepared, and having lighted the flames and having thrust his implements into and cooled them in my flesh, and finally having taken them out and having cut with a sharp blade the same part of my skin that was formerly burned, he pried into me again and again not without the greatest pain. And after they were drawn forth, there did not fail to come out, as the doctor had asserted, along with a great deal of blood, the death-dealing poison. After this, 'Now you are cured,' the doctor told me. I could readily believe it, for much of my frightful fever came out with this blood, and after two nights in which I had not closed my eyes, I at last snatched a little repose."

The doctor's cure was soon supplemented by another even more valuable medicament. On learning of Boccaccio's illness, Mainardo—the same magnanimous knight who had sheltered him after he had been slighted by Acciaiuoli—sent him a vase full of pieces of gold. Boccaccio was overwhelmed by this generosity. This first gift was followed by another one of the same sort and value.

"You have lifted me from a bed of mud, and have freed me from my rustic prison," wrote Boccaccio. "What greater, what more touching thing could you do? I congratulate myself, for I have done nothing to make myself worthy of your friendship. I am happy, no, I am rich, having so good and

generous and great a friend; nay, rather patron; nay, even
further—if you will permit me to say it—lord."

Soon he began really to recover. A year after he was
stricken, he was able to appear in Florence and deliver his
lectures. It was almost a miracle.

Yet it was only a respite, for the lectures were never finished.
Just what time they were broken off and at what point is a
little problematical. The commentary which is interrupted at
the seventeenth verse of the seventeenth canto of the *Inferno*—
in actually the middle of a sentence—seems to give a clew to
the former. Assuming that he assembled his notes just before
he delivered the lectures, he must have spoken on the first
sixteen cantos. It has been guessed that it was sometime early
in December that he was again stricken. In that case he would
have had time to deliver approximately sixty lessons. The
"Commentary" divides itself rather conveniently into fifty-
nine. He withdrew to Certaldo, and he never apparently returned from there. He had but two years to live. These he
passed in his ancestral home.

Of this time very little is known. During part of it he was
in acute agony, but in the intervals he must have worked away
at his Latin writings. On August 28, 1374, he wrote his will.
His heirs were the children of his brother Jacopo, and he
stipulated that from them or from their descendants, his paternal home at Certaldo could never be alienated as long as
there was living a descendant, either legitimate or illegitimate
of his father, Boccaccino. This tolerance he had learned probably for his own bastardy. To his servant Bruna—the same
who had wept so uproariously—he left her bed and bedclothes,
a walnut table, two towels, a wine-cask, and some dresses
which he had apparently bought for her. He asked that all
his debts be paid. He left his books to Fra Martino da Signa,

the monk of Santo Spirito to whom he had already explained his eclogues. Any one who wished to, could copy them, and after Fra Martino's death they were to go to the convent. There was one other legacy which cannot be read of without a smile of amusement. To the convent of Santa Maria del Santo Sepolcro, he bequeathed "all the holy relics which during many years and with great trouble he had collected." To this, then, had come the satirist of Fra Cipolla! One wonders if the feathers of the archangel Gabriel were among them, or even some of the coals from the fire which roasted San Lorenzo! It might well be so.

The loneliness and isolation of these last years is very well indicated by the length of time that elapsed before he heard of the death of Petrarch. His great friend died at Arquà on July 19, 1374, but it was not until late November that any one came to Certaldo to tell him the news.

By this news he was desolated and his last reason for living seemed to be gone. He wrote a long letter to Petrarch's son-in-law, Francesco da Brossano, pouring out his grief, and asking the latter to assist him in attempting to save Petrarch's Latin epic *Africa,* which he said he had heard was to be destroyed. Or rather that its preservation was to depend on the verdict of a committee of lawyers, and Boccaccio feared greatly that this would be the judgment of his old enemies. In this letter he said that grief and his illness had so overcome him that it had taken him two days to write it. He signed it: "Your friend Giovanni Boccaccio, if he still exists."

Nor did he exist long. The letter was written in November, 1374, and thirteen months later he too was dead. He died on December 21, 1375. It is to be presumed that he was carried off by the same painful disease from which he had suffered now for more than three years.

CHAPTER XXX

THAT at least is how, probably, he died, though there is another and a fantastic version of the way his living ended. It was told by the same old wives of Certaldo who, walking past the draughty little house where the moribund humanist lived, and seeing him even in the small hours of the morning bent over his meaningless papers, used to relate that "Boccaccio being in intimate relations with the infernal spirits with whom he held conversation all night, one day commanded the Prince of Darkness to build a hill at a small distance from his house, to which he could go by means of a bridge of glass." And who used to relate, too, that the demon actually did construct the said hill by means of carrying earth thither.

In it, the great romancer was not forgotten by that high, mysterious princess who had once touched him with her love. Nay, rather, she was still enamored of him, and by means of necromancy, they still kept tryst.

"For they tell in Certaldo," it is written in an old manuscript, "as I myself when I was a boy heard more than once from the oldest men of that time, that death came to Giovanni Boccaccio in this way. They say that he used to have himself carried by demons to Naples where he was greatly in love. And they say further that he went thither and returned in two hours. And they say that one evening as he was returning from Naples and was over Pozzuolo, which is a little brook at the foot of Certaldo, at that moment the *Ave Maria* sounded, and he said: 'God be praised!' Then they say that the demons hearing the name of God spoken loosed their hold of him. And they say that, falling into the brook, in consequence he died."

He was buried as he had requested in the same church of San Jacopo and San Filippo at Certaldo which held the ashes of his peasant forebears, and over his tomb were placed four modest lines of Latin poetry. He himself had composed them:

> Hic sub mole jacent cineres ac ossa Johannis;
> Mens sedet ante Deum, meritis ornata laborum
> Mortalis vita. Genitor Boccatius illi,
> Patria Certaldum; studium fuit alma poesis.

"Under this stone lie the ashes and bones of Giovanni. His soul rests before God, his mortal life having been made decorous by the worth of his labors. His father was Boccaccio. His fatherland Certaldo. His only study was beloved poetry."

Later other lines were added, written by his friend and pupil Coluccio Salutati, now Chancellor of Florence and a great man in the Florentine republic:

> Inclyte, cur, vates humili sermone locutus
> De te pertransis? Tu pascua carmine clara
> In sublime vehis: tu montem nomina, tuque
> Sylvas et fontis, fluvios ac stagna lacusque
> Cum maribus multo digesta labore relinquis;
> Illustresque viros infaustibus casibus actos
> In nostro tempus a primo collegio Adam.
> Tu celebras claras alto dictamine matres,
> Tu divos omnes ignota ab origen ducens
> Per te quina refers divina volumina, nulli
> Cessurus veterum: Te vulgo labores
> Percelebrum faciunt, ætis te nulla silebit.

The first of these glowing sentences is a reproach to Boccaccio's modesty. Why should so illustrious a poet speak so humbly of his achievements? The next few give a list of his accomplishments. Only Latin works, it may be pointed out, are noted. The last one is a prophecy:

> Te vulgo labores
> Percelebrum faciunt, ætis te nulla silebit.

"To the people," said Coluccio, "your works have made you greatly renowned. No age will be silent of you."

Very nearly six hundred years have elapsed since the humanist paid this tribute, yet it is still entirely true and still entirely applicable. Silent so far no age has been.

EXPLICIT VITA JOHANNIS BOCCATII
Old Saybrook, Connecticut, December 7, 1929.

BIBLIOGRAPHY

BIBLIOGRAPHY

ANTONA-TRAVERSI, CAMILLO: *Della Patria, della familia e della povertà di Giovanni Boccaccio.*

ANTONA-TRAVERSI, CAMILLO: *Notizie Storiche sull' Amorosa Visione.*

BACCI, ORAZIO: *Il Boccaccio lettore di Dante.*

BACCI, ORAZIO: *La Data di Nascita di Giovanni Boccaccio.*

BACCI, ORAZIO: *Burle e arti magiche di Giovanni Boccaccio.*

BALDELLI, G. B.: *Vita di Giovanni Boccaccio.*

BARTOLI, ADOLFO: *Il Boccaccio.*

BARTOLI, ADOLFO: *I precursori del Boccaccio.*

BERTOLDI, ALFONSO: *Del sentimento religioso di Giovanni Boccaccio e dei canti di lui alla Vergine.*

CANESTRINI, G.: *Di alcuni documenti riguardanti le relazioni politiche dei papi d'Avignone coi comuni d'Italia.*

CARDUCCI, GIOSUÈ: *Ai parentali di Boccaccio.*

CAPPELLETTI, L.: *Studi sul Decamerone.*

CARRARA, E.: *Cecco da Mileto e il Boccaccio.*

CARRARA, E.: *Un peccato del Boccaccio.*

CASETTI, A. C.: *Il Boccaccio a Napoli.*

CIAMPI, SEBASTIANO: *Monumento di un manoscritto autografo di Messer Giovanni Boccaccio.*

COCHIN, HENRY: *Boccacce.*

CRESCINI, VICENZO: *Contributo agli studi sul Boccaccio.*

CRESCINI, VICENZO: *Di due recenti saggi sulle liriche del Boccaccio.*

CRESCINI, VICENZO: *Due studi riguardanti opere minori del.*

CRESCINI, VICENZO: *Fiammetta.*

CRESCINI, VICENZO: *Idalagos.*

CROCE, BENEDETTO: *La novella di Andreuccio da Perugia.*

DAVIDSOHN, ROBERT: *Il Padre di Giovanni Boccaccio.*

DEBENEDETTI, S.: *Per la fortuna della Teseide e del Ninfale Fiesolano nel secolo XIV.*

DE BLASIIS, G.: *Cino da Pistoia nell 'Universita di Napoli.*

DE BLASIIS, G.: *La dimora di Giovanni Boccaccio a Napoli.*

DELLA TORRE, ARNALDO: *La Giovinezza di Giovanni Boccaccio.*

FARAGLIA, N.: *Barbato da Sulmona e gli uomini di lettera alla corte di Robero di Angiò.*

FARAGLIA, N.: *I due amici del Petrarca, G. Barilli e M. Barbato da Sulmona.*

FORESTI, ARNALDO: *L'ecloga ottava di Giovanni Boccaccio.*

FRATI, C.: *Epistola inedita di Giovanni Boccaccio a Zanobi da Strada.*

GEROLA, GIUSEPPE: *Alcuni documenti inediti per la biografia del Boccaccio.*

GIGLI, GIUSEPPE: *I sonetti baiani del Boccaccio.*

HAUVETTE, HENRI: *Boccace, étude biographique e littéraire.*

HAUVETTE, HENRI: *La 39 ème nouvelle du Décamèron et la legende du coeur mangé.*

HAUVETTE, HENRI: *Principe Galeotto.*

HAUVETTE, HENRI: *Recherches sur le de casibus virorum illustrium.*

HAUVETTE, HENRI: *Sulla cronologia delle ecloghe latine del Boccaccio.*

HAUVETTE, HENRI: *Una confessione del Boccaccio.*

HORTIS, A.: *Studi sulle opere latine del Boccaccio.*

HUTTON, EDWARD: "Giovanni Boccaccio, a Biographical Study."

HUTTON, EDWARD: "Some Aspects of the Genius of Boccaccio."

LANDAU, MARCUS: *Giovanni Boccaccio, sua vita e sue opere.*

LANDINI, ANGIOLO: *Il Fratello di Giovanni Boccaccio.*

LOGNON, JEAN: *Boccacce et la France.*

MACCIANTI, G.: *Vestigi etrusche nella Valdelsa.*

MACRI-LEONE, F.: *Il Zibaldone Boccaccesco della Magliabecchiana.*

MACRI-LEONE, F.: *La politica di Giovanni Boccaccio.*

MAGGINI, F.: *Ancora a Proposito del Ninfale Fiesolano.*

MANICARDI, LUIGI, and MASSÈRA, A. F.: *Le dieci ballate del Decamerone.*

MASSÈRA, A. F.: *Le più antiche biografie del Boccaccio.*

MASSÈRA, A. F.: *Sonetti del Boccaccio contro Ignoti Detrattori.*

NICOLINI, FAUSTO: *La lettera di Giovanni Boccaccio a Francesco de' Bardi.*

PAOLI, CESARE: *Documenti di Ser Ciappelletto.*

PINELLI, GIOVANNI: *Appunti sul Corbaccio.*

RADOCANACHI, EMANUEL: *Les oeuvres latines de Boccacce.*

RAJNA, PIO: *Le origine della novella del Frankeleyn di Chaucer.*

RAJNA, PIO: *Le Questioni d'Amore nel Filocolo.*

RENIER, RODOLFO: *La Vita Nuova e La Fiammetta.*

ROSSI, EUGENIO: *Della mente e del cuore di Boccaccio.*

SAVI-LOPEZ, P.: *Il Filostrato del Boccaccio.*

SAVI-LOPEZ, P.: *Sulle Fonti della Teseide.*

SEDGEWICK, H. D.: "Boccaccio, an Apology."

STILLMAN, W. J.: "The Decameron and its Villas."

TOBLER, A.: *Proverbiae quae dicuntur super natura feminarum.*

TORRACA, FRANCESCO: *Giovanni Boccaccio a Napoli.*

TORRACA, FRANCESCO: *Prime impressioni di Giovanni Boccaccio a Napoli.*

TORRACA, FRANCESCO: *Per la biografia di Giovanni Boccaccio.*

TORRETTA, LAURA: *Il Liber de Claris Mulieribus.*

TOYBEE, PAGET: "Boccaccio's Commentary on The Divine Comedy."

TRAVERSARI, G.: *Appunti sulle Redazione del De Claris Mulieribus di Giovanni Boccaccio.*

TRAVERSARI, G.: *Per l'autenticità dell' epistola del Boccaccio a Francesco Nelli.*

TRON, EMILIO: *I Natali del Boccaccio.*

SOLERTI, ANGELO: *Le vite di Dante, Petrarca e Boccaccio scritte fino al secolo decimo sesto.*

SYMONDS, JOHN ADDINGTON: "Giovanni Boccaccio as Man and as Author."

SYMONDS, JOHN ADDINGTON: "Francis Petrarch."

WILKINS, ERNEST H.: "Boccaccio Studies."

WILKINS, ERNEST H.: "The Chronology of the Youth of Boccaccio."

WILKINS, ERNEST H.: "The Date of the Birth of Boccaccio."

WILKINS, ERNEST H.: "Discussion of the Date of the Birth of Boccaccio."

WILKINS, ERNEST H.: "The Enamorment of Boccaccio."

WOODBRIDGE, ELIZABETH: "Boccaccio's Defense of Poetry."

YOUNG, KARL: "The Origin and Development of the Story of Troilus and Criseyde."

ZENATTI, O.: *Dante e Firenze.*

ZUMBINI, B.: *Alcuni novelle del Boccaccio e i suoi criteri d'arte.*

ZUMBINI, B.: *Le ecloghe del Boccaccio.*

ANTONA-TRAVERSI, CAMILLO: *Raffronto tra le peste di Tucidide, di Lucrezio, e di Giovanni Boccaccio.*

DE BLASIIS, G.: *Napoli nella prima metà del secolo XIV.*

DE JOB, C.: *La foi religieuse en Italie au quatorzième siècle.*

EMERTON, EPHRAIM: "Humanism and Tyranny."

FUNCK-BRENTANO, FR.: "The Middle Ages."

GARDNER, E. G.: "St. Catherine of Siena."

MEDIN, A.: *Ballata in morte d'Andrea d'Ungheria.*

PERRENS, F. T.: *Histoire de Florence.*

SAPORI, ARMANDO: *Le beneficanza della compagnie mercantili del trecento.*

SAPORI, ARMANDO: *Le crisi delle compagnie mercantili dei Bardi e dei Peruzzi.*

SAPORI, ARNALDO: *Lettera di Niccolo Acciaiuoli a Niccolo Soderini.*

SISMONDI, J. C. L.: DE: "A History of the Italian Republics."

SYMONDS, JOHN ADDINGTON: "The Renaissance in Italy."

THOMPSON, JAMES WESTFALL: "The Aftermath of the Black Death and the Aftermath of the Great War."

TROLLOPE, T. ADOLPHUS: "History of the Commonwealth of Florence."

VILLANI, GIOVANNI and MATTEO: *Cronica.*

DE SANCTIS, FRANCESCO: *Storia della Letteratura Italiana.*

GEBHART, EMILE: *Conteurs Florentins du Moyen Age.*

GRAF, ARTURO: *Miti, Leggende e Superstizione del Medio Evo.*

GRAF, ARTURO: *Il Tramonto delle leggende.*

SCARANO, N.: *L'invidia del Petrarca.*

TIRABOSCHI, GIROLAMO: *Storia della Letteratura Italiana.*

In addition to the above—which quite obviously represent but a part of the enormous amount of writing which has accumulated around Boccaccio and around his period during the six centuries which have elapsed since he was born—I have drawn frequently on the letters of both Boccaccio and Petrarch. Biographical points having been established, too, by passages in nearly all Boccaccio's compositions—whether in Latin or in Italian, I also have drawn frequently on these.

In regard to quotations: Where I have cited the *Decameron,* I have used mainly the version of John Payne, occasionally modifying his text, however, where his charmingly archaic language seemed to obscure the meaning. Where I have used passages from "Amorous Fiammetta," I have tried to avail myself of the color but not of the inaccuracies of the translation made in England by Bartholomew Yong in the age of Queen Elizabeth. In quoting from the last two books of the *De Genealogia deorum gentilium,* I have used the translations of Miss Elizabeth Woodbridge as furnished in her article on Boccaccio's defense of poetry which has been cited above. In certain of the letters and in all other passages from Boccaccio's Latin works, I have been aided by translations of the original Latin into French or Italian. For the translations of all other quoted passages, I am absolutely responsible. This especially included those occasional instances where the poetry of Boccaccio is rendered into English verse. With the exception of certain passages from Dante's "Divine Comedy" which are taken from the well-known rendering by Cary, all the verse translations are my own.